IX

IAN RIDLEY has been a journalist, author, broadcaster and scriptwriter for the past 35 years, specialising in sport in general and football in particular. His career in newspapers has taken in the *Guardian, Daily Telegraph, Independent on Sunday, Observer, Mail on Sunday* and the *Daily Express*. He was voted Sports Journalist of the Year in the British Press Awards of 2007.

There's a Golden Sky is his ninth book, the first being *Season in the Cold* in 1992. Among his others are the No.1 bestseller *Addicted,* the autobiography of the Arsenal and England captain Tony Adams, which was shortlisted for the William Hill Sports Book of the Year prize, and *Floodlit Dreams,* his account of life as chairman of his home-town club, Weymouth.

Ridley also wrote some 20 episodes of the Sky One drama series *Dream Team* and is a frequent contributor to radio and television.

For Vikki.

Thanks.

THERE'S A
GOLDEN
SKY

How Twenty Years of the Premier League
have Changed Football Forever

IAN RIDLEY

BLOOMSBURY

LONDON · NEW DELHI · NEW YORK · SYDNEY

Published in 2011 by
Bloomsbury Publishing Plc
This paperback edition published 2012
50 Bedford Square
London WC1B 3DP

First edition 2011

Acknowledgements

Excerpts: pp v & 200 'You'll Never Walk Alone' © Richard Rodgers and
Oscar Hammerstein II/Williamson Music; pp 21 & 365-6 'Albert and the
Lion' © Stanley Holloway; p 138 'Ozymandias' © Percy Bysshe Shelley

Bloomsbury Publishing, London, New Delhi, New York, Sydney

A CIP catalogue record for this book is available from the British Library.

ISBN 978 1 4088 3274 5

10 9 8 7 6 5 4 3 2 1

Typeset in Tibere by seagulls.net
Printed in Great Britain by Clays Ltd, St Ives plc

www.bloomsbury.com

When you walk through the storm
Hold your head up high
And don't be afraid of the dark
At the end of the storm
There's a golden sky...

CONTENTS

SPRING

INTRODUCTION
LOOKING FOR GAZZA

THE SETTING WAS the restaurant in the tower block that housed London Weekend Television on the South Bank of the Thames, the date was Friday 16 November 1990, and the diners were six of the most powerful men in English football. After the darkest of decades for the game, they were seeking to set in motion far-reaching changes in its organisation and constitution with the aim of restoring its image and credibility, and by doing so creating new wealth and prosperity for all.

Few would see it like that, however. Rather, ITV's Head of Sport, Greg Dyke, and the men representing the then 'Big Five' clubs – chairmen Martin Edwards of Manchester United, Irving Scholar of Tottenham, Noel White of Liverpool, Philip Carter of Everton and the vice-chairman of Arsenal, David Dein – were viewed as acting in pure self-interest and naked greed, to the detriment of the game as a whole.

'We had had enough and we knew what we were doing was right,' Dein would insist to me 20 years on. 'Football had been beset by disasters and something had to change. The problem was that the voting structure in the game couldn't effect change. The big clubs had to be the ones to do it.'

Indeed, the talks would trigger 10 of the most acrimoniously controversial months in the history of a Football League three years into its second century. At the end of that 10-month period, though, on 23 September 1991, after much wrangling and politicking, the Big Five clubs had gained agreement for what they wanted: a Premier League.

While they might be deemed visionary, the quintet could never have imagined quite what they would be instigating nor what would take shape over the next two decades, given the low base they were starting from. A game and competition at the very centre of British culture, prompting an explosion in media coverage and public interest? The opening up of floodgates to a deluge of foreign players, then to overseas owners? Even the idea of taking League games to overseas cities as its TV appeal went global? In America, they call Major League Baseball 'The Show'. It is a fair description of the Premier League today.

Football was then not quite the monster of 21st-century popular culture that it is today, before every cough, spit, groin strain and sexual indiscretion was covered in newspaper sports supplement (or, if a significant enough story, on front page) and discussed on radio, television and supporters' message boards.

The nation was also preoccupied by 'events, dear boy, events,' as the Prime Minister of the late 1950s and early 1960s Harold Macmillan replied when asked what might disturb his government. Michael Heseltine was preparing the following week to challenge one of Macmillan's successors, Margaret Thatcher, for the Conservative Party leadership. The country was in recession and people were worried about this new poll tax she was proposing. There had been riots in London the previous March.

Inflation, after all, was running at 9.5 per cent, interest rates nudging 14 per cent and petrol was costing, disgracefully, £1.86 a gallon (not a litre). Unemployment was 1.7 million and rising. The average salary was £13,750, the average house price was £59,875 and increasing by a frightening 30 per cent a year. The news abroad was even graver. Saddam Hussein had invaded Kuwait and George Bush was preparing to unleash the might of the United States on Iraq, while promising it would not be another Vietnam. Preparation – called Operation

Imminent Thunder – for the Gulf War was underway in Saudi Arabia, with the British as major participants.

At least the TV was good, as it often is during a downturn when people go out less and the companies have to react. Television itself was in a state of flux, with the Broadcasting Act having just been passed to open up commercial TV. A new company, British Satellite Broadcasting, was merging with a controversial partner called Sky, which was owned by the Australian Rupert Murdoch, whose influence on the British media was growing beyond his ownership of the *Sun* and the *News of the World, The Times* and the *Sunday Times*.

The four main terrestrial television channels were the only ones then available to the vast majority, and the political comedy drama *House of Cards* was proving that art really does imitate life, not least in its title when it came to Mrs Thatcher. Another satirical comedy, *Drop the Dead Donkey*, on the six-year-old Channel 4, was also doing well while a show using current affairs for ready-made laughs was just starting on BBC2. Its name was *Have I Got News for You*, its creator a budding TV genius called Jimmy Mulville.

He also happened to be a friend of mine and a football fan, an Everton supporter who would go on to sponsor them down the years through his company Hat Trick Productions, though he would wisely decline offers to join their board of directors. On the first day of December in 1990, we had lunch on the King's Road in London before moving on to the Chelsea v. Tottenham Hotspur game at Stamford Bridge that Saturday afternoon.

Traditionally, it was one of English football's most hostile fixtures, featuring two sets of London supporters who detested each other. You could watch games safely during the 1980s, if you knew the safe areas and times to travel to avoid confrontational fans, and there was an unwritten code that you would be left alone if with a woman, for example, or simply left the scene of trouble quickly. Even so, you could inadvertently get caught up in trouble – or you feared you might.

There immediately felt a new mood in the air that day, however. It was the one that those six men had discussed a fortnight earlier at their dinner. After the violent, tragic decade for a sport that had become a social pariah, the atmosphere along the Fulham Road was of optimism among the throng rather than gloom, of anticipation rather than menace. The taxi cab was unable to get any nearer than 400 yards from the stadium due to the crowds, whereas a few years earlier you could comfortably have parked your car in a side street nearby.

The reason was a kid by the name of Paul Gascoigne; Gazza to his teammates and now the headlines of both tabloids and broadsheets. A few months earlier, at the age of just 23, the Geordie boy had become the toast of England, his exuberance and sleight of foot having led the national team to a World Cup semi-final in Italy. England lost on penalties to old foes Germany (West and East having been reunited that very year) and Gazza wept iconically in the process. It may ultimately have represented another near miss, with the 1966 World Cup win receding into the distance, but it also brought a perverse redemption for the English.

Hindsight tells us what a good England team it was, with the likes of Peter Shilton, Terry Butcher, David Platt, Gary Lineker, Peter Beardsley and Chris Waddle also in its number, but at the time few gave manager Bobby Robson's team much hope, particularly after dull group-stage draws in Sardinia with the Republic of Ireland and Holland, followed by a narrow victory over Egypt.

As a backdrop, England fans swaggered and rampaged around the streets of Cagliari to heap further ignominy on a country that in the previous five years alone had shown plenty of its shameful side to the world. The newspapers clamoured for the FA to 'Bring 'em home' – both the team and supporters, that was.

It appeared to be merely the latest episode in a catalogue of calamities at the end of a depressing, almost socially schizophrenic, decade that saw huge prosperity for some in the south but the miners' strike and *Boys from the Blackstuff* in the north; 'A Town Called Malice' by The Jam alongside New Romantic pop.

In March 1985, Millwall fans ran riot around Luton ahead of an FA Cup quarter-final before ripping up sections of the ground at Kenilworth Road and fighting running battles with police on the pitch after their side's defeat. Margaret Thatcher, no fan of football, was appalled by the scenes on the TV news. She sought to impose a membership scheme on supporters but the game resisted, even if the Luton chairman, Tory MP David Evans, curried favour with his boss by initiating one unilaterally.

Worse was to follow. In May, a young fan was killed at Birmingham City's St Andrew's ground when a wall collapsed. It received little attention, though, due to a terrible, sickening event some 100 miles north that same afternoon. At first it was just a few wisps of smoke but within minutes, the Main Stand of Bradford City's Valley Parade ground was engulfed in flames, a fire having broken out underneath the old wooden edifice. The probable cause was a discarded cigarette. Fifty-six people died and another 258 required treatment for serious burns. It happened just two days before the stand was due to be razed ahead of rebuilding.

Three weeks later, Liverpool were playing in the European Cup final against Juventus of Turin at the King Jean Baudouin Stadium – better known as the Heysel – in Brussels. As kick-off approached in the crumbling, poorly segregated ground, English fans charged towards the Italians – in retaliation to taunting, it was said. In the crush, 38 Italians and one Belgian fan died. Another 454 were injured. In the shocked and shocking aftermath, English sides would be banned from Europe for six years. It was draconian punishment, but no one dared complain.

When 96 Liverpool fans died four years later before an FA Cup semi-final against Nottingham Forest at Sheffield Wednesday's Hillsborough ground, crushed against fences as South Yorkshire police failed to recognise and avert an unfolding tragedy, one sick school of thought saw it as some kind of retribution, if not for Liverpool in particular then for the English game in general.

Thus did England arrive at Italia '90 as the sick man of world football. Thus did their showing in reaching the last four after the unpromising start pleasantly surprise all. On the players' return to Luton Airport, some quarter of a million people gathered to welcome them home. On an open-top bus, the madcap Gazza wore fake breasts as an example of his puerile but engaging humour. 'Daft as a brush,' was Bobby Robson's affectionate and enduring verdict on him.

Now here we were, here Gascoigne was, in South-West London a few months later playing for Spurs at Chelsea. The boy played another blinder and scored, as did Lineker, whose £800,000 transfer from Leicester to Everton in that *annus horribilis* of 1985 had appalled Mrs Thatcher as an example of a sum that would be better spent on the game ridding itself of hooliganism.

Although Tottenham were beaten 3-2 in front of a crowd of 33,478 (about 12,000 above Chelsea's average at the time), it was a match to uplift – unlike those of the 1970s and 1980s that always seemed to finish goalless or a snatched 1-0 either way, blighted by crowd trouble and with the spectator's main aim being to get away unharmed.

These were shafts of light in a new dawn. And up at the crack of it earlier in 1990 had been another Geordie. His name was Peter Murray Taylor, though it is by a different title that he is best remembered in a game that should be forever in his debt. Following Hillsborough, Lord Justice Taylor was commissioned by the Home Office to look into the events and to draw conclusions. He sat for 31 days and the truth emerged – that this was not due to hooliganism but the dilapidated state of the stadium and fatal flaws in the police operation. Chief among his many far-sighted recommendations would be all-seater stadiums.

These factors all combined to encourage those Big Five into believing they could formalise a positive plan rather than simply, and negatively, threaten breakaways from the Football League. It also prompted me to want to catch a mood by writing about a game on the cusp of major change. Thus, in 1991, at the beginning of the last season before the Premier League was born, I embarked on a journey to take a snapshot of the English game, from top to bottom, from Old Trafford to Hackney Marshes, to try and capture its very essence. It evolved into a book entitled *Season in the Cold* and it began on opening day at Barnet, newly promoted to the Football League, and ended at Wembley with Liverpool winning the FA Cup.

In between, I travelled up and down the country for matches in order to consider the state of youth and women's football, of the England national team, of teams at every professional level and some amateur too. It was the season when Leeds United won the First Division, English teams returned to Europe – struggled to adapt, too – and Hillsborough staged a semi-final again. The backdrop was preparation for the new Premier League after bitter years of internal arguments between the First Division of the Football League and its other three divisions, and external conflict between that Football League and the FA.

As the Premier League closed on the 20th anniversary of that meeting and as the 20th season of the Premier League loomed in 2011/12, I felt drawn back to many of the venues I had visited and people I had met while writing *Season in the Cold* to see how all the promises and premises of that meeting had panned out.

There were new people to meet and new stories to tell too, for the demographic of the audience had changed. Of the 96 people who died on the Leppings Lane terrace at Hillsborough, none was black or Asian, just four were women and only ten of the men were over 35 years of age, illustrating that the game's core audience was still the young, white working-class male. At an FA Cup semi-final now, were anyone to take a cross-section of 96 people in any part of the all-seated stadium, there are likely to be people from ethnic groups – if still not representative given the composition of the country – more women, more older men, and certainly more younger boys.

I also wanted to take stock, to chronicle and analyse the monumental changes to English football – and the nation's culture, indeed – brought about by the Taylor Report and Sky Television, who would soon absorb BSB, win the rights to the new Premier League and go on to put in ever-increasing sums of money.

Clubs were now in mind-boggling amounts of debt, with 'leveraging' – borrowing to buy – the modern way of running clubs. By 2010, two years after the credit crunch had first bitten, it was estimated that the new Big Four clubs of Manchester United, Liverpool, Chelsea and Arsenal were carrying combined debts of more than £2 billion, able to service them through revenue but vulnerable to a continuing recession and the banks increasing interest rates or even calling in their monies.

Beneath them, clubs were tumbling into administration and the game finally recognised it had a problem when Portsmouth became the first Premier League club to go the same way. They were docked nine points, causing their relegation to the Championship – the Second Division in old parlance. There, they were in good company. The majority of the 72 clubs now comprising the old Football League were struggling financially.

You wondered why, for there was more of everything than ever before. Average attendance in the old First Division in 1991/92 was 21,622. In the Premier League's 2009/10 season it was 35,116.

Beyond gate receipts, clubs accrued vast sums through the selling of merchandise. This added to the increased amounts from television money and sponsorship.

Sky's first TV deal to buy the Premier League's rights was worth a then staggering £302 million over five years. A three-year deal from 2009 was worth £1.78 billion to the Premier League. Sky still retained the lion's share of live matches, though other broadcasters had to be granted some rights as part of new European competition laws.

That sum was just for domestic rights. Twenty years earlier, there was a negligible overseas market for the English game. The latest deal brought £1.6 billion from countries with a voracious appetite for a league that had been attracting much of the best playing talent in the world.

The costs were now astronomical, however. Tottenham's playing budget, for example, in 1991 was £4.5 million as part of a combined £75 million for the First Division. In 2009/10, Spurs were paying out £60 million a season, with the total wage bill of the Premier League being £1.378 billion.

Therein was the problem: more was coming in, but huge sums were going out, with Carlos Tevez at Manchester City reported to be on £250,000 a week after a takeover of the club by owners from Abu Dhabi. Gazza had opened the door for players to earn more; a Belgian player by the name of Jean Marc Bosman then kicked down that door. Back in 1995, he successfully challenged in a court football's rule that clubs could retain the registration of players even at the end of their contracts. It meant that players were then free agents and consequently more valuable with no transfer fee needing to be paid to their previous club. The power had switched from club to player and how it would change the financial landscape.

Now agents proliferated, as did new industries growing up on the game's periphery – from public relations to kit suppliers, from merchandise manufacturers to a huge array of betting companies. Astonishingly, in 2011 a quarter of Premier League clubs had their shirts sponsored by gambling concerns.

Once, it was said, the way to make a small fortune in football was to start with a big one. Now there were sizeable sums to be made in the buying and selling of clubs, at least in trading the big ones. Directors could even pay themselves large salaries. The entrepreneur Sir Alan Sugar may have lamented that 'football turns businessmen into idiots' but he did pretty well out of the game when he bought Tottenham. It gave him inside knowledge, for example, of TV deals and he all but ordered Sky, it was reported, to increase its offer for the first Premier League TV deal and see off ITV. 'Blow them out of the water,' were the words apparently used loudly down a telephone line. It so happened that Sugar's company Amstrad was manufacturing satellite dishes at the time.

On top, in return for underwriting Tottenham's debts of £20 million in 1991, he made a total of £47 million by selling his 40 per cent to a company called ENIC between 2001 and 2007. Then at Manchester United, Martin Edwards, who inherited his controlling stake in the club from his father Louis, made £98 million from selling his shares to various parties before leaving in 2003, two years before the Glazer family of Florida instigated an £800 million takeover of the club.

The deal that shook English football the most also came in 2003, when a debt-riddled club in South-West London was sold over a weekend. Having bought Chelsea and its then debt of £1.5 million for £1 in 1982, the chairman Ken Bates made £18 million thanks to a Russian oligarch who had made the bulk of his then reported £7 billion fortune through vast gas and oil concerns in the economic opening up of the Soviet Union. Chelsea cost Roman Abramovich a trifling £140 million, to include £80 million worth of debt.

And then a deal to eclipse even Abramovich's came in 2008, when a subsidiary company of the Abu Dhabi royal family paid out of its fortune – said to be anywhere between £650 and £800 billion – the footling sum of £220 million for Manchester City. The Premier League was relieved, with the disgraced former Thai Prime Minister Thaksin Shinawatra the seller. As somebody once said: 'If you are going to sell your soul, do it at the height of the market.'

There may have been no sign of the bubble bursting at Manchester City, but elsewhere there were warning signs about the game's financial health. Even Chelsea looked to be tightening their belts, with Abramovich's commitment coming under scrutiny after their continued failure to win the Champions League. The bloated son of the European Cup had assumed a growing importance for the biggest clubs since their readmission in 1991 following the Heysel punishment and the Chelsea owner was especially keen to land it, as he would come to reveal in ending his budgeting and putting in yet more money.

It seemed a good time to take stock of the game once more.

Then there was Paul Gascoigne. He was back in the news, as he seemed to have been on and off over those two decades. It began that very week when those six men dined in London. Then, the big sports story was the new England manager Graham Taylor leaving Gazza out of a match against the Republic of Ireland in Dublin. Taylor talked cryptically of the player's 'refuelling habits'. What could he mean? Gradually there unfolded a frightening story of alcoholism, drug addiction, eating disorders and depression.

Later in the 1990s, Tiger Woods would elevate the game of golf to the point where sponsors and television stations all wanted to piggyback his appeal until his sex addiction intervened. Gazza did it for English football, renewing its populist appeal by injecting some showbiz and fun – as well as intriguing controversy through his wayward personal behaviour – into what had been a grim game. And just as every mediocre professional golfer owes part of his increased winnings to Tiger, so every top, made-for-life modern English pro (and vast numbers of those incoming from overseas) owes a piece of his inflated salary to Gascoigne for instigating a boom in the game.

Gascoigne was not, however, initially part of the Premier League. The talent drain after Heysel had not yet been interrupted, TV money not having kicked in, and Tottenham could not afford to turn down a then remarkable fee of £5.5 million from Lazio of Rome in 1992. It would have been £8.5 million, but the Italians had had to wait a year due to Gazza recovering from injury after his headless-chicken performance in the early stages of the 1991 FA Cup final victory over Nottingham Forest which had seen him rupture cruciate knee ligaments.

'It has been like waiting for a baby,' said the president of Lazio, Sergio Cragnotti. 'A very big baby.' In Rome, he promptly broke a leg and failed to fulfil his astonishing potential abroad before joining Glasgow Rangers, under Walter Smith's management. After a spell at Middlesbrough, he rejoined Smith at Everton before gradually sinking down through Burnley, a player-coach's stint at Boston United and 44 ill-fated days as manager of Kettering Town in the Conference.

All the while, his life was plagued by those 'refuelling habits'. And for 20 years, euphemism and denial battled with honesty and acceptance in him. There was Gascoigne, then there was Gazza.

For many, the episodes into which drink led him were laddishly amusing – this was the era of *Loaded* magazine's heyday – and there were indeed some funny anecdotes. Gary Lineker told a story, for example, of their time together at Tottenham when after a night out, Gazza commandeered a London bus and with the agreement of the passengers, persuaded the driver to take them to Lineker's house in a residential road in St John's Wood. Gascoigne sat at the front of the top deck encouraging the gathering to sing along with 'We're all going on a summer holiday' after the Cliff Richard song and film.

Another time, at a swish restaurant in Rome, Gascoigne once ordered lobster. Invited to choose one from a large tank, he promptly climbed in and grabbed the crustacean that had taken his fancy before handing it to the astonished waiter. Dripping wet and beaming, he retook his seat, watched by a dining room part shocked, part entertained.

It also seemed a good joke, when, after boozy episodes in Hong Kong ahead of Euro '96, he scored for England against Scotland on their way to the semi-finals against Germany – and defeat on penalties again – and celebrated with Teddy Sheringham by having water poured down his throat. It was a riposte to the pre-tournament pictures of him in the Far East being plied with booze.

Much of it was not funny, however, the pain very private but the episodes public. He assaulted his wife Sheryl, who would later divorce him as his drinking worsened. And it was no laughing matter at a training camp at La Manga in Spain when he was drunk on the weekend that manager Glenn Hoddle selected England's final squad for the 1998 World Cup. Gazza was omitted, trashing the manager's hotel room in the process.

It was not long after that Gascoigne entered treatment, first at the celebrities' haunt of the Priory in London, which failed to sort him out, then at Cottonwood in Tucson, Arizona, where he seemed to be getting the message. Six months after that, he agreed to an in-depth interview with me at the Everton training ground and we got on well. He admitted, for the first time publicly, that he was an alcoholic, and acknowledged that it was not safe for him to drink 'normally'. An all-or-nothing character, the only way for him was abstinence, he agreed. For a while, his game improved to the point where he was even being touted for a recall to the England squad ahead of the 2002 World Cup in Japan and South Korea. Instead, he began drinking again when Sheryl would not come back to him. Then ITV took a chance and recruited him to their team of pundits covering the tournament.

It did not go well. I went along to interview him again but the sober person who had made such a great spread for my then newspaper the *Observer* a few years before was gone. Instead, he was boorish and defensive. He rambled, his musings sometimes unintelligible as he chain-smoked on the terrace of the South Bank studios. It was all unusable.

It was disturbing, too. As we spoke, he picked at a sore on his finger. When we went out to a nearby bookmaker to film a small feature on him having a bet for England to win the tournament, he was accosted by a collector for a mental health charity rattling a tin. 'He'll need some of that himself,' joked his former Rangers teammate and fellow pundit Ally McCoist. At least, at the time, he and we thought it was a joke.

Gazza was all but finished in English football, although a Chinese club took him on for a while. Soaked in booze, and struggling to get paid, he soon came home to begin some years of scrapes and escapades interspersed with spells in treatment centres. Nothing stuck, however, and he frequently spurned offers of help, trapped in his addiction. As the Premier League grew richer and richer, he grew sadder and sadder, the money he had made when in his high-earning pomp long gone.

Come the summer of 2010 and Gascoigne came again to our consciousness, if in and out of it himself. There seemed to be so many parallels with 20 years earlier. England struggled through their group games at a World Cup – even repeating in South Africa the 1-1, 0-0, 1-0 scoring sequence of Italia '90. They were receiving similar vilification, but this time were out of the tournament all too soon, hammered 4-1 by Germany in the last 16. And to think the FA backed the formation of the Premier League because they thought it would improve the England team.

I wanted to interview Gazza for a third time. What would be his take on it all? What was his current impression of English football and its standards; all the foreign players who had come here – the trickle of his day now a torrent? What did the domestic game's most talented player of his generation think about the money washing about in the game now?

He had just been involved in a car crash, late one night in Newcastle. It seemed symbolic. I phoned an agent Gascoigne once used but after a week of trying, he reported back that he had been unable to track him down. Then, another week on, Gascoigne surfaced in a small Northumberland village called Rothbury. Why? In a story that gripped the nation for a week, a former Newcastle bar doorman called Raoul Moat had gone on the rampage having just got out of jail. Moat had killed the lover of a former girlfriend before injuring the woman with another shotgun blast. The next day, he turned the firearm on a policeman, blinding him, before going on the run.

Moat headed for Rothbury, which held childhood memories for him, and holed himself up in woods before a stand-off with police. Into this, arriving by taxi, entered Paul Gascoigne full of drink and bravado. He had, he told the assembled media, known the man for years and just wanted to talk him into giving himself up. He insisted that as soon as he said: 'Hey Moaty, it's Gazza,' the man would calm down. It was the ludicrous grandiosity of the active alcoholic.

He had, he added, brought along chicken and lager to sustain the man; a fishing rod so that the two could angle together, during which Gazza would talk him round; and a dressing gown to keep him warm. It was tragi-comic, poignant and utterly deluded. Gascoigne was naturally allowed nowhere near by police. Moat soon turned the shotgun on himself and committed suicide. Gazza, probably shocked and shamed the morning after by his own behaviour, headed for yet another treatment centre, this time in Bournemouth.

Gazza was sick again and so was the English game. The echoes of eras 20 years apart were everywhere: back in that season of 1991/92, there was an economic recession going on and a hung Parliament had been mooted, along with the prospect of a coalition with the Liberal Democrats.

Through it all, the national team has usually been used as the barometer of English football's health, often to the chagrin of the FA, which could be doing remarkable work with some of its grassroots initiatives but see it ignored due to the failings of the highly paid professionals over whom it has no real control. Now the question was about the highly paid manager, Fabio Capello, and his running of the squad. His discipline, it was believed, would be an antidote to the laissez-faire regime of the Swede, Sven-Göran Eriksson, England's first overseas manager, appointed in 2001. But after the shock in South Africa, Capello was seen to have feet of clay. Why could the Italian not blend players who looked like world-beaters when playing with their clubs? Why were there no young players of international quality coming through when the Premier League had grown into the most hyped and the most exciting league in the world? While it was widely acknowledged that Spain's La Liga was technically the most accomplished, it was the Premier League that had taken over from Italy's scandal-ridden Serie A as the choice of television audiences around the world, notably in Scandinavia and – most lucratively of all – the Far East.

But, despite all this, there were some uplifting stories, too, and still some wonderful football in the various competitions. There was Blackpool's rise to the Premier League and England's fall from grace; the enduring prowess of Manchester United and the rebuilding of Aldershot; emergence of new exciting players such as Gareth Bale – and the next episodes of a previous Tottenham asset Paul Gascoigne.

Taking stock this time, my aim was to travel from Liverpool to Ipswich, Doncaster to Truro, to visit grounds, matches and people as a way of telling wider tales and truths about the game and the impact on it and British culture of the Premier League, financially and socially.

Did those Big Five back in 1990 know what they were about to unleash? 'I don't think any of us can say we did,' David Dein told me. 'TV deals worth £1.7 billion? In the end, it is a sport and the quality of the football these days is riveting. It's been taken to a new level. I was lucky through my time at Arsenal with Arsène Wenger and all the football we saw.'

Another of those present at that meeting, Irving Scholar, said in 2010: 'No one can say that the Premier League has been anything other than a success and has transformed football.' Was that wholly true of what the legendary football writer Brian Glanville described as the Greed is Good League? As it contemplated playing league matches in foreign cities – a 39th game – it did seem to embody the words of rich-as-Croesus Nelson Rockefeller when he was asked how much was enough money and responded: 'A little bit more.'

Standards of football may well have improved, the game quicker, slicker and more athletic but was it more enjoyable and entertaining? Was the national team improved, as envisaged by the original formation of the Premier League and the FA, the latter quickly sidelined before seeing its name quietly dropped from the title as rows between the two bodies broke out all over again?

What had been the effect on the Football League, with the various name changes of its divisions – now the Championship, League One and League Two? What about non-League – the Conference and below, the women's game, the grassroots?

Is it us, along with our expectations and observations, who have changed most in a less innocent and accepting, more media-savvy modern era? I knew I had changed, for during the period I had crossed a line into involvement in the game through two spells as chairman of my home-town club, non-League Weymouth. After that, it had become impossible to view the game from a fan's perspective any more. Now I knew better what went on within clubs: the rivalries, egos, economics and politics. The dysfunction.

Fans would be asked to contribute ever more, despite a rise in unemployment and a fall in incomes. At the turn of 2011, as VAT hit 20 per cent, Arsenal became the first club to charge £100 for a non-corporate ticket. A survey of 4,000 fans conducted by the Football Supporters' Federation revealed that the average cost of a day at a Premier League game, to include ticket, food, drink, travel and a programme, was now £101.67. Given that most fans at a game were supporting the home side, that was some cost.

Armed with all the information and experience, it prompted a question in me and one I set out to answer on a journey through the 2010/11 season as we arrived at 20 years since the Premier League was first a twinkle in the eyes of the Big Five. Had English football retained its soul or did it now – as Oscar Wilde said in another context – know the price of everything and the value of nothing?

SUMMER

Chapter 1

UP THE POOL

'THERE'S A FAMOUS seaside place called Blackpool, that's noted for fresh air and fun,' Stanley Holloway observed in his monologue about little 'Albert and the Lion'. All of a sudden, the resort was noted, too, for its Premier League football team.

On a glorious May day, with the temperature at the side of the pitch touching 106°F., Blackpool beat Cardiff City 3-2 in the Football League Championship play-off final at Wembley. They would be in the top flight for the first time since 1971.

It was a joyous occasion and a privilege to be present. Blackpool's shirts of tangerine – please, not orange – are among the most distinctive in the English game and one end of the rebuilt stadium was a shimmering sea of replica tops, waving to acclaim their heroes. Their talismanic midfield player, Charlie Adam, scored with a beautiful curling free kick. Their manager, Ian Holloway – no relation to Stanley – had for years been an astute lower division operator, hitherto underestimated due to his Bristolian burr and fondness for a tortured metaphor. Now he was a mastermind. He deserved to dance a jig on his day in the sun.

And there in Wembley's Royal Box, applauding proudly, stood Jimmy Armfield, a reserve here in 1966 for England's World Cup triumph. He was a Blackpool player then, and he first came to this stadium in 1953 as a young professional on the fringe of the first team who beat Bolton Wanderers to win the FA Cup. He would also be a member of the side relegated in 1971 when he played the last of his record 627 games for the club. Now he was a Blackpool vice-president.

His Pool had made history as the first club in English football to win the play-offs out of each division, and in just a decade at that. Down the years plenty have decried the play-off system introduced in 1986, mainly because a team finishing third can lose to a team finishing below them and a near miss means a year's work going to waste. But the enticement of the end-of-season jamboree has enlivened many a season that was otherwise going nowhere. Certainly no one in Blackpool, who had finished sixth in the Championship, will ever again have a bad word said about play-offs.

The last time they had won at Wembley, winning the League One play-off three years earlier, Armfield had watched on television at his neat detached home just a few leafy streets back from Blackpool's Pleasure Beach on South Shore, with a blanket wrapped around his shivering shoulders. The chemotherapy for his cancer of the throat was extracting its vicious toll.

Two days after his more warming experience this time around, Armfield declined an invitation to join the team on their open-top bus ride down the Golden Mile of Blackpool's seaside attractions and boarding houses, all overlooked by the Tower, at the top of which fluttered a tangerine flag. It should be about the players today, he said, illustrating his selflessness. Everyone else in the town's population of 142,000 seemed to be there.

The win would be worth an astonishing £80 million – at the very least – to Blackpool, making the play-off final the world's richest one-off match. The Premier League club who had earned least from TV appearances the previous season, relegated Hull City, still received £32.6 million (compared to Manchester United's £53 million). New Premier League arrangements also meant that any clubs relegated would receive basic TV money – the 'parachute payment' – for four years now, not two. That would mean another £48 million. Then there was increased gate money and merchandise sales...

Blackpool had won football's lottery but the days in the immediate aftermath of victory were about kudos, not cash – that would arrive later in staggered payments. There was something fatalistic about their victory. They had sneaked into the play-offs with a late run and the momentum and force were with them, Holloway's brand of attacking 4-3-3 football taking all by surprise in the season's denouement. There is a team in Sierra Leone called the Mighty Blackpool. Now the adjective applied here.

It was, too, achieved against all odds. The team had cost £815,000 in transfer fees – £500,000 of that for Adam from Rangers – and their budget had been so small that they had been favourites for relegation rather than promotion. 'I come from a council house, so all this money is beyond my wildest dreams,' said Holloway in the euphoria of the Wembley win.

Two months later I travelled to Blackpool as the manager and his squad returned to pre-season training, and it was almost as if the weather was warning of what lay in wait in the Premier League. Rain was driving in from the Irish Sea, the sky slate grey and the wind whipping up white horses on the waves. Families were diving into amusement arcades for shelter and even the weather-hardened donkeys on the empty beach looked to be pining for the stables.

This was July on the Fylde Coast where they hold the Open Golf Championship at nearby blowy Lytham and St Annes and a Japanese journalist once asked why it wasn't staged in the summer. What, you wondered almost gleefully, might it be like when Manchester United came to town in midwinter?

For more than a quarter of a century, Blackpool Football Club had mirrored its environment and reflected the fortunes of the town it represented. Both seaside resort and club had known glory days but they seemed to be just black and white photographs, as colourful changes in English culture and its national sport passed them by.

The arrival of cheap foreign package holidays with their certain sun did for many a bucket and spade shop (which also offered windbreaks and umbrellas). And with the disappearance of the maximum wage in football 50 years earlier came the decline of the small-town club – notably some other Lancashire powerhouses who had been among the founder members of the Football League, in Blackburn Rovers, Bolton Wanderers, Burnley and Preston North End. Blackpool the resort grew seedy; Blackpool the club almost went bust.

'I must say,' Blackpool FC's chairman Karl Oyston admitted to me, 'if it was a choice between an all-inclusive week in a new hotel in Spain and a week with variable weather and queuing up to use the toilet in a hotel in Blackpool, I'd be off to Spain.'

Now a possible revival was in that stiff wind. Recession and a poor exchange rate with the euro meant that the town was becoming a holiday destination once more for some who might otherwise have taken a cheap package abroad. Now it was seeking a more upmarket clientele for short breaks and long weekends while working out a way to retain the stag and hen party income without upsetting either faction and their disparate views of modern excess.

The gains had to be set against losses, though. The political parties had stopped coming here for their annual conferences. Property prices were still below the national average. The scrapping of a scheme for super casinos had also set the town back. Pound shops abounded.

On the cheap seafront stalls, mugs and cushions proclaimed Liverpool, Everton and Manchester United, though not Blackpool. In the Hounds Hill shopping centre, there was a pair of tangerine-coloured underpants on display but they were in a designer men's clothes shop window. The club's success had taken even the merchandisers by surprise.

But not Gypsy Leah Petulengro, a fortune-teller in her booth opposite the Central Pier. As I gazed at the pictures of celebrity clients from days gone by, mainly black and white images of stars such as Cilla Black and Diana Dors, she invited me in to the musty, windowless room. It seemed worth crossing her palm with silver – actually £30 is the minimum for a 'consultation' – to ask her about Blackpool FC's prospects in the interests of research. And to be told that my health will hold out for a while yet and my children will do me proud.

'I predicted the team would win the play-offs,' she insisted. 'And they are going to be fine next season. They are going straight to the top. They will surprise a lot of people.'

The football ground was busy as I passed the statue of Stan Mortensen, the man who scored a hat-trick to win that 1953 FA Cup final. Locally at least it ensured that his name was billed equally with Stanley Matthews, who was nationally more celebrated for his part in the proceedings as at last, after two final defeats, he got his hands on a winners' medal at the age of 38.

The club shop was experiencing the lull before the storm as it waited for new replica shirts to arrive and accompany the lonely 'We are Premier League' flags. Inside the stadium, however, the tempest was raging. The finishing touches were being put to the Armfield Stand while the erection of a new covered stand to bring the capacity up to 17,500 was hurrying along, though it was looking tight for August's opening day home match against Wigan.

The new stand, billed as temporary until the club decided whether it was worth putting up something bigger, would complete the rebuilding of the ground in just 10 years. Although it would be the smallest ground in the Premier League, replacing relegated Burnley, it would at least be modern and tidy.

'Manchester United won't have any reason to complain the way they did about Burnley,' said Oyston as he took me through the dressing rooms on a tour of the ground. Indeed, there was plenty of room for the entourage of a modern-day Premier League club, with all their coaches, physiotherapists and seven substitutes. (As a reminder of lower-division times, mind, the referee's room still bore on its door a sponsorship plaque of the Pump and Truncheon public house.) It might also be a bit of a squeeze, you thought, underneath the pillars outside the main entrance on Seasiders Way, where the latest luxury coaches would debouch visiting squads before they went through the freshly painted reception area and on to the re-laid, lush pitch.

Much of Blackpool's revitalisation was down to the 41-year-old Oyston, who had picked up the pieces in the spring of 1999, having previously run family businesses that included property management and magazine publishing. It brought the Oystons a fortune of more than £100 million and a place in the top 1,000 wealthiest people in Britain. But there was scandal and misery to accompany the money.

Karl's father Owen, who grew up in the surrounding streets, had bought the football club in 1988 and announced grand plans for its future. A flamboyant bearded figure who wore fur coats and fedoras, Owen loved the high life, running a string of racehorses all bearing his surname. He also had a financial stake in a Manchester model agency, a concern that would bring about his downfall.

After a long police investigation, Oyston senior was charged with four counts of rape involving women on the agency's books. He was cleared of three but found guilty of the fourth, the alleged victim a 16-year-old girl, and in 1996 was sentenced to six years in prison. He appealed – and continued to protest his innocence down the years – but served three years.

During that time, his wife Vicki was unable to cope with the demands of running the club and called in Karl. Supporter unrest at Blackpool had reached fever pitch – even though gates were down to around 3,000 at times – with the team mid-table in League One (then named Division Two). The board was threatening to sell the ramshackle ground, which was struggling to get safety certificates and was considered one of the worst in professional football. Mirror of environment. Reflection of town.

'I was not a fan at all. I had only been to a handful of matches,' said Karl, all sober black suit and white shirt as if rebelling against his father. 'I went to a rugby-playing school and had no interest in the football club. I just took it on to help my poor mother out. She was under unjust pressure.' He implemented a series of 'kill or cure' measures.

Oyston junior was astounded by football's practice of paying players through the summer when there was no revenue coming into clubs. Ignoring any discontent, he began negotiating ten-month contracts, immediately cut the playing budget, and began applying for grants from the Football Foundation (a charity set up by the Labour Government in 2000) to rebuild Bloomfield Road. Gradually the strategy worked, though some supporters would resent Oyston's practice of renting out offices on the new premises to local concerns, including the local health trust, with his private company also involved.

After an initial relegation to the bottom division of the Football League, Oyston turned fortunes around to the point where the club became attractive to outside investors again. In 2005, a Latvian businessman by the name of Valery Belokon, who was interested in involvement in English football, bought 25 per cent of the club from Owen Oyston, who had retained his majority shareholding. That state of affairs would prompt the Premier League to seek ownership clarification, given rules about 'fit and proper persons' sitting on the boards of clubs, though in reality they could do little since Oyston senior had been in situ before those rules were brought in.

Belokon's investment was believed to be £5 million of his £200 million fortune and a portion of the money enabled the then manager

Simon Grayson to stabilise Blackpool in the Championship before he decamped to take over at his home town club, Leeds United, in 2009.

In came Ian Holloway, who was given enough money to purchase Charlie Adam, previously brought in on loan by Grayson. And in return for what was a modest investment by modern standards, Belokon got that memorable Wembley day in the sun, resplendent in a tailor-made tangerine suit.

The revenue from the play-offs helped raise Blackpool's income for the season to £8.5 million. Now they were looking at it reaching £40 million at least. The previous year, their playing budget was £4.8 million but even with the new wealth, they – in reality the powerful, parsimonious Karl Oyston – did not plan to spend more than £10 million, preferring to invest the money in infrastructure.

Indeed, Oyston had set a ceiling of £10,000 a week as their maximum wage to a player and it meant that Blackpool would be paying their entire squad around £200,000 a week. Manchester City had just signed the Ivory Coast midfield player Yaya Toure from Barcelona for £25 million. His salary alone was £200,000 a week. 'We can spend every penny we get on transfer fees and salaries and still get relegated, leaving ourselves with a lot of increased costs for the seasons following,' Oyston told me. 'I am absolutely adamant we will not change the approach we have had for the last 11 years and what has got us here.'

The new 5,000-seater stand would replace an open area known among away fans as the Gene Kelly Stand – so called because they were left singing in the rain. The new capacity would more than double their mere 8,611 average attendance of last season and they expected to be full every home game this time around, with 14,000 season ticket holders, 2,000 away fans and just 1,500 kept back for pre-match sales. Season tickets were remaining a basic £355, though fans got only 19 home games compared with 23 in the Championship. None seemed to be complaining, however.

In addition, plans had been submitted to the local council for a swish new training ground, complete with restaurants and rehabilitation pool, to replace the antiquated facility (with its Portakabin toilets just inside the fading tangerine painted gates), and the windswept field next to Blackpool Airport on which Stan Matthews perfected his dribbling 50 years earlier. For now, Oyston saw no reason to spend money to rebuild the spartan canteen, manager's office and dressing rooms. They would also keep their backroom staff to a minimum, just increasing their full-timers from 25 to 30, with the new people on one-season contracts, there mainly to deal with the increased level of media interest. The number would more than double on match days, but compare and contrast with Manchester United. At 75,000-capacity Old Trafford, they were employing some 550 full-time staff; four times that on match days.

Blackpool's kit man, meanwhile, was considering going full-time so that the players would no longer have to wash their own training gear. Even that was causing problems, though, since there had been no laundry room at the training ground.

'The day after we won promotion, the Premier League called us and said they wanted to meet with our eight heads of department,' Oyston recalled. 'We said, "We don't have eight departments, let alone eight heads."' Instead the majority of the administration fell to him and Matt Williams, the club secretary who doubled as press officer. 'We don't want to lose focus and become big-time Charlies,' said Williams, who was relieved to be getting two helpers. 'That's something Blackpool have never been. We don't want to forget everybody.'

That was why, despite new sponsors suddenly wanting a piece of the action, they would retain such local concerns as Clifton Quality Meats. 'Too right,' added Williams. 'Imagine the meat we get through here.'

They would take new shirt sponsors, though, in a company called Wonga.com, providers of short-term loans and one of those growing modern companies instantly recognisable to regular watchers of daytime television – its cash-strapped core market. When it was revealed that Wonga's annual interest rate was the equivalent of 2,689 per cent, Oyston duly took the flak, saying that it was a good deal for the club at least.

'I already had a thick skin before I took on this job,' said Oyston. 'It's a must. I feel a great deal of sympathy for people who take over football clubs with really good intentions but who want everyone to like them. Because the wheels fall off so regularly, being a football club chairman is not a role you should take on if you want universal popularity.'

The team, meanwhile, was left to Holloway, a terrier-like character of shaved head and angular features whose bark was worse than his bite. After a playing career in the midfields of Bristol Rovers and Queens Park Rangers, he had managed QPR, Plymouth Argyle and Leicester City, where he struggled and was dismissed by a serial-sacker of a chairman in Milan Mandaric. After a year out of the game – a year of self-examination – Holloway returned with Blackpool and a determination to implement an attacking playing style that would pay immediate dividends.

'We had got into a mindset that matched people's perception of us,' said Oyston. 'Poor little Blackpool, who will struggle to attract decent players and stay in the Championship. But Ian made us look at ourselves and change our views of what was possible. He made them all better players with his leadership. It was like Wimbledon of the late 1980s when the spirit and everything else all came together.'

Holloway did seem made for Blackpool. His career may have been a hard struggle to reach the top – the lot of the modern English manager who seemed to have to get a side promoted if he was to manage in the Premier League, since he was unlikely to be offered a top-flight job – but it was as nothing compared to the ordeals life had thrown at him.

He had helped his wife Kim through lymphatic cancer. Three of his four children had been born deaf and finding special schools for them had always informed his job choices. He himself had come through a skin cancer on his face. Through it all, however, there was an enviable humour and fatalism.

'He's bright and breezy, like the town,' Jimmy Armfield told me. Or as Holloway said of himself and Blackpool: 'Well, we both look better in the dark.'

Holloway invited me to his office at the Squires Gate training ground. There was a list on the wall showing potential transfer targets, as he laboured to assemble quickly an improved playing staff in the face of new Premier League rules dictating 25-man squads with eight 'home-grown' players. It was a delicate balancing act to bring in the required quality without disturbing the wage structure and the camaraderie he had fostered, which was evident as a jovial group of players outside began the pre-season slog with less gloom than was normal for the first week of vomit-inducing running. In another week, it would be down to the South West for pre-season games against the likes of Tiverton Town. Not for Blackpool nor Holloway yet the lucrative overseas tour.

'We are a little bit different. What that means is when I ring my chairman and I tell him how much players are going to cost, he shouts, "How much? What? I am not paying that. No way. They are all bloody wrong."' By now, Holloway was impersonating the shout. And then he launched into one of his trademark mangled themes. 'We have bitten off more than we can chew but we have got to chew as fast as we can. But what we are realising is that what we have chewed up, we have got to bite off again and make sense of these bite-sized chunks. How we used to deal has changed so dramatically. It's nerve-wracking but it's exciting because if we do it right, we have got no baggage whatsoever and we can end up with a nice new ground and training ground. But I want a really good team. Last season's team was so good it got us this money when it shouldn't have done. What we are trying to do is be very proud of our product that we put out there and be very proud of our unique colour. There is no fear in me because I don't fear losing my job. I didn't have one for a year.'

New signings were needed, however, and the wealth had clearly brought tensions. 'What we are finding is parasite upon parasite out there in the world after the money we have just been given,' Holloway added. 'If you are not careful, all you do is make massive mistakes by bringing in someone who isn't motivated by the right thing and kills your football club stone dead.'

He was, he railed, beset by agents sending in DVDs of their players. 'I have put the discs on a big line stopping the huge horde of crows eating my chickens' food. So thank you some of these agents who think a bloke with one leg hopping about with it videoed on his phone, is good enough for Blackpool. He might have been a couple of years ago but he ain't now.'

It sounded like a giant jigsaw puzzle, I ventured. 'It is a jigsaw and we need far too many pieces and the picture we have got to do isn't on our box,' he replied. 'And we weren't expecting this box.' He was a mix of turmoil and excitement. 'I was fuming at first when people said we wouldn't get 10 points,' he said. 'But when I got the fixture list, even I said, "My God, where are we going to get 10 points from?"'

That echoed Armfield. 'A friend asked me where I thought our first win would come,' he said. 'I asked him: "Where do you think our first corner will come?"'

They reflected the local mood. This was an area where the average weekly wage was £302.50 against a national average of £489. Even more alarming, the average life expectancy for men was just 73.6 years, the lowest in the country. Elsewhere men could expect to average 77.5 years. The comparison for women wasn't much better: 78.8 to 81.7.

'I was an NHS director here for 14 years and the Royal Victoria is a good hospital,' said Armfield, grateful for his treatment there. 'But you do see a lot of health issues. And we do have job problems. A lot of people come here and think life is going to take off for them but it doesn't.'

'Blackpool does have its fair share of social problems and deprivation,' said Hugh Evans, director of policy at the North and West Lancashire Chamber of Commerce. 'Smoking rates are 60 per cent in some of the wards and alcoholism and drug use is very high, along with teenage pregnancies.

'The council has recognised that and there are swathes of the town that are earmarked for major structural change, particularly round poorer hotel and holiday accommodation. At the end of the prom, you can see bed and breakfast for £12 to £15 a night and you just have to wonder how they can survive on that.'

Most of the money coming in to regenerate the town, Evans pointed out, had been public, from central and European government, to create 'a city on the sea'. Now, worryingly, that was drying up. The bonus was Blackpool FC. 'If there is one single thing that would elevate Blackpool, people would say being in the Premier League, even if it's only for one season,' added Evans. 'It's a worldwide exposure and you just can't buy that. The impact will be phenomenal.'

The problem these days, however, was that with Bloomfield Road accommodating so few away fans compared to the old days of the 1960s when the ground held 40,000, the revenue they brought to the town by staying for a weekend was not that significant.

Still, now was no time for rain on the parade. Hugh Evans's optimism was matched by Karl Oyston's. 'My youngest son George is most delighted,' he said. 'I watch *Match of the Day* with him and now we'll be on it so we won't have to wait up for the Football League highlights afterwards.' The relish was evident, too, in Matt Williams: 'Bloomfield Road's great when the wind's whipping in from the sea,' he said. 'I hope there'll be a few teams who don't fancy it.' And in Holloway: 'I feel like Peter Pan. It's that amazing when you look at the list of the teams in the Premier League and see our name there.'

The criticism of the Premier League has been that it has created a huge wealth gap, making bigger clubs richer and smaller clubs poorer. In previous eras, the story went, more clubs could compete for the title; more could rise up through the divisions to the top flight, as did Northampton Town in the 1960s and Wimbledon in the 1980s. Blackpool offered hope anew. 'It is a fairy tale,' said Jimmy Armfield. 'All these smaller clubs will be thinking, "If Blackpool can do it on their resources, so can we."'

Furthermore, the club now had access to the sort of money that could keep a club in business for decades to come and had shown that the Premier League was not quite the elitist organisation it was often deemed. Blackpool became the 44th club to join it in 18 seasons – almost half of the clubs in the full-time professional set-up. It compared with 43 in the previous 18 seasons of the 22-member First Division.

And still newly promoted clubs could surprise the top teams, as had Carlisle in going to the top of the table in 1974. Hull City did the same in 2008. Now, as then, they were also likely to get found out in return matches in the second half of the season. The difference these days was that it was no longer feasible for a newly promoted club to win the title after going up as Ipswich Town had done in 1962, or even challenge for it as Newcastle United had in 1996, since rivals had years more Premier or even Champions League money and thus stronger, deeper squads.

The main challenge for Blackpool was not to become the one out of the three promoted clubs on average who went straight back down. The other challenge was not to squander the new treasure. A season earlier, despite that £32.6 million that had come in, Hull City had gone from riches to rags, relegated with debts variously reported to be between £30 and £40 million after investing too heavily in players and unable to resist the temptation of taking risks to preserve Premier League status. Where Blackpool had been especially fortunate was in going up in the first season of new Premier League financial rules that doubled parachute money and were designed to prevent future freefall.

There were also lessons for Blackpool from the likes of Derby County and Burnley, who began with their own ideals but imploded in the face of the national attention. Blackpool would need to keep their nerve. 'It will be an adventure and as long as people stick with the view, "Look, let's have a good time and let's not get too upset if things don't go our way," it will be fine,' said Oyston. 'With the money this season and with the parachute payments of £12 million a season for the next four years, even if we do go straight back down, this could set up the club forever, if we do it right.'

Therein was the real lure of the Premier League, even for those clubs and their supporters who decried its commercialism. It offered the chance for a club to pay off the past and finance the future. And it offered fresh air and fun, if only for a season, even if they did get hammered regularly and slip back down to a more natural level. For Blackpool, the chill of winter and the winds off the Irish Sea would come soon enough but for now it was still summer, with the season to end all seasons still to savour ahead of them.

Chapter 2

POMPEY CRIMES

As a result of the Taylor Report, around one third of full-time professional clubs in the English leagues have built new stadiums over the past 20 years thanks to a mixture of increased revenue, television money and government grants. The other two thirds of clubs have pretty much all seen major work, either to meet all-seater requirements at the top level or, lower down, to improve capacity. Then there is Portsmouth. Then there is Fratton Park.

Yes, a new stand did rise at the car park end and seats were bolted on to old terracing in other parts of the stadium. Away fans even got a roof over their heads as the Millennium arrived. Otherwise, Pompey's 20,000-capacity home ground was a throwback, straddling the wooden stand glory days of the 1940s and the plastic-seated modern era.

Some see it as an anachronistic delight, a reverberating evocation of a less sanitised era when fans chanted, rang bells and shook rattles to create an atmosphere, unlike many of the clean modern monoliths which housed largely silent middle-class onlookers. It was also, however, a witness to the waste, possibly even corruption, that saw Portsmouth become the first Premier League club to go into administration.

Debts had mounted to £119 million before an administrator put an end to the madness of misguided ambition and back-of-a-fag-packet business plan. Administration led to the loss of their top-flight status, with relegation to the Championship for the 2010/11 season. Their legacy? An example to Blackpool, to the game as a whole, of How Not to Run a Football Club. 'It is only when the tide goes out that you see who has been swimming naked,' said the American economist Warren Buffet. Pompey were left desperately trying to cup hands over their privates.

Relegation marked the end of seven seasons in the Premier League, a period that had yielded some £200 million in television revenue alone but which was still not enough to keep them stable nor to bring Fratton Park into the 21st century. There were millions spent on transfer fees and wages but comparatively little in upgrading a ramshackle ground that, as Hylda Baker might have said, was still stood standing there while over-ambitious plans for a shiny new stadium crumbled away.

With available land scarce, new stadiums were notoriously more difficult to build in the south than the north. But Southampton had managed it and Brighton and Hove Albion were doing so. South Coast clubs from Brighton through to Plymouth had all known their financial struggles but somehow had still managed to improve their grounds significantly.

Yet Pompey were not only anchored in an outdated berth, they were still renting a barely adequate mooring of a training ground from a school up the M27 at Eastleigh. Was it all really worth the FA Cup that the club won under Harry Redknapp in 2008?

Ah, 'arry – one of the most enduring and colourful managers in the English game. An East Londoner born in Poplar, he had played under the avuncular old England manager Ron Greenwood at West Ham, a club that in the 1960s became known as the 'Academy' and supplied Bobby Moore, Geoff Hurst and Martin Peters to England's World Cup-winning team of 1966. Redknapp would go on to manage Bournemouth and West Ham before fetching up at

Portsmouth. Later it would be Tottenham Hotspur, where he would be touted as the next England manager, but it was at Pompey that his reputation became sullied by allegations of under-the-counter financial dealings.

With a keen eye for a player, Redknapp delivered an exciting, expansive way of playing. He could win you things but it was going to cost. And it did.

Pompey trod water for most of the second half of the 20th century, though remained one of the English game's stalwarts. The Pompey Chimes – 'Play Up Pompey, Pompey Play Up' – were a charming forebear of more modern, less innocent chanting, though fans no longer sang the next lines of: 'Just one more goal! Make tracks! What ho! Hallo! Hallo!' The club's mascot, a jolly sailor, was a proper symbol, like Everton's Toffee Lady, rather than the sort of oversized fluffy creatures that have taken over at other clubs.

A great name in the 1940s, when they twice won the First Division title under their legendary captain Jimmy Dickinson, and they also won the FA Cup in 1939 – thus holding it for longer than any club due to the intervention of the Second World War – Portsmouth were one of the many town clubs who would suffer from the end of the maximum wage.

Down and up the divisions they went until, in 1992, they so nearly made the new Premier League, losing out on promotion to West Ham on goal difference alone. It seemed as if it might be the closest they would get. This new competition was not designed for the likes of them. But in the late 1990s, a chirpy Cockney precursor to Redknapp thought otherwise.

Terry Venables had been England manager – and a good one, leading them to the semi-finals of the 1996 European Championships. Before that he managed Tottenham. He had always fancied himself as an owner of a club and got his wish when buying into Spurs in 1991.

He was unable to cope, however, and needed financial help and nous. Alan Sugar, not yet then a Sir or Lord, duly answered the call but soon had Venables out with customary ruthlessness, decrying his nominal partner's business sense.

After England, Venables had bought Portsmouth and its debts for a mere £1 but could not turn the tide. His policy of speculate-to-accumulate – a well-worn strategy in football – did not pay off and in their 1998 centenary season Pompey entered administration for the first time. A new Icarus League was taking shape, a collection of clubs who flew too close to the sun only to burn and fall. It was a sort of Division One and a Half, containing traditional clubs like Middlesbrough and Leicester City: big enough to get up but not big enough to stay up.

Enter Milan Mandaric. Roman Abramovich may be the man who started other wealthy overseas owners thinking about the investment potential of English football but it was Mandaric who first saw the opportunity. Born in Gospnic in 1938, Mandaric grew up in Novi Sad, both towns then in Yugoslavia but now in Croatia and Serbia respectively. As a young man he made money from buying and selling car parts before emigrating to California, where he made more money in technology and investment banking. He sought to marry business with his passion for football and set up San Jose Earthquakes. European football was more appealing, however, and he invested first in Charleroi in Belgium then Nice in France. More passionate English football was more appealing still and his takeover of Portsmouth in May 1999 was a pushover. Though there usually seems to be a mug waiting in the wings at these times, there were not exactly queues to buy the club.

Soon Mandaric and English football discovered his fondness for hiring and firing managers. After Tony Pulis, who would go on to manage Stoke City to the Premier League, then local playing hero

Steve Claridge and former Chelsea coach Graham Rix, Mandaric pushed the boat out in 2002 for Redknapp, who had fallen out with West Ham. With him as assistant came Jim Smith, a veteran bald bon viveur who had managed, well, everywhere.

Redknapp had a canny old-school manager's nose. It scented out places where he would have a chance of succeeding. It scented out money. He knew that money does not guarantee success but lack of it guaranteed failure. Mandaric had money – or at least had access to it with his credit rating. As Robert Maxwell once said: 'It is not money that counts but the illusion of money.' The adage served him well. Until it didn't that is, his empire crumbled and the man who had been a big figure in the game, as publisher of the *Daily Mirror* and owner of Oxford United FC was found dead in November 1991 floating in the Mediterranean, having either fallen or jumped off his boat.

Mandaric determined to buck a trend. In 2001, in an attempt to board the bandwagon that Sky had created, with live football now playing well in pubs, clubs and living rooms, ITV set up a digital channel and agreed to pay a barely believable £315 million for Football League matches. The company quickly lost money, however, and the station went into administration.

Shocked clubs who had budgeted for the money were reining in. Mandaric's decision – on the old principle of investing during a recession if you could get the money together – to spend against the prevailing wind was timely. In came talented but expensive players such as Paul Merson and Teddy Sheringham. Up went Pompey.

Inevitably, Mandaric and Redknapp fell out, as two such strong characters were ever likely to do. Naturally, it was over the size of a transfer kitty. Redknapp decamped pointedly to nearby Southampton, admirably keeping them in the top flight when relegation looked probable. Then the pair fell back in a year later. Redknapp kept Pompey up too.

By 2006, Mandaric sensed the tide was turning. In order to compete with bigger clubs, Portsmouth needed new money that he was no longer willing or able to advance. Besides, post-Abramovich, overseas buyers were plentiful. It felt like a good time to sell.

Mandaric persuaded a young Israeli by the name of Alexandre Gaydamak to part with an initial £20 million. Actually, it seemed more likely that Gaydamak's father Arcadi, owner of the Beitar club in Jerusalem, was the prime mover in the deal but he kept a lower profile in proceedings.

In another six months, Mandaric persuaded the pair to spend another £32 million to buy out his remaining shareholding. It brought Mandaric a huge profit on what was believed to have been a £10 million investment. Avram Grant, previously manager of the Israeli national team, also arrived as technical director. Like Gaydamak, he was a friend of Roman Abramovich. It all became very claustrophobic.

Redknapp tolerated Grant – content to keep quiet and bide his time getting to know English football – in the background because he was now being given money to spend. The manager had as company a can-do chief executive in the rotund shape of Peter Storrie, an Essex man who had been with Redknapp at West Ham. Now they recruited merrily, many of the deals done by an Israeli agent, Pini Zahavi, a friend of Abramovich. 'Appy days, 'Arry days, were here again. Everyone was doing well out of it all.

Redknapp liked his bit of foreign talent but retained a preference for the home-grown. England players such as David James, Glen Johnson, Sol Campbell, Peter Crouch and Jermain Defoe came in on fortunes. Tony Adams, upright former Arsenal and England captain, joined as a coach. The result was eighth place in the Premier League and the FA Cup triumph. No one seemed to be counting the pennies. The pounds were coming in.

But there it pretty much ended. Gaydamak was hoping for more than the Cup. He naively thought that his team might even reach the Champions League, and grew disappointed. His father's business affairs were also unravelling. The funding dried up. Redknapp read the signs and moved to Tottenham.

Tony Adams took on the Pompey job as he was keen to show himself capable as a Premier League manager. He could not halt the decline, however, and lasted just a few months. The understated Paul Hart, elevated to management from coaching the club's young players, then did an admirable job in keeping Portsmouth in the Premier League for one more season.

Against a backdrop of disputes over ownership and who was owed what, Gaydamak ceded control of the club. However, the buyer he found – as Redknapp observed wryly from his new eyrie at Tottenham – was probably the only Arab in the world without any money. Pompey should have known when no less a sporting authority than the former newspaper editor, *Britain's Got Talent* TV show judge and self-acclaimed friend of the stars, Piers Morgan, issued a ringing endorsement of Sulaiman Al-Fahim.

Then would come one Ali Al Faraj, apparently injecting funds. What possessed him, no one knew. Doubts would later be expressed that he ever existed. Next in line was Balram Chainrai from Hong Kong, who was also somehow persuaded to put in money. There was even a local man by the name of Rob Lloyd, apparently fronting a bid from a British businessman who would not reveal himself.

The analogy that sprang to mind was of bald men fighting over a comb. Anyone who followed the saga, and who was wearied by all the talk of finance in modern football, grew sick of the phrase 'due diligence' and the description of a band of interested buyers as a 'consortium'.

With the debts mounting and creditors moaning, Storrie stayed to try and pick up the pieces. But then, he had done much to create the problems as he and Redknapp had accumulated players on high wages that could not be subsidised by crowds of 20,000 and little income from corporate hospitality. Gaydamak foolishly indulged their assumption that he would just continue to fund it.

And so Pompey fell into administration and were docked nine points. The sanction would certainly condemn them to relegation at the end of the 2009/10 season. Recession was blamed. The Premier League was blamed. But it was hard to argue with the organisation's capable, powerful chief executive Richard Scudamore. 'I'm on record as saying that if a club whilst in the Premier League went into administration, then it would be down to bad management of the club,' he said. 'And it is. If you start the season knowing that you're going to get between £30 million and £50 million as a starter from the Premier League through the year, it is entirely possible to get yourself organised so that you don't get into the difficulties that Portsmouth got into.'

An administrator named Andrew Adronikou began running the club, looking as if he was enjoying it rather too much, judging by his ready availability for television appearances.

When Paul Hart was sacked, Avram Grant returned as manager after being sacked by Chelsea. Somehow he guided them to another FA Cup semi-final. Against Tottenham Hotspur. Harry Redknapp's Tottenham Hotspur.

I took a trip to the South Coast. Actually, my first stop was the pretty market town of Petersfield some 15 miles north of Portsmouth. It used to be a bottleneck for holiday traffic on the way to Hayling Island or Southsea but now the A3 bypassed it and there was little reason to stop off – unless your mission was to discover something about Portsmouth Football Club. For in Chapel Street worked John Anthony 'Portsmouth Football Club' Westwood. By day, he ran the family's bookshop, one of those charming, labyrinthine emporiums where barely a word is spoken and middle-aged people browse.

Come match day, however, he was transformed into a dervish figure beloved by the TV cameras, leading the chanting, ringing his bell and blowing his bugle, decked in blue-and-white checked stovepipe hat and waistcoat, with long blue wig and sunglasses. He had more than 60 Portsmouth-related tattoos on his body and PFC engraved on his teeth. His parents probably told him that he would regret them all one day but he was now closing on his 50th birthday and showed no signs of it.

On the day we met, he had just come back from a house clearing and was dressed soberly in a V-neck sweater that almost, but not quite, covered a Portsmouth club tie. Without the blue wig, he was barely recognisable. Neither would you reconcile this man with the message on his mobile: 'Play up Pompey, Pompey play up. Avram Grant's blue and white army. We hate Scummers. Leave a message. If you are a Scummer, don't bleedin' bother.' Scummers? They were Southampton fans, a legacy of bitter days in the 1930s when Southampton dockworkers (Southampton Company of Union Men) took the jobs of their striking Portsmouth counterparts.

Thankfully Westwood was somewhat more restrained now as we found a quiet corner of the shop, behind a couple of bookcases, to talk about his first love. And the dilemma at the heart of every football club soon emerged. Fans want money invested into their team and they wanted to dream. They did not, however, want their club to go bust. 'I think everyone could see this coming but turned a blind eye as long as the money was coming through,' Westwood admitted. It was the Gaydamaks whom Westwood blamed, not Storrie, not Redknapp, who were simply spending the money the owner accorded them without asking too many questions, he reckoned. Not that he was free of issues when it came to Redknapp.

'Fantastic manager, Harry, but I dislike the man for what he did to us by going to Southampton. He soured his time with us by going down the road. He was doing it to get back at Mandaric.' He blamed the fans too. 'Anyone with a brain would know that with 20,000 gates and no corporate facilities, you can't sustain the wages we were paying people,' he added. 'That is the trouble with football – we are driven by success and we are blinkered.

'We love our football club but it has been treated like a rich man's toy and there is a lot of anger out there. Football in this country is driven by the passion of the man in the street. They are the ones who pay for overpriced merchandise, tickets and TV subscriptions and are getting an overhyped product. There are now chairmen, managers and players taking obscene amounts of money out.'

It was the classic lament of the supporter – and more and more of them were sounding it with their own clubs around the time – though Westwood was at least honest in admitting that he happily accepted administration for the winning of the FA Cup. 'We've been in administration before and come through and we will this time. I would still have wanted to do it.

'It's all right for me. I like the old ground but it's disgraceful really,' he said. 'People expect more these days. And a 36,000 capacity would double our revenues. The potential for the club is huge. But I'm not worried about what level we play at. I started supporting the team in the old Fourth Division when I was 12. It's about where you are from; it's about your identity. It's the city, the community. This is what foreign owners don't understand. Pompey is a working-class city. We like football and we like a drink. It's about entertainment on a Saturday afternoon, singing your heart out and watching a game. As long as we have a club to follow, it doesn't matter what league it's in.'

The unquenchable faith of the fan. Many clubs, if of lesser profile than Pompey, were experiencing similar problems with the recession biting but still the core fans remained. Football had always known they would; had always relied on them and would always rely on them.

From Petersfield, it was on to Fratton. Once the ground stood flanked by railway marshalling yards. Now an industrial estate surrounded it, the club offices situated amid the garages, light industry, nearby McDonald's and a budget hotel. There was, too, what once would have been called the club shop, now blown up into the megastore. A semi-final may have been in the offing, but I could have sworn there was tumbleweed blowing across the car park. 'It has been quiet at times over the winter but I don't think that's because of the way things have been here, more the way retail has been in general,' the shop manager Steve Wiltshire attempted to explain. 'But now everyone has a positive attitude. We have got in baseball caps, T-shirts, foam hands, scarves, flags and polo tops. The whole club has pulled together and made progress. People now have a lift, something to look forward to.'

They needed it. The administrator had shut down two merchandise outlets at the city's Cascades shopping centre and at nearby Fareham, and they now operated this one on a skeleton staff, some on wage deferrals, some part-time. Buyer Jane Allen was on a three-day week and said it was almost a relief when all the cuts were made, having lived with uncertainty for so long, but she retained the tired look of someone who had endured a hard winter. 'We have had some very loyal suppliers and people are still supporting us because they have been guaranteed their money by the administrator,' she said. 'It helped when David James and Michael Brown [goalkeeper and midfield player] were in here signing things. We had a queue of people round the block.'

They seemed to have caught the positive, cup-tie mood. Blue T-shirts bearing the slogan so frequently sung at Fratton had even sold out. 'Que Sera, Sera,' they said. 'Whatever will be, will be.' They hadn't reached everyone, mind. Down on the waterfront, there remained a tourist appeal about HMS *Victory* – but the bigger attraction these days was the outlet shopping centre at Gunwharf Quays. There, beneath the new landmark of the Spinnaker Tower – finished after much wrangling in 2005 and at 170 metres high, taller than Blackpool Tower, the local tourist board boasted – as the sun shimmered on the Solent and tourists enjoyed the cafe culture in shirtsleeves, one Pompey fan strolled by. He was wearing an anorak and club scarf round his neck.

From there it was on to the Eastleigh training ground where Avram Grant was holding court. He had earned many plaudits during the winter for seeing the job through in treacherous circumstances, with his wages being withheld and some of his players being released.

With the newspapers on his trail, too. At one point, he was pictured coming out of a, er, massage parlour near the training ground. The response of his wife Tzofit – who described her husband, despite his downbeat manner, as 'fun to steal horses with' – was to say she was not surprised that her husband needed some form of relief given all the problems at the club. Internet message boards were soon overrun with people asking where they might also find such a tolerant woman.

Grant himself had everything in perspective. After Sunday's match – on the Jewish day of Holocaust Remembrance – he would be boarding a plane for Poland, there to join the annual March of the Living from Auschwitz to the killing huts at Birkenau. This year would be even more poignant for him. It was just six months since his father Meir, mentor and inspiration had died at the age of 82. Grant senior somehow survived the Second World War in Siberia but, according to his son, had buried his father, five brothers and sisters and 15 uncles and aunts there.

'It will be a special day. I miss him a lot,' said Grant junior as he gazed out across Portsmouth's green training fields. 'He was at many games of mine. He suffered so much but he never hated anybody. He was such an optimistic man. I learned from him that you need to be strong for yourself. He said to me, "It's always better to be optimistic and foolish than pessimistic and right." I said to him, "It is better to be optimistic and right."'

And, wouldn't you know it, Pompey's patchwork side – missing its best players sold in the transfer window – promptly prevailed, ridiculously, by 2-0, against Redknapp's Tottenham, who had hammered them just a few weeks earlier.

The final against Chelsea would be another matter, however. For a while Pompey rode their luck and it seemed that Grant had personally selected the goal-frame as his 12th man – Chelsea hitting the woodwork five times, including possibly the worst miss in Wembley history, by Salomon Kalou. Then Pompey won a penalty. Kevin-Prince Boateng missed, however, and Didier Drogba went on to score the only goal of the game and bring Chelsea their first Double of League and FA Cup.

Pompey scarf draped round his neck, Grant climbed the 39 steps to receive his loser's medal, lingering to hug along the way his son Daniel, whose eyes said that his father was anything but a loser. After all, surviving as a football club, let alone reaching an FA Cup final, was success in itself for Portsmouth.

In the interview room came a bravura display. Grant's deflation was initially, understandably, apparent. 'It is a sad day, but a very proud day,' he insisted. 'It has been a difficult season but a season I will never forget. This is a fairy tale. This is a story of English football as I knew it.'

Sadly, Portsmouth's was also a story of the modern English game as we would rather not know it. Those who had owned and run the club had not deserved the team who performed so valiantly for them at Wembley. Peter Storrie, the man who negotiated all the inflated contracts and oversaw the spending, still formed part of their official party. Breathtakingly unashamed, Storrie would stay on over the summer as a consultant to the administrator, saying that he might even be in demand from the government if they wanted to investigate football's affairs, given his inside experience of them.

A whole host of expensive players left, however, and Grant moved on to manage in-debt West Ham. Clearly he had not yet suffered enough.

Portsmouth, meanwhile, persuaded those to whom they owed money to agree a Creditors' Voluntary Arrangement (CVA) of 20p for every £1 owed. It was an astonishing list that included the school whose fields they used as a training ground (£40,000), St John Ambulance (more than £2,000) and a whole host of betrayed local businesses and suppliers, including hotels and restaurants.

The CVA was agreed by the High Court despite the objections of Her Majesty's Revenue and Customs. It avoided liquidation and brought the club's debts down to some £25 million but they still had to sell players to find around £7.5 million for the most pressing debts. It did not help that they had already eaten into their first parachute payment of around £6 million from the Premier League back in the spring.

To add to the tortuous scenario, the nominal owner Ali Al Faraj was now well out of the picture, if he had ever been in it, with Balram Chainrai now in charge – reluctantly, as he simply wanted to get back the £17 million he had inadvisedly loaned Al Faraj. Or was it Gaydamak, who now owned the ground and wanted his loans back too? They totalled, he claimed, some £30 million.

The director's loan – the curse of any football club. It helped in the short term when there were cash flow problems but too many and too much meant that the debt became a burden on the club, especially when the director tired of his role, fell out with the board, or came to resent the abuse he would inevitably get from fans. Anyway, if he didn't get his money back, Gaydamak said, he would stop the club playing because he now owned all the land around the ground and would not let them have access.

Fortunately, on opening day of the new Championship season, Portsmouth were away at Coventry City's new Ricoh Arena, where I caught up with them again. Clean and spacious, on the edge of the city with good links to the nearby M6, the stadium may not have had the nostalgic charm of their old Highfield Road ground, but it did show up Fratton Park and showed Portsmouth that to which they should aspire.

Coventry were founder members of the Premier League but had been embedded in the Championship for 10 years now after 34 unbroken years at the top level. After a takeover by a former Manchester City player turned businessman in Ray Ranson, they were hoping for a return. But they were yet to gel under new manager Adie Boothroyd, a soundalike for Bernard Cribbins in *The Railway Children*. Boothroyd had once got Watford into the Premier League. Still, they were certainly good enough to see off Portsmouth, now managed by Steve Cotterill, 2-0.

Restricted by a transfer embargo, Pompey had provided just 13 names for the match day programme, including two in Kevin-Prince Boateng and Danny Webber who were unavailable. In the end, they managed to take 15 players to the game – only four substitutes instead of the current allocation of seven – but four were first-year apprentices. 'It was good to play a game and know that the club are alive and kicking but everyone can see where we are, with 10 professionals and kids on the bench who are nowhere near ready,' said Cotterill.

You feared for him and Portsmouth. In recent years, several clubs had been unable to halt the downward spiral, falling straight through the Championship – among them Leeds United, Charlton Athletic, Norwich City and Southampton – after they had over-indulged in the Premier League.

Portsmouth had become a morality tale for the Premier League, who were now forced to re-examine and tighten their own rules about takeovers, the probity of persons concerned and the transparency of clubs' business affairs. Perhaps some good would therefore come out of it. Perhaps, too, it would do Pompey some good, as they shed a series of questionable owners looking to swap old money for the new riches of the Premier League and got back to the basics of running a club within its means. The CVA deal made them more attractive to possible new owners. But not that attractive.

Would the game really learn from Portsmouth's mad few years, though? Would the authorities take more interest in the source of clubs' cash? Would rules eventually be introduced that limited clubs to spending within their means? Would it make people think twice about trying to make a fast buck from a club without the resources to sustain their involvement?

The answer to all of the above was: probably not. The Premier League may have tightened the odd rule on club ownership but there was no appetite among the membership to revise their financial arrangements any more searchingly along the lines that Michel Platini was installing as president of UEFA. He called it Financial Fair Play, designed to limit spending and debt if clubs wanted to play in the Champions League.

The Premier League was the free market. Portsmouth's wounds were self-inflicted, the League reckoned. This was a one-off basket case. It would take a bigger club in bigger trouble for such sanity as salary caps – the spending on wages being related to a club's income – to be adopted. Also, would supporters become realistic when confronted by moneymen bearing gifts? Many fans were concerned by the debts being racked up and wanted to see their clubs run in new ways. There were still plenty, though, who never stopped dreaming, whatever the evidence.

Chapter 3

THE ENGLISH PATIENT

ALL IS REBUILT now and, as you exit Wembley Park tube station, you are greeted by the stadium's illuminated arch that dominates the North London skyline these days. It's a sight that dwarfs the old twin towers, and inspires feelings of both awe and anticipation – much like your first glimpse of that pitch and those beaming floodlights as a child clinging to your dad's hand. Sir Norman Foster's design was indeed a grandiose new home for the FA and the England team. It was just a shame about the football.

After the end of the Empire Stadium, it had become end of empire for the national side. A supposed golden generation of players – David Beckham, Michael Owen, Rio Ferdinand, Steven Gerrard and Frank Lampard – had come, seen and failed to conquer. To boot, Fabio Capello, who was supposed to be haughtily above all these things as he looked up at the stars and down on the critics, was being dragged into the gutter like all his predecessors as England manager. The Tommy Cooper lookalike was now even being ridiculed, as his considerable reputation and disciplinarian image crumbled.

It is hard to recall now quite how vividly Bobby Robson – revered in his final years as dear old Bobby, the silver-haired sage – was vilified at the 1990 World Cup in Italy. Against a backdrop of hooliganism, his England stumbled through the group stage that pitted them against the Republic of Ireland, Holland and Egypt.

In Cagliari, amid the angst and embarrassment of it all, I met a writer by the name of Pete Davies. He was working on a book entitled *All Played Out*, the premise of which was that England as a nation was on its knees as a result of a decade of Margaret Thatcher's government, and that this was reflected in the sport of football that she so detested. It seemed a valid enough theory.

To the amazement of all, however, England suddenly polished up their act and the tournament opened up. They beat Belgium and Cameroon before losing so gloriously on penalties to Germany in the semi-finals. Gazza wept. Robson came home a hero. His place in English football's pantheon was later secured as he won titles with PSV Eindhoven, Barcelona and Sporting Lisbon before leading his beloved Newcastle United into the Champions League. Arise, Sir Bobby.

It was all achieved with uncomplaining dignity, not least when he was unfairly sacked by Newcastle, and the figure once labelled a plonker by a tabloid newspaper ended his life as a hero. It just went to show: stick around long enough, smile through the abuse and eventually, like Bob Monkhouse or Dennis Skinner, you turn from joke to national treasure.

That status was confirmed as Robson stoically bore his cancer. I was on a table with him at a dinner not long before he died in 2009. Sitting next to him, my partner Vikki talked to him of her own cancer. He asked what kind she had. She had a secondary, she said; they weren't sure if its origins were ovarian or breast. 'Them, pet,' he replied, 'are the only two I've not had.'

In South Africa 2010, Capello had secured the same group stage results as Robson – 1-1, 0-0 and 1-0, against the United States, Algeria and Slovakia – but there the similarity ended. In the last 16, England were thrashed 4-1 by Germany. They returned not to the joyous, ludicrous scenes of Gazza and his fake breasts at Luton Airport and an open-top bus ride, but skulking through a side entrance at

Gatwick almost unobserved, certainly unloved. 'I wasn't happy about that,' one former England captain told me. 'They were like thieves in the night.'

Tonight was a more public homecoming. Tonight England were playing Hungary in an August friendly that must have seemed like a good idea to the FA at the time it was arranged. England, after all, had been tipped to reach the World Cup semi-finals, maybe even to go on and win the tournament. Instead, it had become a game nobody really wanted. Except, curiously, the fans, it seemed.

It wasn't always this way. There were times when some attendances for England friendlies were embarrassingly low. In September 1995, for example, England drew 0-0 with Colombia at Wembley – the game that featured the Rene Higuita scorpion kick. There were just 20,038 present.

Tonight, however, there would be a remarkable 72,024 people taking advantage of the lower ticket prices forced upon the FA. It was still the school holidays so mums and dads were there with the kids. There would also be a fair few wanting to jeer and pillory the summer flops and they would consider it value for money.

But, talking to some of them as they walked up from the tube station to the stadium, it became clear just how tolerant the English could be, in public at least. Annoyingly so, sometimes. For following the national team had often resembled Samuel Johnson's description of a second marriage: a triumph of hope over experience. England followers are usually not from the big clubs, where there is top-class football to watch played by teams who are often better than England. No, the majority are from Hartlepool or Torquay, Carlisle or Colchester, as their flags of St George bearing team allegiances testify. To them, internationals are their chance to see the big names, to feel involved at the highest level. Initial anger having subsided, they usually forgive, even if they don't forget.

There has to be forbearance given that burger and chips cost £6.50, and fish and chips £7, in the food 'outlets' flanking the newly tiled walkways. Even a programme would set you back a cool £6. 'It's cost me about £100 all in,' Jordan Steele, an 18-year-old Aston Villa fan from Birmingham, told me. 'That's £40 for my ticket, £40 for my travel and £20 for my food, drink and a programme.'

It was not the cost that was bugging him, however. 'I'm really angry with these players. They let us down in South Africa. They didn't show enough heart.' So why was he here? 'I'm English, I'm patriotic and I'm a football fan,' he replied. And there in a nutshell was the attitude on which the national team, the national game indeed, has traded for its entire existence.

'I'm not going to boo them,' said David Capicotto from Watford, meanwhile. 'I'm always going to be behind England.'

'No, I won't boo them,' added his travelling companion, Linda McDowell. 'But they did play really badly. I don't think they were trying hard enough.'

Trevor Blake from Bedfordshire had taken advantage of a total price of £55 to bring his three sons along. The 52-year-old was clearly another of the reasonable England fans, unlike the passing group given a wide berth by most as they sang 'No surrender to the IRA' and 'Two World Wars and one World Cup', still fighting battles that belonged to other eras. Like 1990. 'I do feel let down,' said Trevor. 'But I'm here to show my support. My worry is that there is not enough of a sense of pride in these players like there used to be when playing for England was the peak of their careers. Players like Bobby Moore.'

Bobby Moore. A nation turns its lonely eyes to you. The very name conjures up an era when all was good in the game, though it surely wasn't. I interviewed him almost 20 years earlier, when he was working as a pundit for the London radio station Capital Gold. England had reached the 1991 Rugby Union World Cup final and my newspaper wanted his take on what it was like to play in such a match. I will never forget the look of bewilderment that came over his face when I asked him if he had ever contemplated how life might have been had England lost to West Germany that day. 'No, it didn't come into it,' he replied, as if defeat had never been an option. 'No. No. Never.'

He died suddenly of bowel cancer, in 1993. A nation truly did mourn and, while Sir Bobby Robson was lamented, we knew he had had a decent innings. Bobby Moore had only just reached his half-century. The golden boy, fastidious in all he did – 'He was the only player I ever knew who folded his underpants,' his England teammate and my personal footballing hero Jimmy Greaves once said – seemed immortal.

Actually he was. Now outside Wembley stood a bronze statue of him and all were drawn to view it these days, a logjam of people always forming an hour before kick-off. There they could read an inscription, beautifully constructed by his biographer Jeff Powell:

Immaculate footballer. Imperial defender. Immortal hero of 1966. First Englishman to raise the World Cup aloft. Favourite son of London's East End. Finest legend of West Ham United. National Treasure. Master of Wembley. Lord of the game. Captain extraordinary. Gentleman of all time.

What would he have made of the current crop? The prevailing feeling was that these players no longer saw playing for England as the pinnacle of their achievements. Indeed, it was more like a chore. The Liverpool player Jamie Carragher was honest enough to admit it in his autobiography, having missed a penalty in a European Championships quarter-final shootout in Lisbon against host nation Portugal in 2004: 'Fuck it, it's only England... Whenever I returned from disappointing England experiences, one unshakeable, overriding thought pushed itself to the forefront of my mind, no matter how much the rest of the nation mourned. "At least it wasn't Liverpool," I'd repeat to myself, over and over.'

Modern elite players are comfortable at their clubs. The facilities these days at training grounds are opulent. I was once given a tour of Liverpool's Melwood by the then manager Gerard Houllier and saw for myself its manicured lawns, oval-shaped dressing room – designed by him so that there were no corners for players to hide in – players' restaurant and rehabilitation swimming pool. On rough days, there was an outside covered area for training, though without sides so, Houllier said, players could still feel the weather as they would need to on match days.

There, they were among teammates they respected and knew, coached by managers who were among the best in the world. Managers of national teams these days were usually second choices; the first choices like Sir Alex Ferguson and Arsène Wenger would never give up the day job for the England job. The top players also had the Champions League, the all-star competition for Europe's finest. It was clear they felt it to be a far more searching international test.

There was also the question of earnings these days. The minimum for internationals was £40,000 a week, while captain John Terry was on £140,000. When the England captaincy was taken away from him following an off-the-field scandal, he knew that he could always retreat back to the safety and warmth of his club, where his own fans would treat him as a hero no matter the travails on national duty and the contempt of other clubs' supporters.

Besides, playing for England could seriously damage both the players' wealth and their health. If they were injured, they could be out for months and thus miss all the win bonuses. And by not linking up with England, but resting instead during international weeks, they could frequently extend their career and thus earn for longer.

Carragher, indeed, had retired from international football a while back but been prevailed upon to go to South Africa, inadvisedly as it turned out. Manchester United's Paul Scholes had declined the invitation. Now the Blackburn Rovers goalkeeper Paul Robinson had also grown fed up with making up the numbers in training on England trips.

In Moore's day, players announcing their retirement from international football was unheard of. They were retired. 'See you next time, Alf,' chirruped the hat-trick hero Geoff Hurst once to Sir Alf Ramsey after an England match. 'If selected, Hurst. If selected.'

One wonders what Ramsey would have made of Capello. The Italian was often compared to Ramsey for his perceived quiet authority and footballing wisdom. It was hard to argue with his success at club level as he won domestic and European trophies with Milan and Real Madrid, but it was never an image I had personally bought into. It was, though, clearly one that had got Capello the job.

The modern England manager is always appointed as the antidote to his predecessor. After Robson and Italia '90, Graham Taylor was thought to be ideal for the blazers at the FA. He had taken unfashionable Watford to third in the old First Division, then Aston Villa to runners-up. He was articulate, young, up and coming. The drawback was that he had a reputation for direct, long-ball football but the theory was that with better players, he would play more of a passing game.

At the European Championships of 1992, England were beaten 2-1 by the host nation Sweden, prompting a headline in the *Sun* of 'Swedes 2, Turnips 1', with Taylor's face grotesquely merged with a turnip. He had substituted the nation's sweetheart, Gary Lineker, in what turned out to be the striker's last game before retirement. It meant that Lineker was stranded on 48 goals, one short of Bobby Charlton's England record of 49. On the aeroplane home the next afternoon, someone commiserated with him. 'Bobby,' Lineker replied to his credit, 'was a better player than me.'

Earlier that day, Taylor had insisted that, by bringing on Arsenal's Alan Smith, he was trying to turn the tide of the game and so get Lineker another game in the semi-final. Taylor also sought to warn the English game that its so-called stars were falling behind the conditioning and the athleticism of their overseas rivals as new scientific training and nutritional regimes sprang up abroad. He was proved right when overseas players began to flood into the Premier League and eclipsed the English.

Taylor, though, was becoming a prophet without honour. When England failed to qualify for the World Cup of 1994, he was gone. His reputation would be tarnished further by a Channel 4 fly-on-the-wall documentary that gave him too much rope with which to hang himself but that also gave us some of the most memorable quotes in the history of sports television. Among them were: 'Do I not like that,' 'Can we not knock it,' and 'I'm waking up with the usual, pyjamas wet through.'

It was time for a cannier coach. Jimmy Armfield, 1966 England World Cup squad member and respected radio pundit, was entrusted by the FA with canvassing opinion within the game and came up with a popular name. Terry Venables' financial affairs had a whiff of notoriety that even attracted the attention of the investigative BBC TV programme *Panorama*, but he was clearly a cerebral coach and an inspired leader and manager of men. Venables had bought Paul Gascoigne for Tottenham from Newcastle, and the kid respected him so much that he even (at least after a boozy pre-tournament stay in Hong Kong) stayed sober during Euro '96.

England bonded and prospered; the nation was enraptured by hosting a major tournament again and sang along to the catchy 'Three Lions', which suddenly became the national team's nickname.

Venables had England playing a more modern way, based on a sound defence marshalled by Tony Adams but with a fluid attacking formation that had Teddy Sheringham playing off Alan Shearer, as Gazza, Steve McManaman and Darren Anderton formed a creative midfield triumvirate.

The FA had asked Venables before the tournament to wait until after it for new contract talks but he refused. He didn't do auditions, he said. Thus, full of the pride that became his downfall, he departed after England had lost on penalties to the Germans in the semi-finals, again, and a trick was missed when all seemed set fair, for a few years at least, under a popular manager.

As successor, Glenn Hoddle's image was straight and upright, a born-again Christian, though he cherry-picked his religious dogma and used a bit of whatever suited him. He even called on the services of a faith healer, Eileen Drewery, to help players with injuries and even any mental issues. On match nights, she could be spotted, terrified of the press, in a bar at Wembley nursing cigarette and gin and tonic.

She once placed a hand over the curly locks of Ray Parlour, the Arsenal midfielder, as she attempted a diagnosis in one of her sessions. 'Short back and sides, please,' Parlour chirruped, his lack of seriousness reflecting the scepticism of the public.

Drewery's involvement opened up Hoddle to the familiar gathering storm of criticism. He was unfortunate to lose on penalties one of the great England matches – a 1998 World Cup last-16 match against Argentina in St Etienne when a 17-year-old Michael Owen burst on to the scene – but he had few friends in the press when controversy broke.

Journalists – their inflated importance still carrying some sway with the FA's power brokers despite the dwindling sales of newspapers – can make or break an England manager. When it comes to writing about whether a manager stays or goes, it can be a question of whether there are more ticks than crosses in whatever personal relationship exists; a bit like the Peter Cook and Dudley Moore sketch when they debated how you got into Heaven. Hoddle, an aloof, cold fish of a character who often treated correspondents as beneath him, did not have enough of the ticks that came with winning games. He departed after some comments in an interview about the disabled supposedly paying for the sins of a previous life. Something to do with Buddhism, he reckoned.

Next came the chummy Kevin Keegan, quite simply a football man who would bang the drum for England and not bang on about more trivial matters like life and death. Sadly, the footballing methods of the bubble-permed superstar player of the 1970s were a bit too simple. England were appalling at the European Championships of 2000, with even a 1-0 win over an even more appalling Germany unable to paper over the cracks.

When the Germans then came to Wembley in the autumn for the last match at the old stadium, the heavens wept and England slithered to a 1-0 defeat. Keegan, who often wore his heart on his sleeve, admitted he was not up to the job tactically and resigned in the home dressing room toilet.

England, the FA felt, now needed the strong, silent type who would be a tactician, an organiser, rather than just a motivator. Soon, after an astonishing 5-1 win in Munich over the Germans in a return qualifying match for the 2002 World Cup, the nation was in thrall to Sven-Göran Eriksson, England's first overseas manager.

It was reminiscent of the film *Being There*, in which the Peter Sellers character Chauncey Gardiner's quiet air and rare utterances are mistaken for wisdom. Actually, Eriksson came more to resemble Michael Caine in *Alfie*, unable to keep his trousers and platform shoes on. News of his trysts with the former weather girl and fellow Swede Ulrika Jonsson did add to the gaiety of the nation, mind.

Eriksson took England to two World Cup quarter-finals in 2002 and 2006 but we had been told – not least by the FA – that this was a golden generation of players. A quarter-final wasn't good enough. The nation had had enough of Eriksson's indiscretions and dalliances with the Manchester United and Chelsea jobs.

Now, the FA decided, the mood was for continuity and Eriksson's assistant stepped up. Steve McClaren was more of the same, however, too lax and chummy with such players as John Terry and Steven Gerrard, that he called JT – his choice for captain, whom Capello would remove – and Stevie G.

McLaren did try to be tough, as he ditched Eriksson's erstwhile captain Beckham, but England became so insipid under him that he had no choice but to recall the nation's favourite patriot. When we thought we were getting Sven with teeth, we got Sven with whitened teeth. McClaren's injury-hit side lost 3-2 at home to Croatia on a rainy night at Wembley – thus failing to qualify for Euro 2008 – and he became 'the wally with the brolly'.

The next day, as the nation gnashed its teeth again, the FA's chief executive Brian Barwick announced a root and branch review of the ailing English game – that, as the *Sunday Times* sage Brian Glanville once observed, perennially resembles the theatre and the novel: forever in decline.

A few weeks later, Capello was appointed on an astonishing £6 million a year. It was three times the salary of the next highest paid international manager, Marcello Lippi – and he had won the 2006 World Cup for Italy. It was a remarkable coup, the FA insisted. Yet, to many, it always seemed destined for tears before bedtime.

England needed a manager to help a maturing crop of players such as Gerrard and Lampard fulfil their potential in 2010. That manager should also have put in place a much-needed, belated coaching structure that would see a flourishing of younger players who could replace them.

One choice might have been Gerard Houllier, the Anglophile technical director who had done so much to help France win the 1988 World Cup before enjoying five successful years with Liverpool and winning the French title with Olympique Lyonnais. I went to Paris at the time to see him and we had lunch near his home on the edge of the Bois de Boulogne.

Our conversation convinced me that his appointment would have made complete sense, and England would have been getting the best of both worlds. He was a coach who could empower a group of players desperate to fulfil their potential, and who could also instigate a development programme, ensuring that the FA built the National Football Centre near Burton-on-Trent that had been mooted but mothballed for years. 'You need to develop your coaching,' he told me. 'If you want better-trained players, you need better-trained coaches. You need Burton. You need a place where coaches can go, from national to local, to develop a unity of philosophy. It is what we did in France with Clairefontaine in 1988 and the Spanish did with the Ciudad del Futbol outside Madrid in 2003. It is no coincidence both countries became world champions.'

At Burton, strategies could be put in place to bring through young talent. Too many players lauded to the skies at too young an age had fallen to earth, and even many players who had gone on to make the England team had been criticised for their technique. The nation did not know whether it was the coach at fault or the players.

'I would definitely do something with the best young players between the ages of 12 and 15, in terms of their skill levels,' Houllier added, 'but I would need to look more closely at whether that is done on a regional or national level. I would then put in some strong guidelines for academy players between 15 and 19 about how to make a team player. This is very important. There is a huge difference between developing a player and developing a team player.'

Instead the FA went for Capello – a man with no experience of the English game and no feel for its culture, heritage and tradition. He barely spoke the language and appeared to show little interest in how the game might improve or develop in the country beyond his few highly paid years. It looked, at the age of 63, as if he was beating a lucrative path to impending retirement at England's expense, just a gun for hire with little commitment to the country or its players. It also smacked of complacency on the FA's part as they sought to apply a sticking plaster to a gaping wound.

The organisation had grown enormously, like the Premier League, with the advent of Sky and the competition between television networks for live games. The FA had the Challenge Cup and England games to bargain with. For 70 years, it was housed at Lancaster Gate, a rabbit warren of offices in West London, until the new-broom chief executive Adam Crozier, the man who appointed Eriksson, moved it to expensive Soho Square in 2000. There, the number of employees almost doubled to 550 before the move to Wembley in 2009 was made to save costs.

Wembley became a tortuous example of the FA's new vaulting financial ambition under the smooth Scot Crozier. After its closure in 2000, the stadium's replacement was due to be completed in 2003, during which time England games would travel around the country and the FA Cup final be played at Cardiff's Millennium Stadium. Instead, beset by delays and problems over its £800 million cost and funding, bulldozing began finally in 2003 and it was delivered in 2007.

Crozier moved on to the Post Office. An accountant named Mark Palios was brought in to balance the books but left amid scandal when he was revealed to have had an affair with an FA employee by the name of Faria Alam – as had Eriksson, who survived.

Brian Barwick, previously a senior figure with the BBC and ITV sports departments, became the new chief executive in 2005. He was charged with maximising television income and was successful in securing deals that brought turnover of £262 million by 2008. Unfortunately, there was a loss of £40 million on that due to the high interest payments on Wembley. Unfortunately, too, one of the England broadcasters, Setanta, would go bust in 2009, leaving a hole in the FA's finances as recession bit and it struggled to find sponsors.

Almost Barwick's last act was to appoint Capello in haste, leaving England to repent at leisure. A report by Lord Terry Burns in 2005 into FA governance recommended independent directors. The FA only went so far as accepting an independent chairman. However, the Labour peer Lord David Triesman and Barwick struggled to work together, and it was the chief executive who went.

But Triesman was not far behind. After ruffling Premier League feathers during his short tenure, when he declaimed England's biggest clubs for their levels of debt, private indiscretion caught up with him. He was exposed by the *Mail on Sunday* for allegations in a conversation with a female friend about corruption in Russian and Spanish football, England's rivals to host the 2018 World Cup.

By the time of Triesman's resignation, the FA had also lost their latest chief executive. Former civil servant Ian Watmore, appointed by Triesman, plotted the minefield of the game's governance for just nine months. Football, it seemed, was more political than politics – as would be seen when it came to that vote for 2018.

The feeling was growing that English football was becoming the Afghanistan of the world game – beset by factions to the point where it was ungovernable. There was, despite what anyone might have said publicly, a power struggle going on between the Premier League and the FA. The initial alliance of 1992, when it was called the FA Premier League, lasted until 2001. Now it was just the Premier League (having been called the Premiership from 1993–2007), reflecting the overall governing body's loss of influence. Or, as the League preferred it to be known and as an instruction went out to managers to call it in their press conferences, the Barclays Premier League.

The new Conservative-Liberal Democrat government thought it could sort it out, however, and began to mutter about a football regulator. It was an idea floated in the late 1990s when the Tory MP David Mellor was charged by the then New Labour administration with establishing a Football Task Force – a sort of Blair Pitch Project.

As the Premier League had grown in strength and influence, the FA had been forced to cede control of much of the professional game. Instead, it did good, unsung, work with the grassroots of the game by helping with coaching and facilities. Yet most still judged it on the effectiveness of its flagship, the England team. There remained elements within the Premier League, however, who were convinced that it was they who should be running both the FA Cup and the national side.

After a few stuttering friendlies, Capello produced what looked superficially like an impressive qualifying campaign for the 2010 World Cup, sparked by the young Arsenal flyer Theo Walcott's hat-trick in Zagreb as England beat Croatia 4-1. It was deceit by flattery. England's group proved to be a lame one and Capello and his team would be found out in South Africa. It was reminiscent of 2000 and Keegan's England at the European Championships in Holland and Belgium.

When England won that match against Germany in 2000, it was like two tramps arguing over a discarded bag of chips. England also lost to Portugal and Romania, as did the Germans, and went home after the group stages. Crozier insisted that England would not let this happen again. There would be a review into English coaching and a new approach. Once more.

If that review did ever start, it certainly ended a few months later after Keegan's resignation and the appointment of Sven-Göran Eriksson. All would be well. We had David Beckham and in a few years, a wonderkid called Wayne Rooney would come through. The English were failing again to heed the lessons of history, however, and were destined to repeat them. Not so the Germans after Charleroi.

Their federation, the Deutscher Fußball-Bund, went back to their league, the Bundesliga, and agreed a plan for the development of young players through academies. No big deal – Sir Trevor Brooking, we were told, would be working on the same thing with England as director of football development. But the huge difference was that the two parties in Germany had common goals, driven by the acknowledgement that if the national team was successful then so would be the domestic league. Both could prosper. Egos were duly subjected to the greater plan, one to which they adhered even through the dark time of that 5-1 defeat in Munich.

The Germans recovered from that to reach the World Cup final of 2002 and, with an average side before the fruits of the academy system ripened, finished third in their own tournament of 2006. In 2009, their new crop beat England 4-0 in the final of the European Under-21 Championship in Sweden. Then, in the 2010 World Cup, almost half that same team ran riot against England's tarnished group. In the gifted left-footed midfield player Mesut Özil, the Germans included the sort of dazzling flair player with a team ethic that the English struggle to produce – as Houllier had noted.

At tonight's Wembley friendly against Hungary, the public would show their frustration. Still in his job because the FA could not afford to pay him off, Capello was greeted by a mix of lukewarm applause and some boos. Cue the pre-match music being turned up. Louder jeers greeted some of the players. The advance guard of the goalkeepers was spared as they included the new young hope Joe Hart, but not some of the older players.

When the teams were presented before kick-off, it was to three representatives of British forces in Afghanistan – a clever public relations move to quell any revolt in the stands. The thought did occur that the poor trio had surely suffered enough without being forced to go to an England game.

Once the match kicked off, it was the Chelsea pair of Terry and Ashley Cole who were most reviled, but not all of that was due to on-field England matters. Sour at losing the captaincy after an alleged affair with the partner of team-mate Wayne Bridge, Terry, it was suggested, had tried to lead a players' revolt over Capello in South Africa but had received little support. Cole had cheated on his wife, the publicly sainted Cheryl Cole (a singer with the girl band Girls Aloud and *X Factor* judge, m'lud) though we had never heard properly his side of the story nor of Cheryl's foibles.

The jeering lasted only 15 minutes, however, and a banner that read 'Never was so little given by so few for so many' was not held up for long. Capello had given in to public and media pressure and started with a 4-5-1 system, as opposed to his tired 4-4-2, and once England got a corner, applause rang out. Yet muttering returned on the hour when England fell behind to an own goal, and Wayne Rooney was booed when substituted. In South Africa, he had berated England fans on camera for a perceived lack of support. Understandably, fans who had spent their savings on taking in tournaments did not take kindly to such observations. He would take some time to be forgiven. Tonight Rooney looked tempted to flash a gesture but settled for a wave.

Then the yeoman Gerrard – captain in the absence of Ferdinand and one of the few to be cheered – stepped up to score two splendid goals and England escaped another embarrassing, demoralising defeat. Capello remained impassive, as opposed to the frantic, frustrated figure he cut on the touchline in South Africa. It was not impressive, however. Yet again England were playing in straight lines, their movement inflexible, unlike the world champions Spain. Capello had promised all sorts of new young players, such as Arsenal's talented Jack Wilshere, but it was pretty much the usual suspects.

The day before the game, Capello had talked of modern football managers being either monsters or gods depending on the odd result here or there. He had a point and echoed what another England manager, Ron Greenwood, once said about managers getting either too much praise or too much criticism. In the media theatre Capello stumbled through a press conference, his English seemingly having worsened in his two years. God or monster tonight? 'I always have the same name. I always feel the same,' he said. 'I understand you have to write things but for me in the morning, when you shave you look at yourself in the mirror and say, "OK or not OK?", I'm sure what I brought was good. I try to do my job really well. I sometimes make mistakes, sometimes I do well like this evening.'

That raised an eyebrow. And it was clear among the correspondents that much respect for a man who had seemed almost mythically fearsome a couple of years ago had gone. Indeed the mood among the press was almost that he was a laughing stock. Among the players, the word was that the hard man who had earned plaudits after McClaren, for having the players eat together and banning mobile phones at certain times, was now just creating a downbeat atmosphere of tedium. A change in results did that kind of thing.

'All political lives, unless they are cut off in midstream at a happy juncture, end in failure,' said Enoch Powell. The history of the England team showed the same to be true of its managers. Was it fair that so much blame attached itself to them when they were so frequently the victim of circumstances?

Capello himself was soon sucked into the overseas-player argument and paucity of selection choices, which was superficially convincing. After all, Spain had won the World Cup and 77 per cent of players in La Liga were qualified for the national team. In the Premier

League, just under 40 per cent were English. On the opening weekend of the competition for the 2010/11 season, just 91 out of 220 starting players were qualified for England – considerably fewer, too, than in Germany where the percentage was 55.

So much for one of the original aims of the Premier League being to aid the England team. Then again, training and playing with the cream of overseas players was supposed to improve the quality of the elite native players. Besides, when Graham Taylor's team failed to qualify for the 1994 World Cup, more than 90 per cent of players in the Premier League were domestically reared. In 1992, in fact, there were just 11 foreign players in the competition. We should remember, though, that many of the rest were from Ireland, Scotland and Wales.

Capello's choices were dwindling and the situation was worsening with each England manager. Conflict with club managers had also grown. They were not as disposed to the England team as in days gone by when there were fewer fixtures and their playing assets were less valuable. What could he do beyond what any bloke on the terraces could do when faced with such problems?

Actually, a great deal. Given the limitations of the job, recruiting the right man was essential, even if the appointment came with less prestige and respect than once it had. The nation still had enough quality to find a squad of 23 decent players for a World Cup, and the right football brain should be able to organise them in a formation that would bring the best from them. He should also have been able to give them different inspiration away from their clubs so that they did their talents justice. It was why our old friend Harry Redknapp was being touted as a successor. For all his baggage, spotting a player, assembling a team and getting it to perform was what he did best.

Any full-time England manager would also have to oversee the national coaching centre finally being built at Burton and take an interest in the development of young players. Beyond watching games at weekends and having the odd English lesson at his FA desk, it was hard to see what else Capello did with his working week.

The game's governing bodies needed to find common ground, and back up any England manager with the creation of a system to close the gap between expectation and achievement. If they couldn't necessarily help, the FA and the Premier League had at least to stop hindering and cease their conflicts. Rather than be suspicious of Sir Trevor Brooking and keep the FA at arm's length when it came to their academies, the League needed to allow free access and agree standards and aims. Brooking, in turn, also had to recognise that there was good practice already at some of these academies.

Just as the national team needed bright young things, so the administration needed new thinking. We were not holding our breath, however. Post-World Cup, the FA was rudderless without a chief executive and full-time chairman, the acting chairman Roger Burden not wanting the latter post. They did have Sir Dave Richards as chairman of what was now being called Club England (presumably so we could have club v. Club disputes rather than club v. country) and also chairman of the Premier League.

It should have ensured co-operation but instead the charge was of vested interests, with Richards' probity called into question by many. His latest controversy was in being accused by Fulham of intervening in a transfer deal that sent Peter Crouch from Portsmouth to Tottenham instead of them, so as to get more money for strapped Pompey. Eventually, Richards would stand down as chairman of Club England but it would take some months more.

After the World Cup, I spoke to Richard Caborn, sports minister in the previous Labour government and Sheffield United supporter. It was clear he would have put himself forward to be FA chairman and had much to contribute to the national debate. 'The FA has to become a governing body with credibility and influence,' he said. 'It has to assert its authority and bang a few heads together. And it needs to change its mode of governance. It has had four England managers and five chief executives in the last decade and needs some stability. I believe there is a mood for change but I would have to have a clear indication that all parties in English football are willing to change now. The Premier League have been working to keep the FA weak but I think they are acknowledging that something has to be done.'

Naturally he was too combative and challenging for the bigwigs at the FA and Premier League and they went on to elect some months later a safe pair of hands in David Bernstein, a former chairman of Manchester City. It was another opportunity missed when diplomacy of the gunboat variety was more the requirement.

'I wouldn't mind Richard,' one more enlightened member of the FA's international committee told me that night of England's friendly against Hungary as I ran into him on the way into Wembley. He also believed that Capello should have gone after the World Cup. I wondered why he hadn't. 'Money,' came the answer. Capello had two years – about £12 million – left on his contract. I felt sure, I said, that they could do a deal with him for £6 million to spare him further embarrassment and punishment and then get in a better, more reasonably priced man for around £2 million a year, thus saving £2 million over those two years. 'The FA,' the committee member replied, 'is not that clever.'

The answers were not simple, nor clear-cut. But it did need, as a start, vision and experience in the game's administration, a system of coaching and development that was unafraid to learn from elsewhere in the world, and a manager who cared about the future of the nation's talent rather than just his pension plan – along with players who wanted to improve and play for the national team rather than being intimidated by it.

The material was not promising, though, and you were reminded of the motorist who asked for directions in rural Ireland and received the answer: 'If I were you, sir, I wouldn't start from here.'

Hosting the 2018 World Cup was certainly not the answer. Despite the involvement of Lord Triesmann and the experienced David Dein, and the wheeling out of a supposedly winning trio in Prince William, Prime Minister David Cameron and David Beckham, England polled just two votes. One of those was from their own representative on FIFA's board, Geoff Thompson. Russia was awarded the tournament. Eighteen million quid and England were losers again. There may have been some questionable practices within FIFA, antagonised by allegations that proved to have substance in the English media about its probity, but it was clear that once-respected English football was lowly regarded these days.

Now the coalition government, piqued by Cameron's embarrassment in Zurich, would put a tin lid on a miserable year for the FA by announcing, in the shape of the new sports minister Hugh Robertson, that there would be a select committee set up by the Department for Culture, Media and Sport to investigate the governance of the game. It would include looking into the workings of the Premier League, said Robertson, but at the FA, David Bernstein and Alex Horne, the new low-key general secretary (the title presumably so that if he left, he wouldn't add to the list of ex-chief executives), knew that this was really about their organisation. 'If you look across sport, it is very clear to me that football is the worst governed sport in this country, without a shadow of a doubt,' said Robertson. 'The levels of corporate governance that apply to football lag far behind other sports, and other sports are by no means beacons in this regard.'

You wondered quite what Robertson based this immediate view on and how much he actually knew about football, but this was an open goal. There were few willing to defend the FA after its refusal to countenance the major change recommended by Burns and its presiding over the mess that was the England team, despite the fortunes that had been thrown at it.

One Irish rugby commentator once said that the state of his nation's sport was always desperate but never serious, whereas with English rugby it was always serious but never desperate. The same has also seemed to apply to football for many years. As I wandered towards Wembley Park tube station late that night, however, I did wonder whether things were now both desperate and serious. Everything had changed at Wembley, but within it, sadly, chance after chance missed, nothing had.

Chapter 4

OVER TO WEMBLEY

I WAS RELUCTANT to ring up the chairman of Wembley Football Club, Brian Gumm. The last time I had visited them, 20 years ago, I ventured in print that rather than the Venue of Legends – the national stadium's advertising slogan at the time – this ground, just two and a half miles away, was more the Venue of Fag Ends. Word got back to me that Mr Gumm was not amused.

Fortunately, he is not a man to hold grudges. I phoned one Sunday morning to ask if I could come and meet him at their bank holiday home game the next day. 'No problem,' he said between heavy breaths, which did lead me to wonder what he might be up to. 'I'm in the middle of cleaning the dressing rooms,' he explained.

I was, I said, surprised to find him still at the club. It was rare when there was so much turnover in the game, especially among chairmen, who can grow disillusioned by the demands of managers and players or be forced out when their money has gone. 'Still here. Still going strong,' he chimed.

I had wanted to return to the club for an FA Cup tie but they had already fallen at this August's first hurdle by losing 3-0 at Witham Town in one of 201 ties in the extra preliminary round. Wembley to Wembley and all that. Life and football are not quite that accommodating, however.

It was for an FA Cup tie that I had visited previously – Wembley lost 2-1 to Windsor and Eton – just as Gumm had taken over the club.

He was just 37 then with longish, dark hair and I recalled him, in jacket and tie, scuttling all over the ground, keeping on top of match day organisation. He was still developing his feeling for the club then. For his was not a story of buying a club scenting an investment opportunity or even for having some fun. It was of an Englishman protecting his castle.

Gumm lived – still did – just across a park from Wembley's ground at Vale Farm Sports Centre but he had had little interest in them or football, save for watching out for Chelsea's results. Then it emerged that Brent Council were planning to put a travellers' site on the car park next to the park and the football ground. Gumm, a successful, straight-talking builder who ducked out of school at 12 and evaded borstal because his older brother told the courts he had emigrated to Australia, was elected chairman of a residents' group to oppose the plans. 'They chose me because I was a bit rough and ready and I spoke these gypsies' language, I suppose,' he said when we met again these two decades on. His hair was now grey and short, his features craggy, his complexion bearing witness to an outdoor life. The suit was gone in favour of more casual, open-necked, clothing.

Gumm spent fortunes and endured all sorts of threats in taking the case to a government ombudsman, he said. In the end, he won the case, though, and was now proud that the travellers' leader, admiring his fighting spirit, shook him by the hand where once he had wanted to shake him by the throat.

Gumm threw a party in the car park and got to know the committee members from Wembley Football Club, who were naturally grateful to him for keeping their property from being invaded. They were even more grateful to him when he twice dipped into his pocket to help them pay off some debts.

The third time they asked him for money, he decided that he wanted to know where it was going. He started to go to committee meetings. They made him chairman but his involvement only became really hands-on when the committee sacked a manager without consulting him. 'I thought, "I'm not having that,"' Gumm recalled now, as we sat in his small office sipping pre-match tea. 'I said, "Am I chairman or do you just want to borrow another 10 or 15 grand?" I told them I would take over their debts, about 100 grand's worth, and we could start again. I had that kind of money then. My company was working on hotels and it was a good company. Work was plentiful and I didn't drink or gamble.'

His initial experiences were unhappy. He parted company with manager Alan Dafforn over differences of opinion about the budget. Dafforn, he said, wanted a new striker for £200 a week while Gumm wanted a kid by the name of Giuliano Grazioli to be given a chance after scoring plenty of goals in the reserves. Dafforn didn't think the kid was ready, but after going to Barnet as a scout, he soon had Grazioli at nearby Underhill. The player went on to have a good career in the lower leagues and Conference with Stevenage, even scoring for them in an FA Cup tie against Newcastle United.

Then, in the summer of 1992, the main stand at Wembley burned down and had to be rebuilt. 'Most probably it was kids,' said Gumm. 'Some people said we did it ourselves for the insurance money but the stand was wooden and we couldn't get insurance for it. With labour and everything, a new one cost us about £60,000.

'When I first came in I was as stupid as any other silly chairman you could think of,' he added. 'The players were your best mates, you have got money in your pocket and people were patting you on the shoulder saying, "Good old Brian". What a load of bullshit. I was silly as arseholes. That is not the case now.' You believed him – and you sensed a back story of conflicts within the club where he had emerged on top.

Much else had changed, evident in the drive from Wembley Stadium to Wembley FC. For a start, pound shops and Primark were now prevalent in the High Road where, on this bank holiday, the only shops open were those fruit and veg outlets and hardware stores run by the large Asian and African communities in the area.

Having parked at Vale Farm Sports Centre – 'affordable leisure for the whole community' – the 100-yard stroll to the ground took me past the new offices of Sudbury Primary Care Centre and a children's play area and nursery, Partyman World of Play and Twizzle Tops Day Nursery. The latter buildings were owned by the club and leased out to provide a small income. They were derelict the last time I was here, so something had changed for the better. But an Indian restaurant that was also on club premises went bust in its first year, leaving Wembley FC short of £40,000 rental over five years.

Once, the London rugby union club Wasps used to play on an adjacent ground but moved in 1996 to Loftus Road, home of Queens Park Rangers FC, when rugby turned professional, before relocating to Adams Park, home of Wycombe Wanderers. Wasps' old clubhouse was now a Hindu community centre.

A narrow road led alongside some allotments into the football club, where atop a pillar stood a stone lion – symbol of the club since their formation in 1946 when some locals thought that the place that housed the national stadium ought to have a club of that name.

The bar and boardroom had been refurbished but still told the club's history. There remained a signed picture of the England team training there during the 1966 World Cup, 'presented by Mr Alf Ramsey' and beautiful framed old cotton shirts from all the home nations, along with West Germany. There was still, too, a framed newspaper cutting of the day that the flamboyant, innovative Malcolm Allison joined Wembley to take his first steps in management before going on to make Manchester City the champions of England in 1968.

Alongside was a new glass cabinet containing memorabilia from Hendon Football Club, telling of their proud winning of the old

FA Amateur Cup and an FA Cup tie against Newcastle United. For Gumm had done a deal to ground-share with itinerant Hendon, who lost their own ground in 2008, evicted by owners who wanted it for development, and had struggled to soldier on in the Isthmian League.

Wembley also laboured to stay in the Isthmian but Gumm gave up the fight when non-League football was reorganised in 2005 to consolidate the best clubs from Isthmian, Southern and Northern Premier Leagues into Conference South and North. 'There were far more financial regulations,' said Gumm. 'You had to run it like a business instead of a football club, you had to start accounting for all the money and it got too much. My own business was always run properly and above board but to be truthful, I don't think you could run a football club in that day and age without robbing Peter to pay Paul. One month you would try to pay the brewery but if a utility bill came in and they were threatening to cut you off, you paid that. They all got paid in the end.

'We survived but the football went downhill because we had to meet all the ground gradings which were very strict. We couldn't afford to go any higher at that time because we weren't paying wages to players, just expenses. So what do you want? A football club going forward or going nowhere?'

And so they dropped into the Combined Counties League, a collection of small clubs from the London suburbs including AFC Wimbledon, who joined the competition after starting from scratch when the Football League allowed MK Dons to be formed from the old club.

Today, Wembley were at home to Raynes Park Vale from South London in what was an early season bottom-of-the-table contest. The turnstiles were new, all chrome, but the sign above them announcing the club's function rooms, bar and social club was peeling and bore an old 0181 telephone number, the outer London code which was replaced by 0208 in 2000. A hoarding told of the Sun Life of Canada, which was fined £600,000 for pension mis-selling in 1998 before withdrawing from Britain in 2001, only to return in 2009. Like flares, it was back in fashion, it seemed. It just went to prove that it could pay to hold on to your old clothes.

Chris Etherington had. The genial turnstile man and general club factotum was still wearing a replica Wembley shirt from around 20 years ago, all red and white zigzags. These days, it would be described as vintage. Then, as with many jazzy, crazy designs of the time, it just looked like a video on the blink.

Wembley's shirts were now more sedate, as throughout football, thankfully, with plainer designs unlikely to detract from sponsors' messages in these highly commercial times. Their livery resembled the Dutch side Ajax, though inverted with a broad white band on the front of the red shirt. Some shirts had the logo of the sponsors Dial-A-Cab, some did not.

The teams ran out to just a smattering of applause. Chris had not been busy on the gate. There were only 24 paying adults at £6 a head (plus one non-paying, who was watching it from the top of the children's slide at Partyman World of Play) and 10 children and senior citizens at £3 each. That was a grand total of 34, yielding revenue of £174.

Among them was a quartet of groundhoppers, strange creatures, usually single men of 30 upwards, who probably still lived in their mum's back bedroom. They travelled the country notching up grounds they had visited. You could tell them by their conversation as they discussed road works and train timetables and the quality of match day programmes, which they kept pristine in polythene bags.

'Crowds are poor because the team is poor,' said Gumm without frills as he made his way to the directors' box of sorts where there were some plastic chairs under cover, though he preferred to watch the game standing next to the dugouts. It was no wonder, given the gate money, that the players were not being paid. 'I'm talking with them about some expenses, though,' said Gumm. 'It's not fair really because they're training on Tuesdays and Thursdays and playing Saturdays and not even getting any petrol money.'

Clearly they were on a starvation diet. Apart from the time-honoured corpulent goalkeeper, Wembley's players were distinctly thinner than Raynes Park's. There was also the fattest linesman you had ever seen. The ground was neat and trim, the rebuilt stand containing 300 seats in a ground with a capacity of 3,000 looking well kept. Through the trees could be spotted the arch of the national stadium.

Boards dotted around proclaimed Hendon FC and Wembley FC side by side. As for advertising hoardings, you wondered why they all told of Flora and BUPA and Vittel until you remembered that a director of Hendon was David Bedford. Bedford, the shaggy haired and moustachioed former British 10,000 metres record holder – who once successfully sued the 118 118 directory enquiries company for pinching his image in their advertisements – was director of the London Marathon. 'He's a straight guy like me,' said Gumm. 'I don't think Hendon would be here without him.'

Hendon even had their own club shop, in a Portakabin next to a tea bar that was selling egg and bacon rolls this morning for a bargain £1.20. You worried about the toilets being adjacent but they were luxurious for this level, all tiled and with a big mirror. There was even a Tesco anti-bacterial handwash.

It was a decent game. Striker Kobi Osei put Wembley into a two-goal lead but it was wiped out just before half-time. Then a minute before the interval, defender Antoine Djerrou rose to meet a corner from player/manager Ian Bates and Wembley led again. 'It's exciting isn't it, Dad?' said a small boy, showing that you don't have to take kids to the Premier League. They could still have fun at their local club.

'Yes, and there's more goals in this game,' replied Dad. But fathers are not always right, you come to learn. Wembley fought a rearguard action and held on for 3-2, heeding the exhortations of an old man instructing them to tighten themselves up and not stand around like statues.

Gumm was left pleased with his three points as he sought to keep the club in the Premier Division until times picked up. Not that there were any signs of it. In fact, he reckoned times were getting distinctly harder. The Premier League, you ventured, was supposed to inject money into the game that would trickle down through it and thus improve everybody's lot. Had he not found that?

'Not at all. It's got worse,' he lamented. 'I don't feel the powers that be feel they need non-League clubs like us any more. Things are just dying. The game's all about money and we are just a burden to the game. There are grants available from the Football Foundation but you need a degree these days to fill in the forms. We put in new floodlights at a cost of £80,000 but they would only give us 50 per cent when some people get 70 or 80 per cent. After about four months of me moaning, they gave us another five per cent just to shut me up, I think.

'As for grants from Brent Council, we have got no chance, even though we are the largest club in the borough and we help improve things for local youth. All their grants go to other social and ethnic groups and it's gone in a year before they are back for more.'

Any benefits of being close to English football's seat of power had also disappeared, according to Gumm. 'We used to have England training here but that stopped years ago,' he said. 'The last international team we had was Poland three or four years ago. And in the old days, the big clubs like Chelsea and QPR used to come here for friendlies or the Middlesex Senior Cup. Now, if they do come, they send a team of kids who don't draw a crowd.'

Wembley's last appearance at Wembley was in 1988 for the Middlesex Senior Cup final when Russell Grant, TV astrologer and dedicated to keeping the county's name alive, campaigned to have the final there. 'And I don't think we'll ever play there again,' said Gumm, though the chairman had personally made a couple of visits.

'I phoned them up when the old stadium was coming down and said, "We are your local football club. Any chance of having some of your old gear?" They said to come over and we liked an old carpet with "Welcome to Wembley" on it and a physio's table but they wanted £400 for the carpet and £3,000 for the table. They wouldn't let us have them for nothing. We did have their chief executive Brian Barwick down for an FA Cup tie just before he resigned and he was shocked we'd never been invited to the stadium so he left me two tickets for an England game.'

Wembley still received phone calls from people trying to get through to the stadium. 'The last England game we couldn't get any work done, the phone was going all the time. I tried to get 118 118 to sort it out. We could have earned a fortune taking people's pin numbers. I could have been a millionaire.'

As it is, he had, he said, put in 'a quarter of a million easy' down the years to keep Wembley going – quite apart from the time he has invested – and that it had taken 10 years off his life. Then again, perhaps it had put years on his life, given football's capacity to keep grown men at this child's game, to keep them energised.

And he did embody the love–hate dilemma of anyone involved in football, where no matter how gloomy a picture he painted, he revelled in its maddening appeal. As someone once told me: 'When you're in the game, you want to be out of it. When you're out of it, you want to be in it.'

'It's what you get out of it, isn't it?' said Gumm. 'I am fortunate that I can do the pitch and all the groundwork because I have time on my hands. This club doesn't owe a penny to anybody. I set myself five years to achieve that but it took me a lot longer. In the early days, I was as green as grass but those days are long gone. If I had done it straightaway, Wembley wouldn't have been struggling now.'

The club was treading water, he admitted, but one part of being a fan and chairman would never leave him: there was always next week, always next season. 'I might start paying wages again after this season,' he said. 'We might have a right good go next year.'

AUTUMN

Chapter 5

THE GOONERS SHOW

JUST 15 MILES or so around North London from Wembley, from Jubilee to Piccadilly Line, is the tube station of Cockfosters. I used to feel about it the way I did when finding a smashing little hotel that none of the upmarket Sunday newspapers had reviewed yet.

To explain . . . Years ago, it used to be relatively easy to park around Arsenal's atmospheric art deco Highbury ground with its four distinct, two-tiered stands in a valley of North London. There were side streets and a system of double-parking on nearby Drayton Park, out of which chaos a yellow-jacketed steward or two somehow brought order. Then came all the residents' parking bays, with Islington council needing to augment their income and able to charge large sums to the nouveau riche who had moved into what became in the 1990s an up-and-coming area. Even then, you could still find little schools or churches that had parking space and charged only a few quid.

But, in 2006, the club's new stadium arrived, a four-tiered bowl that dominated the view towards Central London from Highgate Hill a few miles away. On a much larger site at nearby Ashburton Grove, its £357 million cost was part-financed by selling off Highbury for apartments. Parking became tighter as crowds increased from the old ground's 36,000 to the 60,000 of the new venue, now billed as the Emirates due to the Middle East airline paying £100 million for 15 years of naming rights. It meant that more people were having the same idea and joining those who had never wanted to drive in anyway. London Underground it had to be.

For anyone arriving from north of London, as plenty of Arsenal's support did, Cockfosters at the end of the Piccadilly Line in Hertfordshire was the smart access point. Its copious car park cost just £1 and it was only 10 stops, the first few of them overground, to Holloway Road station. That delivered you to the side of the stadium for the box office and press entrance. For those who wanted the other side, there was still Arsenal station, which the legendary and visionary Gunners' manager of the 1930s, Herbert Chapman, had persuaded London Transport to rename from Gillespie Road back in 1932.

That was all very well until more people cottoned on to Cockfosters, to be joined by supporters of northern clubs, who now arrived in their droves off the nearby M1 and M25 for their games at Arsenal. Curse them. Fans of rival clubs even started swapping travel info on their respective internet message boards. Now anyone wanting to make it into the car park had to get there ridiculously early. So, dear reader, we should now keep it to ourselves.

Tonight, three hours before kick-off, it was already filling up even though there were no away fans to be seen. Arsenal were playing the Portuguese side Braga in the Champions League and it appeared that few from the Iberian peninsula had made it through the roadworks round the western side of the M25 from Heathrow to junction 24 for Potters Bar and Cockfosters. Then again, many with better local knowledge sometimes failed to make it through that Bermuda Triangle of roadworks which always seemed to have signs saying they would be finished in three years' time.

It was funny. The older I was getting, the earlier I set out for games. I used to poke fun at my mum for hoarding plastic carrier bags under the sink 'just in case' they might be needed. Now I left home ludicrously early 'just in case'. Of traffic. Of a panther on the tracks at Southgate. Family ridicule seemed worth enduring for those triumphant moments of finding a space just before the car park was full, of hearing on the radio about delays once beyond them. For a lifetime of experiences of football breeds savviness. Those who are early at Holloway Road beat the crowds and the crush for the lifts, thus avoiding having to schlep up the 139 steps.

Besides, it was also no great hardship spending a couple of hours before the game in the new, vast media lounge at the Emirates, with its comfortable furniture and spacious work stations. And excellent food: tonight, sea bass and teriyaki, to be followed by Ben and Jerry's ice cream. (A vegetarian option was also available along with cold meats, salads and fruit.) By popular consent among the press – one of the few things that the *Daily Mail* and the *Guardian*, for example, would agree upon – Arsenal provided the best fare of all English clubs, all served by happy, helpful staff.

There were times, indeed, when, due to attend a Saturday match, I had been tempted to ask if I could book in on a Friday night, with just a little egg, bacon and coffee and the newspapers on a Saturday morning, thus avoiding Cockfosters with its mile-long tailback and the angst of wondering if the car park would be full by the time you got there.

Arsenal also serving up the best fare on the pitch these days made much effort worthwhile. For some time now, Manchester United had been the most rounded of teams, combining style with steel, and Chelsea the most powerful, but Arsenal had been the most artistic. If any neutral could have picked a venue for a season ticket, it would surely have been here. By general consent, they passed and moved with a fluency unrivalled in the English game.

The whole package was largely down to one man, certainly on the field and probably off it as well. His building of a successful team enabled the club's board to attract the money needed to build the club and stadium, into whose design he also had an input, if not quite as much as he had had in the modernisation of the training ground.

Arsène Wenger arrived at Arsenal in 1997 to succeed the hapless Bruce Rioch, whose upright demeanour and disciplinarian streak, gained from his father's military background, ought to have suited the Gunners (or Gooners, as the vernacular had it) but instead rubbed the players up the wrong way. They were used to George Graham, winner of eight trophies but who had been forced to quit after being found to have received a 'bung' from an agent in the transfer of two Scandinavian players.

Graham insisted on strict standards of organisation on the field, not least in building a back four of a defence whose ability to catch opponents offside was immortalised in the film *The Full Monty* as an example to the cast's male strippers of synchronised forward movement. Off it, though, he gave the players latitude to enjoy the drinking culture present in the game in the early 1990s. He was an adherent of the old Bill Shankly principle that you had better treat players like men as you were going to have to ask them to play like men. Arsenal duly did, taking on the powerhouses of the north like Liverpool and Manchester United and matching them physically. Many of them could also drink for England.

Wenger, a masterpiece of recruitment by the Arsenal vice-chairman David Dein, that prime mover of the Premier League, was seen as professorial and scientific, with his studious look and immediate changing of the players' regime to a healthier diet that precluded alcohol. No more fish and chips on a Friday night and sausage sandwiches on Saturday morning for the captain Tony Adams, whose recovery from alcoholism coincided with Wenger's arrival.

With his large round glasses – prompting the nickname of 'Windows' among the English players – Wenger also gave off an unworldly air. Once, not long after joining the club, Arsenal were playing at Crystal Palace when the floodlights failed during the warm-up, though rumour said that there might be an explosive in the ground. The team trooped back to the dressing room, where Wenger was surprised to see them return as he prepared himself to come out for kick-off. He wondered what was wrong. 'There is a berm,' said Ray Parlour in his best Inspector Clouseau impersonation. 'A berm?' said Wenger. Cue team collapsing in fits of laughter.

Wenger was born in the Alsace region of France, near the German border. There was attention to detail in all he did, using statistics to formulate strategy, but he also liked his football to have an attacking swagger and spontaneity. In producing the potent blend, he imported World Cup-winning countrymen such as Patrick Vieira, Thierry Henry and Robert Pires. They accompanied his fortunate defensive inheritance of David Seaman, Lee Dixon, the totemic Adams, Steve Bould and Nigel Winterburn as well as the sublimely inventive Dutchman Dennis Bergkamp, signed by Rioch.

Very quickly, the English players accepted Wenger's methods. They could see that their careers might be extended by a couple of years and this could mean an extra few million pounds to them. As well as silverware. In his first full season, Wenger led them to the Double of Premier League and FA Cup. In the next eight years, another five trophies were accrued. His 2003/04 team even went a league season unbeaten in winning the title and so emulated Preston North End's feat of 1888, though the achievement actually eclipsed theirs given that those Invincibles played only 26 games compared to Arsenal's 38.

Then, however, the Arsenal board of directors, which included the wonderfully named Sir Chips Keswick and Lady Nina Bracewell-Smith, decided on a change of strategy that triggered concern among fans and a power struggle within the club. Wenger wanted the training ground at London Colney in Hertfordshire reappointed to take in all the latest facilities, including injury rehabilitation pools, weight rooms and indoor pitches. (And such a control freak is Wenger, that he was said to be always first to arrive on cold, dark winter mornings to turn on the lights and ensure that the heating was the right temperature for when the players arrived.)

That completed, the board also wanted a stadium with a much bigger capacity to bring in the revenue that would enable them to compete longer-term with Manchester United. They were a good mix at the time, it seemed. The chairman Peter Hill-Wood, Lady Nina and Sir Chips may have sounded like throwbacks who embodied Arsenal's traditional virtues but they were forward looking too, along with modern businessmen such as Dein and the influential Danny Fiszman, a diamond dealer.

It meant borrowing £470 million for the project, to include buying up land and small businesses around the site on top of the building costs. Paying it back would mean putting a brake on investment in Wenger's squad. Players would have to be developed rather than bought. Now there came conflict among the board. Dein wanted to encourage new investors so that competing for trophies was not put on hold due to construction costs. He was all for encouraging the American Stan Kroenke and Russian Alisher Usmanov, who were buying up shares to give them a stake in a club that would soon be making huge profits.

The board did not agree, however, with Hill-Wood even declaring when it came to Kroenke that they did not want 'that sort of person'. Dein became the first casualty of a change in dynamic at the club, to general surprise. Despite being thought central to Arsenal as a bosom buddy of Wenger, he was clinically cut adrift.

Dein's worry was that Arsenal were falling behind the big clubs of Europe, borne out by Wenger's teams now failing to win trophies after the FA Cup of 2005. The board were not to be rushed, however, and Dein found himself isolated and forced to walk in 2007. As revenge and consolation, he aligned himself to Usmanov, selling his 14.5 per cent share in the club for a cool £75 million.

A year later, Lady Nina also fell out with the board, believed to be over the appointment of the American Ivan Gatzidis as chief executive, and left. The board had all entered into a 'lockdown' agreement not to sell their shares but now she put her 16 per cent shareholding up for sale. Neither Usmanov nor Kroenke, though, were yet ready to build up their stake to the 30 per cent threshold for triggering a full takeover.

Against this background of uncertainty in the running of the club, the fans were growing impatient. They continued to love Wenger for the football he offered them but some began to doubt the 'Arsène Knows' banner usually visible in the crowd. Why had he failed to buy a better goalkeeper than Manuel Almunia? Why was he so parsimonious with the club's money, with £50 million now said to be available after four years of increased revenue from the Emirates and the easily serviced debt halving to £200 million? Why was he buying from Tesco when they should be able to afford Waitrose?

Defenders such as Laurent Koscielny and Sebastian Squillaci looked decent, if frail for the English game at this stage, but totalled only £12 million, while striker Marouane Chamakh came on a free transfer from Bordeaux. It was part of Wenger's policy of not spending beyond the club's means, even if the board might have wanted him to appease supporters further. With the hauteur of an old French aristocrat, the manager had a distaste for the spending habits of first Chelsea and now Manchester City when it was not money earned but the cash of sugar daddies.

He was a firm believer in clubs not spending more than they took in – 'financial doping', he called it – and thus a backer of his compatriot, Michel Platini, now president of UEFA, who had instigated new financial 'fair play' rules being adopted for the 2012/13 season. The rules meant that owners could not simply make loans to clubs to underwrite losses but had to invest as equity and were limited in how much they could advance. The idea was to make clubs sustainable in the long term to replace the chasing of short-term success.

At least Wenger had held on to his talisman Cesc Fabregas, a World Cup-winner with Spain that summer of 2010, after which he had spent his holiday agonising over a move to his beloved home-town club of Barcelona. Fabregas was the shining star of Wenger's night sky. The manager had spent the last five years nurturing young players and was not about to change course. Trust me, was his message. He was, after all, the most successful manager in Arsenal's history, overtaking both Chapman and Graham.

It was some history, too, as evidenced by film shown just before the teams walked out at the Emirates to the strains of Elvis's *The Wonder of You*. There were the old Chapman teams of the 1930s in black and white, with shirts tinged red thanks to modern technology; there was Charlie George scoring the FA Cup final goal against Liverpool that gave Arsenal the first leg of the Double in 1971; there was Michael Thomas pinching the 'it's up for grabs now' title-winning goal at Liverpool in 1989 (the last time, incidentally, that the title had been decided on goal difference despite the annual importance that seemed to be placed on it). Then there were the legends, great goals by Bergkamp, Henry and Adams. And Bob Wilson's voice emoting: 'You were wearing this gun on your chest and, my goodness, everywhere you went you felt proud to be wearing it.'

Wilson's back, with his goalkeeper's No. 1 on it, could be seen on a giant mural outside the stadium, linking arms with Bergkamp. It was one of eight that enveloped the Emirates, featuring 32 of the club's top players in a massive huddle embracing the arena. It was all part of what the club was describing as the 'Arsenalisation' of their newish home, which might otherwise simply be another modern bowl lacking individualism – the curse of latter-day stadium design. Another feature was the restoration of the huge clock that used to be such a trademark of Highbury.

Putting the clock back was one of the reasons I had come to watch this particular Champions League game, even though it featured one of Portugal's lesser lights in Braga. Neither was the Emirates particularly attracted by them, it seemed: the previous Saturday at a game against Wolverhampton Wanderers, the tannoy man had advised, unusually, that tickets were still available. And though the gate would later be given as 59,333, it was clear that this included season ticket holders who had not shown up.

The English usually supported the early games in the Champions League as no other nation but the worrying signs for UEFA were growing. Tickets were now easier to come by as fans hit by recession were getting bored by this early group-stage sparring that featured some of the lesser lights of the European game rather than the major club names. It all seemed designed simply to spin money and fill television time ahead of the serious stuff of the knockout stages after Christmas, and fans were seeing through the expansion of the competition.

When English teams returned to European competition in 1991 after the six-year ban following the Heysel disaster, Arsenal were champions of the old First Division and thus accorded a place in what was then still known as the European Cup, or the Champions' Cup officially. At the time, it was England's only place, as opposed to the four that would gradually evolve over the next 10 years with the competition developing into the Champions League as TV demands grew. It would mean also, among many other spin-offs, that the results that used to take up a page in the *Rothmans Football Yearbook* now occupied 15 pages in its successor, produced by the omnipresent Sky Sports.

That year of 1991, the tournament featured leagues for the first time. After two qualifying rounds, eight teams would be divided, with the winners of each group going on to the final, which was to be at Wembley that season (as it would be 20 years later). Having beaten FK Austria comprehensively on aggregate in the first round and drawn 1-1 in the away leg of their second round in Lisbon against the celebrated Benfica, Arsenal were favourites to reach the lucrative league, with its guaranteed three home games and financial windfall.

In the event, they were beaten 3-1 by a cannier side more versed in the sort of contain-and-counter football that wins in Europe. George Graham's Arsenal huffed and puffed but lacked the subtlety to unlock the Portuguese when the scores were level and they conceded twice on the break in extra time.

It would spark a debate that was dormant when English clubs were winning six European Cups in a row in the 1980s through Liverpool, Nottingham Forest and Aston Villa. Resurrected, the debate centred on not just how far the exile from Europe had set back the English game, but also whether its more direct, less technical style was outmoded. 'I had experienced the international game with England but never European club football,' Tony Adams recalled when I asked him for his memories of the Benfica game. 'Their technique was better and the game was different, with more counter-attacking and keeping the ball. The referee also handled the game differently, more strictly.

'I think we learned quickly, though,' he added. 'Within three years we won the European Cup-Winners' Cup.' Indeed they did, but it was based on that absorbent defence and pinching a goal on the break to bring them the tag of boring Arsenal. I remember a banner at an away game of theirs in Europe: 'One life, one love, one club, one-nil.'

Wenger changed all that with his progressive methods and quicker, slicker style of football, though it would be Manchester United in 1999 who would be the first English club to become European Champions since the ending of the ban. That year, they played 11 games to win the trophy compared to the nine of their 1968 triumph and the 13 nowadays.

United's victory would herald a resurgence by English clubs that would see Liverpool win the tournament for the fifth time in 2005 and United again, for a third time, in 2008, as part of a run that had an English club in the final for four consecutive seasons. By now, though, the clubs were stacked with overseas talent and the debate about the quality of the English player had shifted to the national team.

For all Wenger's prowess in Europe – qualifying for the Champions League 11 years consecutively – none of his teams had ever won it, though they came close in 2006 when they led Barcelona 1-0 in the final in Paris before succumbing 2-1. Indeed the criticism of Wenger's teams now was that they needed a bit more of the George Graham grit.

Not that any would be needed tonight as they again encountered Portuguese opposition 20 years on. The teams' differences were marked. Braga's history told of them being the Arsenal of Iberia, with an expat having introduced them to those red shirts with white sleeves and giving them their nickname of 'Arsenalistas', but they were a lame, overawed team that bore no resemblance to the one that had overcome Celtic and Seville in qualifying rounds. They confirmed that Portuguese teams, in the Premier League era anyway, did not enjoy travelling to England. None, indeed, had won in the country since Benfica at Highbury.

Quick and slick on a rain-moistened pitch – which didn't stop Wenger having it watered until 10 minutes before kick-off, as he liked a fast surface – Arsenal were ahead within seven minutes. Fabregas, wearing a beard and suddenly looking like a man, stroked home a penalty, though it took them another 22 minutes to double the lead, prompting a glimpse of that supporter impatience when the mutterings began.

One criticism levelled at Premier League stadiums now was that their all-seated areas and increased capacity had brought them new, 'gentrified' audiences – the sort who called it 'footy' – as the game reached out beyond its working-class roots towards the more moneyed. It was more evident than anywhere else at Arsenal, where the clientele of Islington wine bars sometimes seemed to outnumber the regulars from the old spit-and-sawdust pubs on the Holloway Road.

There certainly seemed to be fewer of that bloke down the caff in *Fever Pitch* who impressed on a young Nick Hornby that Arsenal were 'fucking useless last year, fucking useless this year and they'll be fucking useless next year.' While you were unlikely to get many observations like that these days, however, elements of the old moaners remained. 'Come on, liven up,' shouted someone with Arsenal only a goal up as the half-hour approached.

The Russian Andrey Arshavin's goal shut the bloke up before a neat little backheel by the left-footed 18-year-old Jack Wilshere – an outrageously promising product of the academy – created the chance for Chamakh to make it three.

A fourth arrived with Fabregas adding his second to gild the lily of his flowery performance. 'Get him off, he's rubbish,' shouted a WIC (the old football writer's standby of Wag In Crowd – usually another journalist in the press box but, on this occasion, a proper supporter). Instead it was Chamakh who was substituted. So long Marouane, as Leonard Cohen almost sang. His replacement, the Mexican Carlos Vela, added two more goals to make it a 6-0 rout.

By then the crowd had dwindled to fewer than 20,000. Despite the virtuosity on show, taken for granted by many these days, most were eager to beat the rush. Leaving any later would mean a long walk to the Victoria Line stations of Finsbury Park or Highbury and Islington as the smaller Arsenal and Holloway Road stations would be shut by the police until an hour after the final whistle to avoid potential crowding.

Those left in the ground urged each other to 'stand up if you hate Tottenham'. Another constant.

Wenger was a contented man that night when he arrived to talk to the press in the media theatre, the backdrop these days a board of Euro sponsors plainly visible on television: beers, credit card companies, computer game manufacturers and car manufacturers. 'The way we played the game was the way we wanted to play the game,' said Wenger. 'That was to play at a high pace with a lot of quality and good attitude and good collective spirit. It is the philosophy of our game.'

There was praise for Fabregas and for Wilshere, one of the few Englishmen to enjoy Wenger's confidence. In his 13 years as manager, Wenger had always seemed to have a mistrust of them after the retirement of those he had inherited. It was as if he did not believe them to be as hungry as the imports from Africa, as dedicated as those he brought in from France nor as talented as South Americans.

Indeed, he had only ever signed six English players in (note the names for quiz question purposes) Richard Wright, Sol Campbell, Matthew Upson, Francis Jeffers, Jermaine Pennant and Theo Walcott, with only Campbell having been a real success and the jury out on Walcott. We were still waiting to see whether he was more than a flying winger and if he possessed a footballing brain. Wenger hadn't expected Wilshere to come through so early, he said, 'but football teaches you to be open minded.'

As ever, there was a caveat as the question came in whether Arsenal were physically and mentally strong enough to win the tournament. 'We are in the top eight in the rankings year in, year out,' he said, his English – good before he came to the club – now having grasped its nuances and colloquialisms. 'But as long as we have not won it, people will question the way we play. I believe you win the Champions League with quality.'

This was Wenger at his most civilised and communicative. When in the mood, his Friday press briefings were the most entertaining and informative in the game. You could ask him about any issue and receive a forceful and intelligent view rather than mere platitudes. I have been tempted on down days to ask him the meaning of life.

Would he sleep well tonight, he was asked. 'I will have the Sunderland game on my mind,' he said with a smile. Knowing him, he would be up at his home in leafy Totteridge, not far from Cockfosters, watching games from all over the world on his multi-channel television system, his family long since asleep.

He would indeed be plotting the forthcoming weekend's Sunderland game, though it would not turn out as expected, with Arsenal conceding a late equaliser to reveal their soft side. Wenger revealed his curmudgeonly one too and would be banned for one match by the FA for pushing the fourth official. It illustrated the frustration that seemed to come over him every autumn when he began to have doubts about his side, having been so optimistic in the summer. His body language began to mirror Basil Fawlty, regressing into a childlike ball, beating his clapped-out car with a twig or wringing his hands in frustration when Sybil discovered he had been gambling.

'Now he has joined the nutters. In fact he is one of the key nutters,' said Harry Redknapp of a man who seemed so at peace in his early days in the English game, as might be expected from someone who had come from Japanese football with Grampus 8 of Nagoya and had absorbed Zen Buddhism. Now he was the Nutty Professor. Wenger would also come down further off his pedestal when it was revealed a few weeks later that he had been carrying on an affair with an 'exotic dancer' in Paris, she blowing the whistle to an accommodating English press when he sought to end it. As part of a miserable period for him, Arsenal also somehow contrived to lose the return match in Braga 2-0.

It all echoed what the former England and West Ham manager Ron Greenwood once said of those in his profession: in the end, it gets to us all. Still, unable yet to give up this mistress of football, Wenger would soon be signing a new contract that would take him to 2014 and almost to his 64th birthday. Would they still love him, would they still need him? He had to win something beyond plaudits and admiration in the near future.

The way Arsenal played, the Champions League always seemed to offer the best bet, though they had been unfortunate the previous season to be drawn against a magnificent Barcelona side. Even Barca were beaten, however, by the cannily crafted Internazionale team of Jose Mourinho, who disposed of the Catalans in the semi-final and Bayern Munich in the final.

In total, it earned the Milan side a breathtaking €48.75 million – £41.5 million – for their Champions League campaign. Such were the riches on offer in the competition, it was no wonder that such a fuss was made these days in the Premier League about finishing fourth, even if it was, in pure sporting terms, a sideshow. Just for qualifying, there was €7.1 million (£6 million) with the equivalent of £680,000 for a win in the group matches and £340,000 for a draw. Reaching the last 16 brought an extra £2.55 million, the semi-finals £3.4 million more.

The problem for the English game had become that it was in danger of creating a self-perpetuating elite, with the same few big clubs qualifying each year, able to afford to buy up the best players and thus continue the cycle. Wenger and Platini may have had a point about financial fair play but there still had to be room for a club wanting to invest to break the cartel.

The old concept of the European Cup being contested by the champions of each country in a knockout competition was long gone. The Champions League may be a misnomer but there was no going back to the former format no matter how much traditionalists pined for it. There was simply too much money washing around. The most likely change would be to benefit the big clubs even further with there being a risk that the main names in England, and their counterparts in the most profitable European television markets of Spain, Italy, France and Germany, would break away to form a European Super League.

Now that there were signs of people losing their appetite for the early stages of the Champions League, a move to form a league of, say, 16 of the most glamorous clubs would surely be tried sooner rather than later. It would give 30 midweek dates, home and away, and surely prove more of an attraction than, say, Braga. Everyone knew anyway that by and large the bigger clubs were going to make it out of the group stages to the last 16.

The probability, though, was that those bigger clubs would need two teams, one for domestic competition and one for European. The discernible desire among supporters was still for internal weekend competition in most nations alongside meaningful, rather than mournful, European nights. That was certainly evident in England with a depth of professional football, from Arsenal down, not matched anywhere in the world.

Chapter 6

DONS AND MASTODONS

In the 1991/92 season in the old First Division, Luton Town beat Arsenal 1-0 at home with their rugged old England centre forward Mick Harford scoring the winning goal. How different the paths of the two clubs had been since then. Arsenal, all elegance and class matched by their home venue, now bestrode a world stage, moving like haughty Afghan hounds. Luton were yapping dogs desperate to be heard in their own scruffy backyards.

From the lofty peak of the top flight, Luton became another morality tale of football and its finances, falling all the way through the Football League to gain the dubious distinction of being the first FA Cup finalists to slip into the Conference, the fifth tier of the English game. There they discovered a club who had been FA Cup winners in another existence, AFC Wimbledon having been formed in response to the League shamefully allowing the previous bearer of the London suburb's name to move to Milton Keynes and become MK Dons. Now on the way up, AFC had met the Hatters on the way down and the two were coming together in an early season promotion contest.

For the non-League game, the Conference was its version of the Premier League. There were the big, traditional names with fan bases to match, such as Luton, Wrexham, York City and Grimsby Town. Then the medium-sized, more usually associated with the level, in Kettering, Barrow and Bath City. Below that came those who made it through for a season or two but fell back when the revenue from

their smaller support found them out, among them Forest Green
Rovers from Gloucestershire and Histon, a village on the outskirts
of Cambridge.

There was usually, too, a club being bankrolled by wealthy
backers. This season, it would be Crawley Town, recently taken
over by two local business people but with, they said, backing from
investors in Hong Kong too. Boggling the mind at this level, they
had paid some £500,000 for new players in the summer, including a
Conference record £275,000 for the York striker Richard Brodie. It
was all the more surprising given that many in the competition were
reining in. Most clubs were now full-time, but some were having
second thoughts.

In addition, just as there was a gulf in earnings in the Premier
League, where Yaya Toure was earning £200,000 a week at Manchester City and Charlie Adam £10,000 at Blackpool, so it was in the
Conference. Brodie was believed to be on £2,000 while some players
at Hayes and Yeading – average crowd a few hundred – received £100
a week.

The mix arrived as a result of the reorganisation of football's
pyramid. It was 1987 when automatic promotion to the Football
League for the Conference champions was first, finally agreed and
2003 when a second place for the play-off winners was introduced.
That meant, correspondingly, that two were relegated from the League
each season.

Thus did the Conference now have several former lower-division
stalwarts such as Mansfield Town and Darlington, while the lower
divisions of the Football League contained some less traditional
names who had risen with money and momentum, before hitting
a glass ceiling and rebounding. Kidderminster Harriers and the
Northamptonshire club of Rushden and Diamonds, manufactured
by the Doc Martens footwear founder Max Griggs before he sold the

club in 2005, sprang to mind. Dagenham and Redbridge, along with Stevenage, might be joining them in the near future, you suspected. The differences between League Two and the Conference were more blurred than ever. More Conference clubs could beat their supposed betters in a one-off cup game but more League Two clubs would still come out on top over the course of a season due to stronger squads assembled with more sponsorship and TV money.

At its inception, the Conference was meant as a national competition for the semi-professional elite like Altrincham and Worcester City who had outgrown their regional confines, not League cornerstones like Luton. Nor towns and grounds as big, even if Luton's home was a relic. For despite all the grandiose plans for new stadiums, even a dome, at various junctions of the M1 through its Bedfordshire stretch down the years, the club remained rooted at antiquated Kenilworth Road, hemmed in by terraced streets. The ground had gradually been converted to seats but its shell told still of how it used to be when men finished at the factory – perhaps making the hats that gave the club its nickname – at midday on a Saturday, enjoyed a couple of pints and a pie and walked to the match.

The surrounding Bury Park area had remained predominantly Asian these past 20 years, though despite the best efforts of Luton – as at many clubs – the abutting community was still the great untapped market of the English game. You might have seen four men in turbans on the front row in television pictures from Manchester United but they were rare season ticket holders.

'The town has gone through many changes,' the veteran Labour MP for Luton North, Kelvin Hopkins, told me. 'We have always had large waves of immigrants. In the 1930s, people would walk from Wales and hitchhike from Scotland. Then came people from the West Indies and East Africa, after that the Asians, mainly from Pakistan, Kashmir and Bangladesh. Now there are more Africans.'

The reason, quite simply, was jobs. In the boom of 1973, Hopkins pointed out, there were 38,000 people employed in the car industry through Vauxhall and General Motors. 'People would come to the town, get the promise of a job at Vauxhall and go and rent a room on the strength of that. The sons and daughters are still here but there are only 2,000 employed in the industry now.'

The descendants of the Scots, Welsh and Irish still went to the football, he agreed, but not enough of the Asian community. 'We have a big black community too, but not enough from that go to games either. You do see more at the big clubs, and it is good to see them in a mixed group of friends. I hope that could happen more at Luton.

'I know the club has made overtures for youngsters from the black and Asian communities to come in,' added Hopkins. 'And it's not true that the Asian youngsters don't like their football. You see them around Luton in parks putting down their jumpers for goalposts like we used to. We also have a really enthusiastic local character in Butch Fazal who runs the Luton United club.'

There was, though, an undercurrent of apprehension, according to Hopkins. This was not surprising in the town where the new right-wing English Defence League (EDL) which had staged heavily policed demonstrations was based, to the concern of locals. 'I think there is a discomfort going to an event where it is almost an all-white audience,' said Hopkins. 'Five or 10 years ago, white racists were prominent and even though there might still be a small number of EDL, the overwhelming majority have nothing to do with them.

'But that feeling may still be about in the Asian community. There is a gap between perception and reality. It only needs a few racists in to put people off. Football is about going with your mates and it starts when two go together. If white, black and Asian friends start going together, then it will take off. I hope that players of Asian origin come through in a few years and that the community will support them.'

That community, many from generations of immigrants from the Kashmiri city of Kotli, according to Hopkins, was certainly on the football club's doorstep. In one corner by Luton's main reception, next to a bridge over the Hatters Way bypass, there was a mosque and community centre. Near here, too, was the Bury Park Islamic Centre where Taimour Al-Abdaly studied, the suicide bomber of Stockholm this autumn of 2010, before he was ostracised from the centre for his extremist views. Down on the Dunstable Road, meanwhile, just past the UK headquarters of COGIC (Church of God In Calvary) in the old cinema and past all the Asian textile and kebab shops, was the Nadeem Shopping Plaza.

At the Oak Road end, for visiting fans, there were turnstiles still between the terraced houses that even bridged the pay stations. At the other end of the ground, the entrance to what was now called the Kenilworth Stand still had a row of turnstiles ahead of the turnstiles, a legacy of the mid-1980s. In 1986, following the riot involving Luton and Millwall fans the previous year, the then club chairman David Evans MP was a lone slave to Margaret Thatcher's wishes in introducing identity cards for home supporters and imposing, for what would last five years, a ban on away fans. It held, too, with some strict policing, even if a few visitors did sometimes make it into home areas, usually keeping quiet to avoid ejection.

Linking the two ends, an alley still ran alongside the back of the old Bobbers Stand, so called because it used to cost a shilling to stand there back in 1905 when it was erected. It all added up to a picture of a club – the first fully professional in Southern England, back in 1890 – left behind by the modern game. Luton Town, in fact, felt like the club that football forgot.

The demise had almost mirrored the local car industry and loss of jobs but Kelvin Hopkins MP for one believed it was less to do with local economics or changing demographics and more to do with the management of the club for at least a decade.

Luton were certainly one of the most unfortunate in the modern history of the English structure. For back in 1990, when they were in the old First Division, they voted for the new Premier League before doing the most damaging thing imaginable: they contrived to get themselves relegated the season before the competition began. This time, there was no last-day reprieve of the sort that saw the then manager David Pleat memorably gambolling across Manchester City's old Maine Road pitch in beige suit and loafers in 1983. (Loafers which would raise £4,000 at a charity auction in 2010, indeed.)

Luton had never been back to the top flight since. That was 20 years without any Premier League money. During that time the club spent plenty trying to return, mind. Even as recently as 2006, when they reached fifth in the Championship, they were paying sums they didn't have. It caught up with them and by 2007, a series of chairmen had grown weary of putting in or borrowing the money and Luton were relegated to League One.

I caught up with them later that season, in January 2008, when they were drawn at home to Liverpool – who always used to hate coming to Kenilworth Road in the 1980s when a little-lamented synthetic pitch was another of David Evans' bright ideas – in the third round of the FA Cup. That was the good news. The bad was that Luton had gone into administration and looked like being relegated to the bottom division of the Football League, thanks to a 10-point deduction.

'This club has rested on its laurels too much, allowed too many people to pass them by,' said the manager at the time, Kevin Blackwell, who grew up on the Luton terraces and recalled being passed down to the front in the late 1960s when the powerful England striker Malcolm Macdonald was banging in the goals. 'It's just been stuck in a time-warp,' added Blackwell, a chirpy character who had lost his chirp.

'I wasn't surprised by the level of debt', said the administrator Brendan Guilfoyle – yes, the same man who would go on to sort out

Portsmouth, then Crystal Palace, having already been in to Leeds when the hapless Blackwell had been manager there a couple of seasons previously. 'At £4 million, with £2.5 million of that due to the Inland Revenue, it was very low when you compare clubs like Coventry and Leeds,' added Guilfoyle. 'But I was surprised by the losses of £3 million to £4 million every year and the wage bill of £3.6 million.'

Also that day I spoke to Nick Owen, former breakfast TV host with Anne Diamond and now a news anchor for the BBC's regional show in Birmingham. It was a curious experience sitting down with someone whom your mum once described as 'dishy'. Owen had the ultimate accolade for any fan of having a lounge named after him, just like the comedian Eric Morecambe, Luton's most famous and loved fan, who did so much in the 1970s to give the club some affectionate publicity. Owen grew up in the Hertfordshire town of Berkhamsted, about a dozen miles from Luton, and was first taken to Kenilworth Road by his father. His first game, he remembered, was at home to Leeds in 1958. It had been a 6 p.m. kick off to fit the match in before darkness fell, he remembered, because the floodlights were so poor. 'So much so,' he said, 'that when we had a big Cup replay a couple of years later against Manchester City, they refused to play at night so it had to take place in the afternoon.' It was the tie where Denis Law scored six on the Saturday and it was abandoned 20 minutes from time, with City winning 6-2, he recalled. 'Law scored again in the replayed match but Luton won 3-1 this time, so he scored seven goals but ended up on the losing side.'

His earliest memories were of walking into the ground 'and having my breath taken away. I know that it's not the most glamorous sporting venue but to me as an excited youngster it was utterly magnificent.' Anyone who has ever supported their local, unglamorous team would surely recognise that feeling.

Owen remembered England internationals Ron Baynham and Syd Owen, who became the Footballer of the Year in 1958/59. 'Those guys were gods to me,' he said, remembering too the top scorer Gordon Turner and Northern Irish international Billy Bingham. 'They reached the FA Cup final that year but I was unable to go to Wembley because I was away at boarding school.'

His best moment? 'We've had quite a few but winning the Littlewoods Cup in April 1988 against Arsenal has to be the very tops. We had a fabulous team – Mick Harford, Brian Stein, Ricky Hill, Steve Foster, Mal Donaghy . . . It was a cracking game too. Andy Dibble saved a penalty which could have put us 3-2 down but we came back to win 3-2 with virtually the last kick of the game. A truly wonderful day.'

Soon after an FA Cup game against Liverpool in 2008 – won excitingly 5-3 by the Premier League club – Owen would be proudly taking over as chairman of the club. Guilfoyle found buyers, a consortium of local fans and businessmen with access to funds, and Owen was asked to be its public face. 'I was flattered to be asked,' he said. 'I had to consult with the BBC about taking the position because being a newsman plus a football club chairman, particularly in controversial circumstances, could be a compromising position. I think it went pretty high up at the BBC before I was given the go-ahead.'

It was somewhat of a bitter-sweet position, however. The previous chairman David Pinkney, businessman and part-time racing driver, had arrived with great ambition and promises of the new stadium that the club so badly needed; had always needed it seemed, according to Owen, who could remember as a boy reading a headline in the *Evening Standard* saying 'Luton Town to build country's best stadium'. But Pinkney found the financial mess too much for him, notably in a £3.8 million lawsuit from Mike Newell, a manager sacked by a previous regime, and the club went into administration yet again.

Next, Luton were hit by more than 50 FA charges relating to transfer dealings under that previous regime, led by chairman Bill

Tomlins and chief executive John Mitchell. The punishment would be drastic, the FA imposing a 10-point deduction and the Football League adding 20 more for Luton being serial financial basket cases. Relegation to the Conference was inevitable. When I spoke to Owen again, he recalled starting the 2008/09 season with a 30-point penalty as the worst moment of his time supporting the club. 'The sense of injustice, cruel and vindictive as it seemed, was overwhelming,' he said. 'The powers that be said they were preserving the integrity of the game but did it really do that? Did it have to be so severe? It was described as the harshest penalty any club had suffered in Europe. The 20 points for the third administration I can understand but why a further 10 from the FA for a technicality?

'We had apparently paid a handful of agents about £160,000 in total through our holding company and not the football club. Nothing illegal, no bungs, no corruption. Could the 10 points not have been suspended? Could not the FA have talked about this with the League? Minus 20 would have given us a chance, albeit slim, but minus 30 was a killer. Equally grim was dropping out of the Football League. And the people who suffered were totally innocent of any misdemeanours – the new owners, the club staff, the players and of course the supporters. Devastating.'

When relegated, all clubs considered big by Conference standards seem to think they are going to bounce straight back until they realise how physical and competitive a lot of the football is at that level. Luton's demanding fans thought it too but in their first season, the club finished runners-up to Stevenage and were thus consigned to the play-offs. It proved an unhappy experience and ugly scenes returned to Kenilworth Road as Luton were eliminated by York. Home fans invaded the pitch, forcing visiting players to take refuge in the back of the Oak Road end before they could reach the dressing rooms with police help.

It was nasty but nowhere near as serious as that 1985 riot involving Millwall fans that attracted the interest of government. Indeed, in many ways it reflected the difference in the gravity of hooliganism over 20 years. Once it had been the central issue of the English game; now it existed only seriously in pockets and without the extremes of confrontation and violence of the 1980s and early 1990s.

These days, trouble within grounds is rare due to the widespread use of closed circuit television that enables police, who now had their own offices and boxes within professional grounds, to identify miscreants and prosecute. It came at a cost to clubs, who had to pay expensive bills for officers inside though not outside, but more organised police methods certainly made watching the game safer.

The foolish did occasionally still fancy their chances inside stadiums, as with a League Cup tie between West Ham and Millwall in 2009 when a man was stabbed outside Upton Park, but condemnation is quick and widespread these days. At its worst in previous eras, violence was considered barely worthy of comment. There was also a school of thought back in those days that it should not be reported, so as to deny its shameless exhibitionists the publicity they craved.

There was anecdotal evidence to suggest that hooliganism still occurred between rival factions but away from grounds so as to avoid police interest. As a spectator, it was usually easy to avoid if you were not looking for it and not interested in the internet websites where opposing 'firms' would organise their confrontations. It was as it should have been: private business between like-minded hooligans, leaving the rest of us to get on with the primary business of football.

Tonight, on this September Friday five months on, trouble was never likely. Indeed, there was optimism in the air, along with planes taking off from LA – Luton Airport. Luton were also back *on* the air, with the game against AFC Wimbledon being televised. A new satellite station called Premier Sports had done a deal with the Conference (now sponsored by the betting company Blue Square, in another sign of the times) following the collapse some 15 months earlier of the Irish-owned station Setanta, which was back in its recession-ravaged homeland with tail between legs.

There was a spruceness to a ground that may have been an anachronism to most but was still too good for the Conference. The glossy programme – 'Blue Square Premier Programme of the Year 2009/10', it told us – recalled 125 years of 'history, pride, passion' from 1885 to 2010 and the front cover had a picture of old heroes such as Kerry Dixon and David Preece. Inside was a feature on the innovative David Pleat, who had created that fluent side of the mid-1980s. When times are hard and your situation sad, football fans have a knack of regressing to their club's history, the nostalgia that comforts them, when defenders never made mistakes and strikers took every goal chance.

Luton were among those ridiculed in the 1970s for being in the vanguard of executive boxes – with *Foul* magazine, a *Private Eye* of the terraces at the time, even offering a cash prize to any player smashing the Perspex frontage – but they had become de rigueur now. These in the Bobbers Stand had hardly changed and still looked like old gas showrooms, but they were far superior to any facilities of the smaller clubs in the league like Eastbourne Borough. At Eastbourne's Priory Lane ground, basic single-tiered stands told of a history in the Sussex League, the club's rise cannily financed by an indoor bowls centre, well used by the local market of retirees. Tonight, 18 of Luton's 28 boxes looked to be occupied. The clock at the end of the stand was even working, which it had not been on my last visit. It was surely a sign that the club was less impoverished.

Luton's orange shirts were a good match for easyJet, the budget airline based at the nearby holiday airport, and thus a good sponsorship fit, as huge touchline hoardings illustrated. There was even a board for the University of Bedfordshire, one of those faux new unis which had grown out of the Luton College of Further Education. That in turn became Luton University, where the aforementioned bomber Taimour Al-Abdaly had been doing a degree in sports therapy.

The pitch was immaculate after being relaid in the summer. It was a far cry from those ludicrous days when David Evans incurred the ridicule of the game – and how the governing bodies agreed, heaven knows – by installing that plastic pitch, which made for a distorted, bouncy, game.

'It's a big night tonight. Let's hear it for Luton Town,' screamed the public address announcer, which seemed poignant when you recalled that the ground had hosted the likes of Manchester United, Chelsea and Arsenal, as well as Liverpool. Still, it was a top-of-the-table match. The old money of private ownership gone to waste was up against the very model of a modern club who embraced fan ownership in the shape of a supporters' trust organisation. Capitalism v. socialism. (Not quite the best billing to a game that I have seen, mind. That came at the 1982 World Cup finals in Spain, when Scotland fans brandished a banner for the match against the Soviet Union proclaiming: Communism v. Alcoholism.)

AFC Wimbledon may have been one of the game's newer names but there was great tradition behind them. A Southern League club until 1977, winners of the FA Amateur Cup, Wimbledon were elected as champions to the Football League on the back of some remarkable FA Cup results, notably a 1-0 win at Burnley and a draw against then mighty Leeds at Elland Road. Suddenly, London SW19 was famous for something other than tennis.

Under Dave Bassett's vibrant management, and the colourful ownership of the Lebanese Sam Hammam, they proceeded to move up through the divisions. Then, with the ebullient Bobby Gould inheriting the side, they won the FA Cup in 1988 by beating Liverpool at Wembley – having beaten Luton at Tottenham's White Hart Lane ground in the semi-final.

Following the Taylor Report, the Dons moved to Crystal Palace to share Selhurst Park, not having the money to update their Plough Lane home. Eventually, Hammam grew tired of low attendances and wrangling with the London Borough of Merton about coming home. Opportunely, fortuitously, he sold a decaying outfit to a Norwegian concern for £26 million in 1997. They, too, struggled to make a go of it, however.

Then in League One, it seemed the club might die around the turn of the Millennium, or so those who wanted to move the club elsewhere declared. Actually, other groups might have been able to take on and restructure the club to retain its South London roots. In 2002, an entrepreneur based in Milton Keynes called Pete Winkleman, who had been trying for years to entice a Football League club – including Luton – somehow got the FA and League to agree to him relocating the club 61 miles north of Wimbledon. MK Dons began playing at a hockey stadium, which summed up the whole soulless episode.

Football was appalled. The franchise system of moving clubs where the money is may work in the United States, and may enrage locals there but square with their free-market ideals, but it conflicts seriously with the community ethos of English football. MK Dons indeed. Some would never forgive.

A new Wimbledon club was formed in 2002. Among the founders was Kris Stewart, who too became an early chairman, and had been a supporter since the club reached the old First Division in 1986. He remembered the day he heard of the move to the Buckinghamshire town of concrete cows, whose new grammatically challenged stadium:mk would become more colloquially known as the Moo Camp as a twist on Barcelona's Nou Camp. 'It's hard to describe how horrible it was when we heard they were stealing our club, even though we were sort of expecting it,' Stewart told me. 'You can kid yourself in these situations that you've prepared for the worst but when the worst happens, it still hurts like fuck. That's where the "a pessimist is never disappointed" thing falls down for me. I was very close to tears. I was a bit late to work that morning.'

After hastily arranging trials on Wimbledon Common, AFC's first match was a friendly at Sutton where they drew a crowd of 4,657. 'We got smashed up 4-0 but we were all so happy it didn't matter,' Stewart recalled. The first win came against Bromley, the winning goal scored by one Glenn Mulcaire. The *News of the World* reported the match at the time by crowing that Mulcaire worked for the paper's 'special investigation unit'. He would be jailed in 2007 for his role in tapping the phones of the rich and famous, which was exposed as going on at the Sunday newspaper.

Starting in the Combined Counties League that embraced Wembley FC, Wimbledon gradually worked their way through the non-League pyramid, winning four promotions in seven seasons and at one point going 78 games without defeat, the longest unbeaten record in English senior football. Their superior crowds facilitated a bigger wage bill than any other club at the various levels.

The club's administrative body was formed as 'The Dons Trust' under the auspices of Supporters Direct, an organisation suggested by the Labour government's Football Taskforce and set up in 2000 to help fans participate in their clubs, or run them where appropriate. The model was the Industrial and Provident Society set up by Northampton Town supporters in 1992 to rescue their ailing club after its meteoric rise to the old First Division in the 1960s was followed by its falling star of a decline back to the Fourth Division in the 1970s and 1980s.

Wimbledon's Trust – one of 10 in non-League football controlling their club, along with two in the League at Brentford and Exeter City –

committed itself to retaining a 75 per cent shareholding, though it did sell off a stake in order to help finance the buying of the Kingsmeadow ground they shared with Kingstonian FC for £3 million.

Following promotion from Conference South in 2009, they enjoyed a promising first season, finishing eighth, and now came to Luton as leaders under an astute manager in Terry Brown, who had led Aldershot from their own non-League rebirth back into the Football League after falling out of it 1992.

Tonight, though, you could only agree with the Luton fans in the Kenilworth End who sang 'Top of the League? You're having a laugh.'

Playing the vogue 4-3-3 – but badly, as they became stretched, with their defence lying deep and becoming exposed – Wimbledon should have gone behind after just seven minutes when Matthew Barnes-Homer hit the post with an overhead kick. No matter. Midway through the first half, George Pilkington headed home Andy Drury's corner, and before half-time Zdenek Kroca doubled Luton's lead with another header.

'E-i-e-i-e-i-o, up the Football League we go,' sang the Luton fans in the healthy crowd of 7,283. There were some black faces among them if not Asian, but mostly they looked to be the descendants of white grandparents who moved out of these town streets to suburban semis long ago but who came back to support the club handed down through the family.

Meanwhile, the confined press room, all but deserted before the game where once it heaved, served welcome tea and sandwiches at half-time. Brian Stein, scorer of those two goals at Wembley in the Littlewoods Cup final against Arsenal, was here doing some scouting and regaling the local press with tittle-tattle dressing room tales of the good old days.

Within three minutes of the restart, Barnes-Homer had driven home Luton's third from the edge of the penalty area and Wimbledon were already well beaten. It might have been even more had Luton not effectively declared.

'Go into attack mode, Luton,' shouted a fan with outdated charm during the lull of the last half-hour. 'It's the best form of defence.' It almost conjured a vision of Eric Morecambe smiling and puffing on his pipe, something that would never be allowed now in the wooden main stand post-Bradford. The 3-0 defeat was a rude awakening from the early season reverie for Wimbledon. Terry Brown was even grateful. 'It would have been an absolute nightmare if we had won,' he said. 'Supporters would have been saying, "Well, here we go". We couldn't cope with Luton's direct approach and we have got to be stronger. Can we go to York on a freezing cold midweek? Probably not. It is all very well playing nice football but what you need is a mixture to get out of this league and we haven't got it right yet.

'But we are a work in progress. I am in a lovely position as the manager as I have been given time to mould the team. We are trying to build, like Dario Gradi did with Wimbledon when they were in the Southern League. At the moment, we have a non-League ground which holds 4,000 and we are averaging 3,300. We could go up to League Two, and even League One. Dagenham and Redbridge have shown what you can do.

'Long term, we need to get back to SW19 if we can and it is down to the council to make that happen. We have to get some revenue streams or we will hit a ceiling. People talk about a benefactor with £1 million to come in but do you want that to happen? You lose your club if you are not careful. We have turned down rich people saying they will take this on board and drive it. That's not what it is about. It's about proving a fans' club can work.'

Luton, taken on by a group of fans though not Trust-run, were happy tonight, but would turn again in a few weeks after a home defeat by Crawley, who did have those benefactors. Almost perversely then, to show how fickle the game was at this level, Wimbledon would beat Crawley in a week's time, despite their annual playing budget of £400,000 being around one third of Crawley's. It would be the start of another Dons unbeaten run and refute tonight's evidence of over-achievement.

For now, the Luton manager Richard Money – his name better suited to Crawley, perhaps – was safe despite the machinations inside a deeply political club. Results were quelling the noisy message board of the Luton Outlaws, whose members were muttering about the club already beginning to run up new debts as they sought to rise through the divisions again.

'I hate the politics which seem to be present all the time but that is the price you have to pay when you're involved with an institution which arouses such intense passion,' said Nick Owen. 'But I'm happy in the knowledge that all of us involved in running or backing the club are doing it for one thing only – the good of Luton Town FC.'

The game in general, he agreed, got him down, too, these days. 'English football today is not the game I grew up to love. Money is such a defining part of it. It has become far less compelling at the top level for me than it was. The big have got so much bigger. The divide is cavernous and it is simply less interesting.

'The players and officials seem remote from the ordinary fan. The soul of the game seems to have been blown away. It was far more enticing to think that any one of about 10 to 15 clubs could win the League. I find the lower divisions far more interesting. Perhaps the world's financial meltdown will correct things a bit.' Perhaps, he added, a club producing and developing its own young players was the answer.

Owen was clearly desperate to see Luton escape from the embarrassment of the Conference up into those lower divisions, which may be ignored by Premier League fans but remained appealing, even exotic, to the non-League. Not that the Hatters' fans saw themselves as non-League. They were just out on loan to it.

'Yes, there has been a dramatic decline,' Owen mused. 'I find it very sad and wonder what our great players from the past make of it all. I have seen loads of promotions and many relegations so I am hardened to highs and disappointment to some extent, but it still hurts. I do feel angry with past regimes at times, yes. Our latest situation could definitely have been avoided.'

He still rued the previous owner turning down financial help from the people who eventually took over the club. 'That one dismal decision cost us our place in the Football League,' Owen lamented. 'Now we need a ground with much better access, much better parking, much better facilities, greater crowd capacity and the ability to make money up to seven days a week.

'We have a good location and catchment area, with all the smaller towns around us. We are just off the M1, 30 miles from London with an airport and rail links. So many people tell me they would come to watch Luton if they could park, see properly and be comfortable. We have to do something. Who knows what we can achieve? Even now, it is not impossible to rise up the divisions to Championship level.'

Luton were not alone in sinking so low but at least they had avoided going out of business, the fate that befell Accrington Stanley in 1966 when they were unable to compete any more after the demise of the maximum wage for players six years earlier. With so much competition around them in the bigger Lancashire towns of Blackburn and Burnley, it seemed they would never be a force again, but after reforming in 1968, they finally made it back into the Football League from the Conference in 2006.

Accrington's story had been inspiration for many after them, including Terry Brown's Aldershot, as communities would not let their football club die after demises caused by changing circumstances and bad management. More recently there had also been Maidstone United, Halifax Town and Chester City, all reformed in new guises and seeking to work their way back up through regional leagues, as Wimbledon had been doing.

All – embodied in Nick Owen and Luton Town, Kris Stewart and Wimbledon – clung to that addictive spirit, the dream, belief and optimism keeping those involved in football hanging on in the present in the hope of a future that their past insists could be so wonderful. The metaphor often used is of a phoenix rising from the ashes. There was a place central to the modern history of English football, though, where that analogy was actually rather more literal.

Chapter 7
THE UNFORGETTABLE FIRE

NO ONE COULD know it at the time, but it was the beginning of the end of probably the most brutal decade in English football. In fact, none of us even knew how serious it was. As news filtered through, we even joked – shamefully, in hindsight – that the chairman had probably torched the grandstand on the last day of the season to claim the insurance money for a new one. Very quickly, though, we knew the gravity of the events at Bradford City's Valley Parade ground on 11 May 1985. There can be no levity when 56 people lose their lives in fire and smoke and 258 more require treatment for serious burns. Realising that this was a touchstone moment for the English game would take a little longer.

Not that much longer, though. The shock that spread from the old wool mill centre across the nation, throughout the world indeed, had barely abated when, a mere 18 days later, 39 fans, mostly Italian, lost their lives in the crumbling Brussels stadium named the Heysel ahead of the Liverpool v. Juventus European Cup final. The English game was confirmed as the outcast of Europe, its stadiums antiquated, its followers barbarians. In the words of letter writers to newspapers (in those days before internet message boards): something must be done.

Sir Oliver Popplewell was commissioned to investigate the Bradford fire, which was started by a match or cigarette end dropped onto rubbish that had accumulated under the wooden main stand, and his report insisted on new safety standards for grounds. Timber edifices had to be replaced, said Sir Oliver; stewards had to be more plentiful and better trained. There should be closed circuit television to monitor crowds.

Then after Heysel, UEFA banned English clubs from European competition until it was deemed that their followers had civilised themselves. It was six years before the governing body decided that the English had made acceptable progress, with the Hillsborough disaster of 1989 postponing the process. Ninety-six Liverpool fans died when crushed against fences at Sheffield Wednesday's notorious Leppings Lane end. When the truth emerged later, it was clear that this was nothing to do with hooliganism and everything to do with stadium inadequacies and a botched police operation. Now the admirable Lord Justice Taylor surpassed Popplewell's attempt to rehabilitate English football by insisting on stadium rebuilding to encompass all-seaters over the next decade.

Yes, Hillsborough was the rock bottom for the national game and Gazza's tears the beginning of a recovery that would stir the founders of the Premier League, but Valley Parade started the process. As perhaps the real beginning of modern football, it deserved to be acknowledged in any journey. I wanted to remember the event with some of those who were involved and to pay some respects. Bradford now found themselves in League Two – to which Luton and Wimbledon were aspiring – and I wanted to see how or if the club had transformed with the changes that the fire had provoked.

As the 25th anniversary of the fire approached – to be marked by a gathering around the memorial in Centenary Square and a service in the cathedral – I drove to the Yorkshire city, negotiating the new dual carriageways and ring roads, passing signs for Little Germany, a mill area built by European merchants. Suddenly there, towering unexpectedly, stood Valley Parade.

Roads snaked around the ground, which was still perched amid suburban streets, its modern cantilevered stand a curious rebuild of the gutted structure that lingered in the memory. Spanning only three-quarters of the distance along a touchline, it was as if, like some unfinished bridge or road in a third world country, the money had run out before completion. Still, with a capacity of 25,000, the ground renamed by sponsorship as the Coral Windows Stadium was too good for the level of League Two.

Up high outside the executive boxes in this main stand, I sat almost directly above the point where the fire began in the old construction, which, poignantly, had been due to be demolished on Monday 13 May, 1985 – just two days after the fire. There I heard the testimony of some key figures of the fateful day.

David Baldwin was now Bradford City's chief executive but had been a 14-year-old on the club's books as an associate schoolboy player those 25 years ago. He had been taken by his father to witness his beloved claret-and-amber Bantams receive the trophy as champions of the old Third Division ahead of the final game of the season against Lincoln City. They were two of a crowd of 11,076.

The score was 0-0, the game five minutes from half-time when Baldwin began to realise that something was wrong. 'I was on the Kop, about 30 yards away from where it started in the main stand,' he recalled. 'I just saw a bit of smoke, very localised, and thought they would get the fire extinguishers on it.

'But it started to build. They cleared out the section but less than a minute later, the whole end of the stand was engulfed. Then it started to roll to the other end like a wave. People were pouring out on to the pitch. I saw a policeman's hair catch fire, maybe from spitting bitumen. It felt like a lifetime but the whole stand went in a few minutes.'

In fact, it took just four minutes for the blaze to dash its destructive way from one end of the stand to the other. 'I could feel the intense heat on the right side of my face where I was, up against a temporary

TV gantry, which was there to show the highlights later that night,' Baldwin added. 'We were all huddling together to get away from the heat before we got out of the ground.'

Mark Ellis, now a coach at the club, was then Bradford City's left winger, a diminutive local lad of 23 with fair hair. 'We got the trophy before the match and it was a strange atmosphere,' he said. 'It was a poor game, like a friendly in some ways. Nobody was really bothered. There wasn't the normal pressure to get three points.'

Then, with everyone thinking about their interval refreshment, he was waiting for the ball to be returned to him from the crowd for a throw-in. 'The ball didn't come back and then I spotted a little fire halfway up the stand,' he remembered. 'But I didn't think any more about it and thought it would get put out and we would keep on playing. That fire got bigger and before you knew it, people were panicking and jumping around. Within seconds there were policemen on the pitch and stewards dragging the players back to the changing rooms at the other end of that stand.

'Some of us didn't realise how severe it was and some tried to get up into the bar where they had family. I got shepherded out of the stadium and round the corner where amazingly I bumped into my mum and dad and the girl I was going out with then. I looked up and saw the stand blazing. Heard people screaming and saw them crying. It's 25 years ago and blurry but I'll never forget it.'

Ellis walked up to the Belle Vue pub at the top of the hill on Manningham Lane and, stunned, watched events unfold on television with his teammates. They were all still in their kit.

By now, Baldwin and his father had edged their way out of the back of the Kop and they stood for 10 or 15 minutes, he reckoned, talking with other fans about what to do. 'You weren't sure if you should stay and help or whether being here you were a hindrance to the emergency services,' he said. 'At that age, you look to your dad, don't you? My dad was in the Army and was used to crises. He thought it best to get me home. So we walked the two or three miles.

'As we did, we could see it. The ground sits on a stage in the middle of the valley. Wherever you are in Bradford, you are looking down on it. The smoke was billowing. We got home about 6, maybe 6.30 p.m. We may have dived into a pub on the way home. My mum, brother and sister were frantic. They hadn't heard from us. There were no mobile phones then. They had seen it unfold on the TV. Not until then did we know people were badly injured or had lost their lives.'

How curious is memory in the random way of recall. Baldwin remembered on the Monday afterwards asking a teacher at the Hanson School he attended, and which looked across to a ruined Valley Parade, if they could shut the blinds of the classroom window framing the charred main stand.

Then, 18 days later, the family moved to Coventry due to a posting for his father. It was the day of the Heysel disaster. 'We got there with one portable TV and put it on a kitchen worktop. We sat down with a couple of chairs and couldn't work out why the game hadn't started. I remember sitting there thinking, "Not again. Not another one."'

Mark Ellis remembered going back to Valley Parade four days after to retrieve his car, its roof blackened. Another memory came to mind, too, of a 'very, very weird, eerie' reserve team game that somehow was allowed to be played at the stadium in front of the skeleton stand at the start of the following season. (The first team played at other venues – the city's rugby league ground Odsal, Leeds United's Elland Road and Huddersfield Town's Leeds Road – until December 1986.) 'I think we won 6-0,' Ellis recalled of that reserve match in the way footballers always remember games and results.

Meanwhile, on that night of 11 May, with the emergency services heroically busy in taking the worst cases to the specialist Pinderfields Hospital in Wakefield and the rest to the Bradford Royal Infirmary

(BRI), Professor David Sharpe grew curious. Then 39, he had been a consultant plastic surgeon at the Royal Infirmary for just over four months and was the only one on call that night.

Someone turned up at the hospital from the football stadium with a burned hand. He thought it was odd. But very quickly, it was 'pandemonium' at the BRI. 'I knew there had been a disaster,' Professor Sharpe said. 'But the great thing about the hospital was that it used to run a burns clinic every week and they were used to doing dressings.'

Once the operation was in full swing, he decided to visit Valley Parade. 'I suppose it is why politicians visit scenes, not only for the public relations but also to see what you are dealing with. In my case, I wanted to know if we were dealing with cloth or foam, for example, which can affect smoke inhalation cases. It was 8 p.m. and the stand was still smouldering. I went to speak to the fire officers. It was pretty horrendous. There were human remains and all sorts of things.

'But,' he added with the necessary professional detachment, 'in terms of disasters it was straightforward. If it was a bomb blast, you would get limbs shattered and smoke inhalation. The 258 I saw over a number of months mostly had burns to their scalp and the back of the hands from protecting their heads. It was a cold day, so a lot were wearing wool, which is a brilliant protection. A lot of steel workers wear wool.

'Around 15 surgeons came to Bradford from around the country and we operated on about 80 patients in the window for treatment between days two and five. We had the perfect opportunity. If we had waited for the skin to rot off, and bandaged and grafted three weeks later, they would have ended up with stiff hands.

'We cleared four wards and allocated four surgeons to each of the four operating theatres. It was easy to work out what we needed – tangential excision – that is cutting off the burn tissue and immediately grafting. We knew to within 20 minutes how long it would take. By operating aggressively and early, it worked out. If it hadn't, I guess I would be doing something else now.'

It was all, he insisted, routine. 'Nothing ever happens that easily. I am the recipient of a lot of credit I don't deserve. That's not false modesty. All surgeons have massive egos and I have got a bigger one than most but it was teamwork and the patients were all in it together. We were a family.

'Most of the patients stayed about three weeks. I am proud of the fact that 90 per cent of the burns victims had 100 per cent graft and 90 per cent of them walked out healed. It made more sense to have them in wards dedicated to this and they could share their experiences. Morale was so much better. Maybe that was why there were not so many psychological or psychiatric problems afterwards.'

In the immediate aftermath, Professor Sharpe had to deal with journalists 'climbing through the windows' but the media soon became 'fantastic' in their offers of help. Robert Maxwell, then proprietor of the *Daily Mirror*, turned up with his customary fanfare. He may have proved to be a crook in raiding his employees' pension fund before his death, may have been using his newspaper and the football club he owned, Oxford United, as vehicles for his self-aggrandisement, but Sharpe had reason to be grateful to him at the time. 'He asked us what we wanted,' said the professor. 'He put in beds and got us equipment, such as left-handed graft knives. He went to the Lord Mayor of Bradford's office and started off the fund. He was a big man. He put the fear of God into his journalists. Whenever he walked into the room they crapped themselves.' You could not see Professor Sharpe being intimidated. Upright and distinguished, his bearing is that of authority.

Until the disaster, he had had little interest in working on a burns unit. 'I worked on one in Glasgow. Lists were always being altered.

It was not physically unpleasant but the level of reconstruction techniques you could use was crude. Ultimately it was a question of dressings and skin grafts. Robert Maxwell helped establish the Bradford burns research unit, however, and skills developed. We developed a lot of techniques as a result of the fire, using adhesives and tissue glues and things like this, and I hope there is a heritage that people will benefit from in the future.'

As a result, it had, said Professor Sharpe, who still practiced in Bradford, 'followed me around'. Indeed, he would go on to help with the Piper Alpha disaster of 1988, when 167 people lost their lives in a fire on a North Sea oil rig. Then, on 7 July 2005, he found himself in London for a meeting, when he was one of a group of people evacuated from King's Cross. A bomb had gone off on an underground train, one of four on London transport that day. It became known as 7/7.

He made his way to University College Hospital and was put in charge of one of six teams of specialist burns workers. Late that night, an ambulance dropped him at the foot of the M1, where his wife picked him up to take him back to Bradford. For this, and his work at the city's burns research unit, he was awarded what seemed a meagre reward of an OBE.

In 2010, the unit suddenly found itself short of £100,000 to keep its work going. The money was quickly raised in Bradford. City led the way by staging a match featuring such playing favourites as Dean Windass and Stuart McCall, whose father suffered serious burns in the disaster. Professor Sharpe remained amazed by the city's capacity for generosity of spirit as shown in the raising of the money. 'The people of Bradford have shown themselves to be very proud of the research unit,' he said. 'And we are very proud of the people of Bradford.'

David Baldwin is proud of his city, too. After the fire, he played for the club on schoolboy forms until he was 17. He went on to study hotel management and catering in the Lake District, playing for Carlisle and Berwick Rangers part-time until he was 22, and later started his own recruitment company that did so well that he could sell it in 2003 and retire to Spain. A few years later, an old friend, Mark Lawn, bought into Bradford City and asked him over for six weeks to look at the club and how they could improve it. Baldwin has been here ever since. 'I get a remuneration but not the normal commercial rate. I can afford not to,' he said. 'I do it for my passion for the club. It keeps me in the city. I think back to what this city and this club did for me. It moulded me as an individual. I feel I had success in my work life due to the proud foundations of where I come from, with my grandfather and father being so passionate about the club. I believe that a football club doing well changes the face of the city.'

For a while after the fire, once Valley Parade was rebuilt, City did do well. They even reached the Premier League in 1999 under a promising young manager in Paul Jewell. The drawback was having a bombastic chairman in Geoffrey Richmond. It emerged that the club were paying wages that they could ill afford, with the Italian Benito Carbone reported to be on £40,000 a week and the maverick striker Stan Collymore on £25,000. It was even said that the wage bill was 115 per cent of income.

When they were relegated after just two seasons, beset by financial troubles as a result of the excursion they couldn't pay for, they went into administration in 2002. The club sold Valley Parade for £5 million to ease the crisis and were now having to pay £1.2 million a season in rent, leading to them considering a partnership with the Bradford Bulls rugby league club in a redevelopment of the vast natural bowl that is Odsal stadium.

Their slip through the divisions to League Two had been alarming but it was beginning to dawn on them that it may not even be finished yet. These were tough times for Yorkshire football in general, as the county was without a Premier League club for the first time since the competition was set up and had once featured three.

Bradford's neighbours Leeds United were champions of the old First Division 20 years previously in the season before the Premier League began, their manager Howard Wilkinson being the last Englishman to lead a side to the title. They had also been through turbulent times since, however. In 2001, they reached the semi-final of the Champions League under David O'Leary's management but the chairman Peter Ridsdale had invested heavily in players and high wages by borrowing against future revenue. Failure to qualify for the Champions League subsequently led to financial meltdown and relegation in 2004. They would even slip into League One.

By then, Ridsdale was long gone, becoming one of a new breed of financial footballing nomads who would go on to run Barnsley and Cardiff City and to advise Plymouth Argyle when they went into administration in 2011. The former Chelsea chairman Ken Bates, grizzled, grey-haired and gruff, paid £10 million for Leeds and they were now, finally, chasing promotion from the Championship.

Another of the Premier League's founder members in Sheffield United – who scored the Premier League's first goal in 1992 through Brian Deane in a 2-1 win over Manchester United – were in the Championship, too. They were, though, threatening to join their fellow founder members and city rivals, debt-riddled Sheffield Wednesday, now taken over by Milan Mandaric of Portsmouth notoriety, in League One. The game's ownership issues had become very tangled.

There was hope in Huddersfield mounting a League One promotion campaign but Barnsley were annually fighting against relegation from the Championship, in which Doncaster Rovers were overachieving. Nearby, Rotherham were mounting a promotion challenge from League Two despite having lost their traditional home at Millmoor and been forced to play home games at the soulless Don Valley Stadium in Sheffield. Out east, meanwhile, Hull City were still recovering from debt after relegation from the Premier League, Scarborough were trying to get through regional leagues after going out of business and York City just could not get themselves back up from the Conference. It was a league into which Bradford City were suddenly in danger of dropping.

Six months after my trip to Valley Parade, I caught up with them in leafy, suburban Barnet, the Hertfordshire club a different world from the industrial heart of the north. City were now managed by Peter Taylor, the former England Under-21 manager, who, in a spell as caretaker manager for the senior team, had perceptively made David Beckham captain when few saw leadership potential in him.

I also wanted to see how Barnet were doing, having attended their first game in the Football League after promotion from the Conference in 1991. It was a distinctly memorable 7-4 home defeat by Crewe Alexandra, although Barnet had bounced back from that to reach the promotion play-offs. They went on to lose in the semi-final to a club who, at the end of the 1990s, began a decade-long rise as Bradford began their descent over a similar period. Their name was Blackpool.

Barnet were then managed by Barry Fry, who went on to oversee Southend United and Birmingham City before settling in for the long-haul as director of football at Peterborough United. His colourful, controversial chairman Stan Flashman, with whom Fry had a hate–love–hate relationship with at least three sackings and reinstatements a season, died in 1999. 'Fat Stan' had been forced to resign from Barnet in 1993 when the club went bankrupt and were threatened with expulsion from the League.

Since then, Barnet had bounced between Conference and League and were looking at the possibility of a return to the former, languishing in the lower reaches of the table along with Bradford. City had been among the promotion favourites at the start of the season, with a playing budget of £1.2 million – more than double Barnet's – among the best in the division, thanks to an average of 10,000 fans staying loyal at Valley Parade. Cheap-as-chips season ticket prices helped too.

Not much had changed on the way to the ground at Underhill, though some had had their chips there. The Blue Fin fish and chip shop where Fry used to get free fare for directing visiting teams after games was now the Curry Cottage. Now, too, Barnet had a somewhat more enlightened chairman in Tony Kleanthous. The former business partner of Theo Paphitis, the old Millwall chairman and occupant of the BBC's *Dragons' Den*, could not resist taking over impoverished Barnet in 1994 after their post-Flashman period in administration, and became the youngest chairman in the League at 28.

Since then, Kleanthous had risen to become a representative of the lower divisions on the FA's 12-man Executive Board and an outspoken critic of the Premier League. 'I draw back from using the word impotent but they lack the teeth they need to have,' he said of the FA. You would have liked to have been an observer at his first FA board meeting, which included three representatives from the Premier League, after he had publicly aired his views about the modern top flight. 'The Premiership clubs now control everything in football but I have yet to see them take any decision that can be construed as being good for the game as a whole,' he said. 'The small clubs are just there to prop up the football pyramid and are considered no more than an irrelevance.'

That wasn't the half of it. 'In my opinion,' he added, 'the Premiership has become a cancer, slowly devouring the purists in the game and seeking to consume everything in its path but wielding a huge wallet which divides its clubs from the rest of football.'

Now he had a chance to do something about it on the FA board and, after several meetings did admit: 'In fairness, Premiership clubs themselves are starting to recognise that there needs to be change.' Perhaps it was something to do with increasing wages in the Premier League, the clubs starting to get twitchy. After all, as Kleanthous said: 'If someone is earning £1 million a year, they are not going to become a better player if you pay them £2 million a year.'

Kleanthous had certainly made a difference at Barnet. The ground had been upgraded, not only due to his £1 million investment but also with the revenue from Arsenal, whose reserves played here and who therefore provided a groundsman to prepare a perfect pitch. No matter all the work, the pitch still sloped.

Around the green sward, the terracing and stands looked neater and tidier, crush barriers freshly painted in club colours of amber and black. There were new, natty floodlights and offices at the bottom end of the ground behind what was now a seated stand. The road down, going past the 1st Barnet Scout group and allotments, was now properly tarmacked. At the top end, however, there remained netting to prevent the ball ending up in the gardens of the semi-detached houses behind the terracing, houses which precluded any real expansion of the club.

An engaging and benign autocrat of the old-fashioned variety who used to run football clubs, Kleanthous had made many attempts over the years to move the club into a new-build stadium elsewhere in the borough, but either the land was not available or the local council would not co-operate. Instead, he had created a splendid new training ground and academy well used by the community and all its youth teams at Edgware, a mile out of the borough.

Called The Hive – Barnet's nickname is the Bees – the facility also had enough land on which to build a stadium. In another two years, the freehold of Underhill would revert from the council to the football club. Then would be the time. They needed to remain in the Football League, however, for the finances to add up. If relegated, funding for the academy, in which they placed so much store as they sought to develop their own players, would damagingly dry up. They badly needed a result today.

Peter Taylor's need was even greater, however. An hour before the game, he came to sit up in the stand to watch the warm-ups and admitted as much to me when I joined him. 'Yes,' he said. 'I've been around long enough to know that if we lose today, my position will come under scrutiny.' Bradford was a big club with great expectations, he added. But, with the eternal optimism of the football man, he reckoned his Bantams – hitherto not pulling their weight – were just 'one touch away' from being a decent side. 'I'm still thinking about promotion, not relegation,' he insisted.

A crowd containing David Gill, the Manchester United chief executive whose son Oliver was on loan at Bradford, and John Motson, the BBC commentator who used to report on Barnet for the local paper, witnessed a grim, goalless first-half. There was more action at half-time when the Barnet mascot Bumble was presented with his trophy for having won the recent Grand National race for football club mascots.

Then Bradford – led by Zesh Rehman, captain of Pakistan and one of the few players of Asian extraction in the English professional game – turned it around. Midway through the second half, Tommy Doherty sent through Leon Osborne and he fired home a fierce low shot. There was patent relief on the Bradford bench and among the 424 travelling fans in a crowd of 2,435 (compared with the 5,090 who had witnessed that Barnet game against Crewe 19 years earlier). Within six minutes, Omar Daley, a Jamaican international, put Tom Adeyemi clear and he duly converted. Bradford had sealed the game.

If Bradford's story was about fire, Barnet's was about water and keeping their heads above it. Kleanthous was urging the Premier League to rethink its distribution of TV money. He wanted their relegated clubs to get less parachute money, which he believed gave them the edge on their rivals in the Championship and had the potential to create a yo-yo effect of the same clubs going up and down. Others in the division would stagnate, he claimed, while those lower down could not expect to get up and compete. 'This is all a recipe for disaster for an industry that has survived for over 100 years, and which now has more income than anyone could have imagined yet is in danger of failing in the long term,' he said, urging the Premier League to 'help the sport, help the industry and do something good for a change.' It was heartfelt but would fall on ears not quite deaf but in need of a hearing aid.

One touch away from being a decent side, said Taylor of Bradford (though no one had yet hit on the nickname of Barbara) meanwhile. In the event, two touches was all it took. The thought occurred that the year 2010 had been an important anniversary for one of the most resonant of names in the English game and that 2011 would mark another, being 100 years since they won their only FA Cup.

Goodness knows, City needed something joyful to celebrate rather than just something tragic to commemorate. The more immediate concern, however, was to avoid becoming the FA Cup's first winners – after Luton as the first finalists – to be relegated to the Conference. It had, after all, been only just over a decade since they were in the Premier League and competing with the very biggest name in English football . . .

Chapter 8

THE CRÈME DE LA KREMLIN

Where there's a will, there's a way: Sir Matt Busby Way. When I drove down it 20 years earlier for a meeting with the then Manchester United club secretary Ken Merrett, it was still known as Warwick Road North. It offered an unpromising route to Old Trafford through an industrial wasteland on one side, terraced housing on the other. Renamed in 1993 after the man who made the club into the national and worldwide phenomenon it had become, the road now felt more of a boulevard to a land of hopes and dreams.

Turning the car off the Chester Road again, I immediately became aware of the new buildings and businesses that had sprung up in this regenerated area. It was as if all these hotels, offices and shopping outlets around Salford Quays wanted to be close to success and greatness, hoping it would rub off. None of them was yet as tall as Old Trafford, however, which could now be seen from the M60, some five miles away. It had spread upwards and outwards to its near-76,000 capacity, making it the biggest club ground in Britain.

Those two decades ago, I could park on the main road in front of the forecourt and entrance to the club offices for my meeting with Ken Merrett. Not any longer – United had bought up acres of land around the stadium to accommodate their audiences and so parking had moved on. I settled for the vast tract of tarmac known as Car Park E behind the bronze statue of the thrilling 1960s triumvirate of George Best, Denis Law and Bobby Charlton.

Opposite was the forecourt that has served as a focal point for fans ever since they came here, baffled and desperate for news, in 1958 when the Munich air disaster cut down eight Manchester United players so prematurely. The area had been eaten into by expansion but it remained busy with people even when there was no match, not least due to a cavernous outlet selling merchandise way beyond the old scarves and bobble hats and which had every right to call itself a megastore.

Above its doors currently was a mural depicting 100 years of building up Old Trafford to its current dominant state. It almost seemed to be sending out a message to the rest of English football, and the words of Shelley's poem sprang to mind:

My name is Ozymandias, king of kings:
Look on my works, ye Mighty and despair

Another reason for the human traffic being generated was one of the many commercial ventures that made United the financial monolith it had become. The club was compelled, after all, to wring out every possible penny of income, not only to finance its playing ambitions but also to service the huge debts incurred by its American owners, the Glazer family. They bought the club in 2005 for £790 million, the majority of that sum borrowed.

For someone like me, wishing to scratch beneath the surface of what was for a journalist and writer a notoriously closed community, it was a bonus to discover that, like everything at United, getting inside the club could be bought. You could even book it on the internet – another big change from the avuncular Ken Merrett's day when he used to take calls from fans in Scandinavia and South America wanting score updates. Now they simply went online or watched the TV, with every United game televised overseas.

United called their Museum and Tour Experience: 'The greatest football story ever told' and no one was believed to have reported them to the Advertising Standards Authority. It cost £13 (plus £1 booking fee, plus £3 for a brochure, plus £3 for the headphones). It was open seven days a week and did a tour every 10 minutes, with up to 50 people on each. That added up, I worked out, to around £200,000 in income a week. About the weekly wage of Wayne Rooney, the latest in a line of marquee players for United.

The museum opened in 1986, the year Sir Alex Ferguson arrived as manager, and, housed in the West Stand, it now occupied three floors. As the manager said amid the commentary, 'No one can fail to be impressed with the history of the club and the Theatre of Dreams.' Now there was a rare and encouraging thing to start with for a writer: a quote from Ferguson.

The Theatre of Dreams. No one quite knows for sure who coined the term. The former football correspondent of *The Times*, Geoffrey Green, is often cited, though he himself attributed it to Charlton, now Sir Bobby and, in a masterstroke of public relations, an ambassador for United. There was now a special exhibition showing how the ground had been rebuilt, mostly in the last 20 years following the Taylor Report.

All the greats were accorded their place in the museum, notably the No. 7s of the modern era, the shirt having become synonymous with the club's talismanic player, like the No. 9 at Newcastle United and the No. 10 for Brazil. From Best they went through England's lionheart captain Bryan Robson, the thoughtful Steve Coppell, poster boy David Beckham, the turbulent Frenchman Eric Cantona and the posing Portuguese Cristiano Ronaldo.

A personal favourite shirt, though, was that of Billy Meredith from the 1912 FA Cup final. His name and presence lingered on in various corners of Old Trafford but the scarcity of mentions of him hardly reflects his pioneering effect on United in particular and football in general. He was the original superstar and the support's demand for a maverick, a player who embodied the ethos of the club as a cut above, could be traced back to him.

Born in the mining community of Chirk, North Wales, in 1874, Meredith was a sickly baby kept alive, according to folklore, by his mother placing him in a warm oven. He became a pit pony driver at the age of 12 and played for Northwich Victoria before being spotted by Manchester City. He scored twice on his home debut at the age of 20, though City were beaten 5-2 by Newton Heath Lancashire and Yorkshire Railway – the first incarnation of Manchester United. He was soon awarded the soubriquet of 'Merrylegs'.

Meredith, a right winger who always appeared on the field with a trademark tooth pick in his mouth, was deemed guilty of bribing an opponent to lose a game in 1905 and banned for 18 months, though he always denied it. During his time out of the game, amid huge controversy, he signed for the club now named Manchester United. Thus began a 15-year association with them during which he won both League and Cup. Still going at the age of 47 – thanks to a revolutionary fitness regime that included such new-fangled ideas as Turkish baths – he returned to City and became the oldest player ever to figure in the FA Cup when he played a semi-final for them aged 49 years and 245 days.

Off the field, Meredith also helped form the Professional Footballers' Association in 1909. He died in 1958, two months after Munich. Some player, some story for the modern superstar to contemplate. The explosion in media may have created the celebrity of Best, then taken Gazza and Rooney to new highs, and lows, but Meredith's tale in many ways topped them.

Having negotiated the museum, I joined the 40 or so people on the tour. They were young and old, men and women, from all corners of the globe. Our guide was Alan, clearly a United fan of many years standing, and he led us up into the North Stand, the largest cantilevered stand in Europe, capable of holding 25,000 people. In keeping with the commercialised atmosphere around the club, his first statement was to tell us that seats here worked out between £30 and £50 a game if you bought a season ticket and that it was £56,000 a season for a hospitality box for eight people. (There were 179 in the ground in all.)

We were then led across to the West Stand, where a man was carrying out a very important job for the day. In advance of a Champions League game, he had been deputed to remove the hoarding at the front of the edifice bearing the Nike swoosh logo. The different coloured seats in the stand making its pattern had also been covered up. The sportswear and shoe company, you see, were not sponsors of the Champions League.

From there we were taken out of the ground, past the memorial of that snowy Munich day. Due to the rebuilding work of the past decade, it had been moved from the front of Old Trafford to its position on a wall round a corner. A nice touch now were the red and white roses beside the plaque, which reminded us that three club officials also died, along with the co-pilot, a steward, a travel agent, a supporter and eight journalists, including the former Manchester City goalkeeper Frank Swift.

There was due reverence for a moment and I couldn't help thinking of the moving match in 1992 against Everton that I was privileged to attend. It was the first after the death of Sir Matt Busby when George Best – who would himself be accorded much reverence in 2005 after his sad demise due to alcoholism at the age of 59 – shed a quiet tear and a lone bagpiper played.

I was fortunate, too, to be able to interview survivors on the 50th anniversary of Munich. I thought I knew everybody's story, the most vivid being that of goalkeeper Harry Gregg's heroism in pulling teammates and a pregnant woman and her daughter out of a burning fuselage. But I did not and discovered a tale new to me.

Kenny Morgans was just 18, a Swansea-born right-winger who had broken into the United team just six weeks earlier. He recalled looking out of the window and seeing the wings being de-iced. He recalled, too, the three attempts to take off, the plane hitting the fence at the end of the runway – at 3.04 p.m. After that, he remembered nothing except the story told to him when he awoke three days later. 'About 8.30 or 8.45 p.m., two German reporters went back to the burning plane and they found me,' he said. 'I was still there. I was the last to come out. I was caught underneath a wheel. They got me to hospital and I didn't wake up until Sunday morning. I had a cut head and a lot of bruising. I had lost 10 pints of blood.' Imagine that these days – journalists, anybody, being allowed back to a crash scene. But there was no trace of bitterness in Morgans' voice that he had laid undiscovered for so long.

I remembered the tale as our tour guide led us down the Munich tunnel, a thoroughfare under the South Stand, and past the Treble Suite (marking the notable feat of League title, FA Cup and European Cup in 1999). In the tunnel a series of murals telling the history of the club adorned the walls. Alan informed us that the greatest player he ever saw was Duncan Edwards, who died at Munich aged just 21. All who saw Edwards, a kid from Dudley in the West Midlands, told of both skill and power, his sheer specialness. He and Meredith were the two I wished I had seen in the flesh.

You couldn't blame them, I suppose, but the younger and overseas visitors had something and somewhere else on their minds. Excitement duly increased in the group as we entered the players' lounge – smaller than I thought it would be – where there hung an honours board bearing the name of every United player who had played for their country. Here Coleen must have sat with baby Kai to sip champagne. There must be where Rio Ferdinand tweeted his in-depth, 140-character observations after matches.

Then the dressing room, scene of so much magical history down the years involving all the greats. Magical history such as Ferguson projecting a boot that caught Beckham above an eye. In the corridor outside, the young upstart Cesc Fabregas once hurled a pizza at Ferguson after one particularly feisty United v. Arsenal encounter. Priceless moments indeed.

Wood-panelled, the room was windowless and soundproofed. On one wall was a giant screen so, Alan told us, Fergie could show replays from the first half to the team and point out the error of their ways while the players were munching on interval bananas and Jaffa cakes and drinking energy drinks from the fridge in the corner. What happened to oranges and hot tea? Presumably the latter was stopped on health and safety grounds due to the potential danger from Ferguson hurling cups, though it seemed he did have a caring side. According to Alan, the manager personally checked the players for items of jewellery, which could injure them and opponents, before they ran out for the game. Bless.

On the other three sides of the room were the pegs bearing the 25 shirts of the first-team squad in the places in which they changed on match days. While the two central defenders, Ferdinand and Nemanja Vidic, were side by side, the two then first-choice strikers, Rooney and Dimitar Berbatov, were in opposite corners. It might have explained their lack of closeness on the pitch sometimes. Alan told us that as players left, new ones simply took over their spots but surely the two could have been put together if they requested it? Instead, Rooney had Ryan Giggs and Michael Owen, mature professionals, on either side.

Naturally, under each place was a plug socket for hairdryers – though you might have thought the players would have wanted to avoid them, given that Ferguson's habit of standing in their faces and sounding off when displeased with them was known as the hairdryer treatment – or even, these days, the charging of iPhones. Equally naturally, there was a full-length mirror.

We were fortunate that outside at pitchside, the TV people had all but finished setting up for the next day's game and we were allowed down the wide tunnel in a corner of the ground. From there, we could take the walk along the touchline to the halfway line and the managers' and substitutes' areas, which at United are neat, raised brick constructions. We could even sit in those leather seats resembling those in airline first-class sections – of course bearing sponsors' logos – that were a requirement in the Premier League now. Never had it been more cosy and comfortable to be a sub. Perhaps too much so – some players seemed content these days to occupy them in the Premier League and make a squad member's salary rather than take a pay cut to play every week in the Championship.

Between the opposing areas was the old tunnel to the former dressing rooms, the only area left standing after German bombing in 1942 had forced United to share a ground with Manchester City at Maine Road until 1951. Those old dressing rooms, Alan told us, had now been turned into a wedding chapel where many a couple were United.

The tour ended at the back door of the megastore, into which we were urged by our guide. No surprise, really, given that any tour of a stately home or National Trust venue deposited you in the gift shop. It shouldn't have been any surprise, either, that here amid the replica shirts and general tat – from slippers to Christmas decorations – bearing the United logo (it had long since become more than a badge) was a group of people from overseas hungry to acquire merchandise.

What did have me raising an eyebrow and smiling was the group of eight all dressed identically in plum-coloured robes. They were, one told me when I inquired, Tibetan Buddhist monks from the Himalayan village of Ladakh in India, based at the Tserkarmo Monastery. They were on a European tour talking about their faith and that night they would be appearing at St Peter's House in Oxford Road.

There was a banner that hung inside Old Trafford proclaiming United as 'The Religion' but this was certainly the collision of two worlds. 'We know all about United,' added my man. 'We see them on TV.' Another monk nodded in between bursts of speech on his mobile. He seemed to be seeking the shirt size of a mate in the monastery.

What also surprised me was that the shop was not doing the kind of business that might have been expected. For these were strange times at United. The devotion may have remained but it was no longer blind, as was being revealed this season above all others in recent history.

I had taken the tour, to be honest, because another entry into the club had been denied. Those 20 years ago, Ken Merrett, who had stayed on as an assistant secretary, had been informative and insightful, telling me an abiding truth about football that has always stuck with me: lose three games and everything is wrong, from holes in the stand roof to the temperature of the meat pies; win three and all anyone writes to you about is getting tickets.

Meeting with his successor, I thought, would be a good compare-and-contrast exercise about the growth of the club and its staff of 550, which rose to some 2,000 on match days. It would reveal how United had become the cynic's epitome of why the Premier League was formed: to facilitate England's biggest club in making more money and in keeping more of it away from the redistribution process to clubs with less earning potential. And, of course, to use that money to become champions again, which duly happened after 26 fallow years in 1993 and made them the Premier League's first winners.

It helped, I thought, that the new club secretary was an old friend. Well-respected in football's administrative circles, John Alexander had just moved from Tottenham Hotspur to Manchester United. We had played in the same college team together at London University, where he was a more than decent pacy, rangy striker. He went on to have a good professional career and put his geography degree to good use by finding his way from Millwall via Reading – for whom he once scored four goals in a game against Grimsby Town as the Royals won the old Fourth Division title in 1979 – to Northampton. Sadly for the Scouser – a Liverpool fan, whisper it around Old Trafford – his playing career was ended by a broken leg.

I emailed him and a reply came back a few days later. Sorry, he said, but after checking with the powers that be, it was 'not club policy to get involved with this kind of project'. But come in to the training ground at Carrington for an off-the-record cup of tea next time you are up north, he said. He even invited me to his Cheshire home when I pointed out that the newspaper I was then working for was banned from Carrington for something or other to which the omnipotent Ferguson had taken exception, as the manager was wont to do.

There were no hard feelings on either side. I half-expected it – no money in it for the club, I guessed. Such is modern Manchester United, which often has the feel of a Kremlin. For journalists, access and information is limited, which only matters because of its effect in keeping supporters in the dark. These days, Sir Alex was refusing to talk to the BBC, after it cast aspersions on the business dealings of his agent son Jason, or to attend the manager's supposedly obligatory press conferences after matches, for which the Premier League apparently fined him during the 2010/11 season, though refused to publish details. Instead, you had to get the quotes off United's own in-house television station, MUTV. He would not even speak to them on occasion if he had said something the previous week that got him into trouble, such as a comment about a referee.

Being a football writer in England these past two decades has therefore often meant being a Kremlinologist – sometimes as well as psychiatrist, economist, even war correspondent – and developing expertise through reading the runes on how United is run. This season such skills were coming in very handy, as the club was enduring one of its internal agonies with a talisman player – the kind of drama that had gone on ever since Meredith.

Wayne Rooney was the heir in an elite line of such players since Merrylegs, the most notable in modern times having been George Best. The benign but puritan and patriarchal Sir Matt had struggled to understand the Belfast Boy's self-destructive, addictive personality. Busby, after all, was used to dealing with more malleable young men in simpler times. His Babes were surely going to win the European Cup until the return trip from a semi-final in Belgrade against Red Star was interrupted on that airport runway. Ten years after Munich, in 1968, Busby did finally and famously win the European Cup, Best playing a starring role in the 4-1 win over Benfica at Wembley.

Alex Ferguson followed in Busby's footsteps. He was from Glasgow, Busby from Bellshill 10 miles south, and after being recruited following a successful spell at Aberdeen, Ferguson very quickly grasped United's core values established by his fellow Scot. The need was to match style and steel, to build teams that won by entertaining expansively. It was why he survived his first four years without winning a trophy, an indulgence unlikely to be granted to his successor, and he was accorded the chance to turn from fresh-faced enthusiast to ruddy-cheeked *éminence grise* over 25 years.

Ferguson's first Best test came in the form of the telegenic David Beckham, blessed with a more equable temperament than the man whose fame he equalled. Ferguson grew weary of the pop star culture that surrounded Beckham and his Spice Girl wife Victoria, however, as celebrity obsession took off with the turn of the 21st century. The manager eventually sold him to Real Madrid.

Then there was Eric Cantona, seen snobbishly as somewhat of a yokel in France but as one cool character in England for his playing mix of muscle and subtlety, threatening demeanour and 'when the seagulls follow the trawler, it is because they think sardines will be thrown' philosophising. Cantona was piqued and pushed into Parisian exile by an eight-month FA ban for kung-fu kicking a Crystal Palace fan in an astonishing episode in 1995 amid the Premier League's burgeoning popularity, but Ferguson persuaded him back.

Next Cristiano Ronaldo, a 'Portugeezer' with sublime skills and who brought the art of dribbling back to the English game. Not only that, he scored goals too, 42 of them in one season even. But the man fond of pranging expensive cars always seemed to be on the brink of leaving, until in 2009 Ferguson reluctantly granted him his wish to go to Real Madrid.

Now the manager was busy bringing his experience of all of that to bear upon a character who embodied elements of all of them: fame, notoriety even, earning power and the ability to produce something different on a football field. Like Meredith, like Best and Beckham, this one was a zeitgeist figure, too. He may not have had the looks, but in an age of austerity, he was somebody for working-class kids to aspire to be. This was the age of the Wayne.

Ferguson had always given the impression that what he loved best was players such as the red-haired Paul Scholes – the carrot-topped Cantona – and Ryan Giggs, who like Meredith was a Welsh wing wizard. Both – at least in public image – were dedicated products of the youth system – players he could control. As both student of United's past and creator of its modern history, however, Ferguson knew that there had to be a place for the player who could conjure the unpredictable on the field and who made a team special. It meant that usually he came with issues and problems. Rooney was one such player.

As a kid with Everton – one who I saw light up the FA Youth Cup final of 2002 – Rooney was hot property and had agents scrambling for his favours. There developed a struggle for him between one Paul

Stretford, who had formed his own management company, Proactive, and the original agent, Peter McIntosh. A messy, murky row erupted, which ended in court with Stretford claiming he was being blackmailed.

When it emerged that Stretford had indeed poached Rooney and lied about times and dates, the case was thrown out. Stretford was then fined £300,000 and banned from football for nine months by the FA for improper conduct. He still retained the trust of Rooney, however, and Sir Alex always felt he could deal with him, particularly as Stretford delivered the player to United from Goodison Park for a transfer fee of £20 million in the summer of 2004.

This autumn six years on would come as a shock to United's system, though, and football went into media frenzy for 10 October days amid claim, counter-claim and speculation. There was even a clutch of balaclava-clad heavies at the gates of Rooney's Cheshire mansion that he still just about shared with his wife Coleen.

And, as was the way now with WAGs, Coleen was a huge character with a big say in the story. She was the Scouse sweetheart carving out a career of her own in advertisements, mainly for the clothing catalogue company Littlewoods (another of Stretford's deals, which may explain why the couple stuck with him). As with Wayne and young lads, a whole generation of teenage working-class girls seemed to aspire to be her. Very marketable.

Rooney had had a terrible year, mirroring the English game. He had suffered an ankle injury as United slipped out of the Champions League in the spring then laboured through the World Cup, his frustration evident in that berating of England fans to camera at the end of another limp performance.

He was carrying a secret, though. A Sunday newspaper claimed to have proof of him having paid prostitutes, this time younger and more photogenic women than the 46-year-old grandmother he had allegedly used when a teenager. A tape of him in the brothel was said to exist and was much sought after on Merseyside by criminal elements looking to make money from its sale or distribution. The *News of the World* had been sitting on this latest episode, though, so as not to damage England's World Cup campaign. This autumn the paper felt constrained no longer.

George Best's dalliances in the anything-goes 1960s always had an element of charm about them, even style, as he stepped out, or stayed in, with actresses like Susan George (even the *Carry On* films' Barbara Windsor, she revealed in 2010) and Miss World winners before they became politically incorrect. Rooney's were simply tacky. One detail had him giving a hotel porter £200 for fetching him a pack of cigarettes. On the eve of the season, Rooney had also been pictured alongside a nightclub in the early hours of the morning puffing on a tab and urinating in an alleyway.

Ferguson was believed to be angered by Rooney's behaviour which was tarnishing the club. He kept him out of the spotlight, claiming the player had an injury. Rooney, though, told journalists after an England game that he had no injury. It was believed that he felt he was not getting enough love from his manager. A story emerged that contract talks between club and its prize asset had broken down. Rooney wanted to leave Old Trafford. Cue the modern equivalent of the Chicago press pack frantically rushing for the phones at a twist in a juicy murder trial of the Al Capone era. These days it was hold the front page, as well as back.

On the eve of a Champions League game against Bursaspor of Turkey, Ferguson fought back, using a press conference he was duty bound to give. In six riveting minutes, when no question needed to be asked, he offered a virtuoso performance in front of live cameras, part pained, part determined, outlining Rooney's refusal to sign a new contract. The decision had left him dumfounded, he said. There was a rare sympathy for the manager.

Rooney's people, including a former *Daily Mail* news editor Ian Monk, sought to retaliate the next day. Stretford thought it would play well with United supporters if a statement talked of his client's concerns about the club's transfer dealings and ambitions, thus heading off any idea that Rooney (or Stretford) might simply be after a fatter contract. The supporters, after all, were worried by the huge debts that the Glazer family had inflicted upon the club in borrowing to buy it – 'leveraging' was the official euphemism – and there had been growing protests over the club's financial position ever since the Americans had marched into Old Trafford in 2005. Rooney's statement would backfire, however, not just because it came hours before the Bursaspor match, where a banner reading 'Who's the whore now Wayne?' was unfurled.

The speculation grew more intense. Had Rooney been tapped up by newly moneyed Manchester City, now owned by the Abu Dhabi royal family and dubbed by Ferguson 'the noisy neighbours'? Would Roman Abramovich relax a spending embargo he was reported to have imposed at Chelsea? Was Jose Mourinho at Real Madrid interested?

The next day, Rooney and Stretford met with the United chief executive David Gill for talks which also included the Glazers on a conference call. Rooney appeared to be wavering in his desire to leave.

Another day on and United made an announcement. Rooney had agreed a new five-year contract. No figures were made available but it was believed he would be getting a basic of £160,000 a week, with bonuses if United won trophies likely to take it up to an average of £200,000 a week over the term of the contract. It wasn't quite the £250,000 that Carlos Tevez was reported to be earning across at Manchester City but at a minimum of £40 million over those five years, it was not so much a pretty penny as a drop-dead gorgeous one. And it meant that the revenue from 7,407 fans paying for the cheapest tickets – 10 per cent of United's average home crowd – would be needed to pay Rooney's weekly wage. Or that revenue from a week's worth of stadium tours.

I spoke to Kevin Rye of the fans' organisation Supporters Direct. 'For a long time, any story about money has been regarded as a good news story,' he told me. 'A player signs – good news. A new contract – good news. A new TV deal – good news. Except what people have realised now is that this money has to come from somewhere and it comes from them.

'The fans end up paying in some way and in the constant race to the top, the fans are subject to a race to the bottom. The effect each time is to create another tipping point for individual fans and this will tip some over the edge and they won't renew their season tickets or go to matches at Old Trafford as a result. It has in the past and will again.'

As counterpoint to Rye, an AFC Wimbledon fan who believed in the concept of supporter ownership, I had already had lunch with Keith Harris, a lawyer with a London firm called Seymour Pierce. A former chairman of the Football League, he had become the market leader in a new footballing industry – brokering the buying and selling of clubs.

Greying, urbane, 57-year-old Harris's reputation took off when he was involved in the deal for Ken Bates to sell Chelsea to Roman Abramovich in 2003. Soon after that Harris would put together Doug Ellis and the American Randy Lerner at Aston Villa as the old autocratic British order gave way to new money and overseas raiders. Harris was also engaged to sell Newcastle for Mike Ashley but, like many others, found the owner of the Sports Direct sportswear chain somewhat volatile.

Harris was also a Manchester United fan and switched from the hard-headed businessman to the pained supporter when it came to his own club. Indeed, though they came from opposite ends of football's market, Kevin Rye and Keith Harris both believed in a collective ownership of their own club. It was just that Harris's collective, who called themselves the Red Knights, was rather more minted.

Indeed, they were a group of superfans led by the Goldman Sachs chief economist Jim O'Neill and they claimed they had access to £1.2 billion in pledges from companies and other wealthy people in order to buy out the Glazers. The family had always turned them down, though it was believed they might deal at £1.5 billion, almost double what they paid.

The club, Harris believed, was just not worth that, however, as it was using income to service debt. Indeed, the autumn's financial results would show that, although the club had made a trading profit of £100 million, there was an overall loss of £80 million due to the paying off of interest on loans. It meant that in the last year – one which saw Ronaldo's departure for a world record fee of £80 million – United had spent more than four times the amount on servicing debt than they had on buying players.

This was on top of the poor season ticket take-up in the summer, when they were forced to advertise them for sale after selling 'only' 50,000 ahead of the new season, 14,000 short of the usual amount sold. United were not saying how many of the 8,500 premium seats, which brought in 40 per cent of their match-day revenue, had been sold.

'There is no change in our motivation of changing the regime,' Harris told me at the time. 'The news about season tickets is significant. If the sale level is below their budget and expectations, then that will clearly have an impact on the Glazers' business plan. Their margin for error is not huge.'

It was indeed clear that United were suffering due to a boycott by some, with the Independent Manchester United Supporters Association urging fans to withhold funds. The Manchester United Supporters' Trust, however (yes, it did sound like the People's Front of Judaea and the Judaean People's Front at odds in Monty Python's *Life of Brian*) could not bring themselves to recommend damaging the club financially.

Harris and Co. were popular, though, among Trust members – and United's Trust was the biggest of the lot, with 163,000 members signed up. The promise was of a stake for fans' groups – and a 'golden' shareholding that would give them power of veto on any future change of ownership. Others were more sceptical, calling them the Red Dwarves or the Barren Knights. Indeed, Harris was now persona non grata at Old Trafford.

But with every financial figure, every scrap of damaging news, the Red Knights advanced a little on the Kings at Old Trafford and nearer endgame, which might just have flushed out other would-be buyers, perhaps from the Middle East. The rulers of Qatar were said to be interested in increasing a portfolio that included the 2022 World Cup and may be willing to put the upstarts of Manchester City-owning Abu Dhabi in their place.

That the ownership of United was such a public concern and topic of debate illustrated how the game had changed. For years, few cared that the club's owner Louis Edwards might have been an autocrat who exploited his players. When those players were Best, Law and Charlton, nobody noticed the chairman much. Edwards was one of the few, indeed, who had any profile at all – the old autocrat Bob Lord at Burnley perhaps, gruff Sam Longson, sacker of Brian Clough, at Derby County – but chairmen were largely anonymous men.

Gradually, however, such figures grew in profile and significance as coverage of the sport increased. Louis passed the club on to son and heir Martin, a tall, distinguished figure who developed a feel for the game and the club. Edwards junior performed his best act when refusing to sack Ferguson with the manager under pressure for not winning the title, a feat that took seven years of grace to achieve.

Martin tried to sell the club a few times, first in 1989 to the ludicrous Michael Knighton, who juggled the ball on the pitch prematurely without having the £20 million asking price, and ended up owning Carlisle United. Then it was to Robert Maxwell before Dave Whelan, who went on to turn Wigan Athletic from a non-League club into a Premier League one, and even to Rupert Murdoch, whose Sky TV had a 10 per cent stake at one point. In the end, a successful sale was concluded in 2005 to that family of American businessmen, headed by father Malcolm Glazer with his sons Joel and Avi being his eyes and ears.

It was remarkable to think that at one point Martin Edwards was ready to take 'just' £20 million from Knighton. A decade later, Sky's offer was £680 million, though it was blocked by the Monopolies and Mergers Commission (why is there only one of those, by the way?). In between, in 1991, Edwards floated the club on the stock market, opening the way to the modern Manchester United. He made £5 million but retained a 50.5 per cent shareholding. Bit by bit he sold it off, accumulating almost £100 million for himself in the process, with Irish horse racing tsars J.P. McManus and John Magnier becoming majority shareholders in 2002.

At first friendly with Sir Alex Ferguson, they became embroiled in a dispute with him over the ownership of the thoroughbred horse Rock of Gibraltar, racing being the manager's passion on the side. They attempted to force him out of the club but the board resisted and invited new investment, the Glazers arriving to take on McManus and Magnier's 28.7 per cent shareholding.

It explained Ferguson's backing for the Glazers as owners through all the criticism of them. To join in would not only have been to bite the hand that fed but also to open himself up to accusations of ingratitude after they had rescued him from his dispute with the Irish power brokers. To boot, he also no longer had to endure the layers of red tape of the club being a public limited company, with a football board and a company board, and was able to get quicker answers when it came to buying players.

For all the grief heaped upon Edwards, perhaps through not spending enough on players, it was as nothing compared to what the Glazers would receive due to their leveraging. For there were still many unacquainted with the ways of high finance and the City – as shown by the revulsion at bankers when it came to them reclaiming their snouts-in-troughs bonuses so quickly despite having created the credit crunch. Many did not quite understand how the Glazers were allowed to buy a football club with borrowed money, then get that football club to pay it all back out of profits.

It all resulted in protests by fans wearing green and gold scarves representing the original Newton Heath. The irony was that that club went bust in 1902 and were bailed out by a brewer named John Henry Davies, who saw the club's support as a captive audience for his product. He was not the last owner, or sponsor, to spot that potential.

There was a by-product of protest, too, with the formation of a new club in 2005 by disaffected supporters who wanted to get back to their roots. They called it FC United of Manchester and it was part of the growing movement that had spawned AFC Wimbledon. Membership of FCUM was £12 a year and the club was run by a democratically elected board. Comparisons with Barcelona were furthered as they refused to allow their team to wear a sponsor's name on their shirts. They shared a ground with Bury FC of League Two, often bettering their landlords' gates despite being in the Northern Premier League – the seventh tier of the English game.

There was even the possibility during this season that they might be drawn against Manchester United in the FA Cup. After beating Rochdale excitingly in the first round proper, FC United drew at Brighton in the second round but lost the replay. There were echoes for Wimbledon, who would have been sent to MK Dons if both clubs had won replays. In the event, Milton Keynes lost to Stevenage, who went on to beat Wimbledon then, remarkably, Newcastle United in the third round. For both FC United and Wimbledon there was relief, even if the media thought two such contests might be spicy. Neither wanted to put money into the coffers of concerns they still resented.

'Looking at the Rooney saga, I'm glad I'm out of it, not paying these millionaires and not paying Glazer's interest,' Mike Turton, a founder member of FC United, was quoted as saying. 'I followed United for 30 years and I was a season ticket holder but the Premier League is less interesting for me now. There is a lack of soul and quite a few mercenaries just passing through.'

He represented the feelings of many. It was nothing new that people were disillusioned with the professional game. Many a neutral seemed to have been decrying the amount of money in the game and the state of its finances ever since the first time Corinthians were knocked out of the FA Cup. The difference now was that so many diehard supporters who had invested so much in the game, emotionally and financially, were so fed up. If many at the most successful club in the country's core were wavering, what hope for the rest?

Wavering they certainly were, as shown by the sheer number of those green and gold scarves. They disliked the Glazers, for sure, but now they were none too keen on Rooney and their club's handling of him either. It, he, had become a modern footballing morality tale. People were sick of the disloyalty and the intrigue. And in a time of recession, they would become sicker still.

Even the chief executive of the Professional Footballers' Association, Gordon Taylor, normally a staunch defender of his members even through many an issue that attracted public contempt, grew concerned during the Rooney saga. 'It wasn't the best of times to have such a dispute airing at such a time for many of the fans on whom the game relies,' he told me. 'Of course people will pay to watch the top players and it's not for me to condemn a player earning what he can for a short career but the game does need to show more social responsibility. I deal with clubs at all levels and about two-thirds have financial problems. I don't want football to go like banking, where everything looked good on the surface but they were paddling furiously to keep their heads above water.

'Rather than just pay fortunes, with the balance of payments going abroad, the game has a duty to give the next generation a chance and I'd like to see managers given more time to bring young players through. I'd also like to see the Premier League looking at rules from American sports, such as no club being allowed to have more than 20 per cent leveraged debt.'

There was an irony here, of United being outstripped financially across town at Manchester City, which was not lost on many. Suddenly the balance of financial power had shifted. United were far from down and out, though. Indeed there were those who admired the Glazers' business model, which kept producing revenue despite dark forecasts. Sponsorship, for example, had almost doubled to £80 million in the previous four years and a United commercial team in London had now moved into 11,500 square feet of new offices at a cost of £80 a square foot. When it came to needing to raise funds, indeed, the family had little trouble in getting the financial institutions to fork out £500 million in a bond issue. It took attractive interest rates to lure the investment houses, mind, meaning annual payments of £43 million.

The owners then surprised everyone when the pressure was building on them as winter approached by announcing through United's holding company, Red Football Joint Venture Limited, that they were paying off £220 million worth of the debt incurring the highest interest. Where had it come from? It sparked new speculation among Kremlinologists. Was it a down payment on the club from the Qatari royal family? The Glazers would surely prefer to sell to the Qataris with their guaranteed money rather than those upstart Red Knights, whose funds they believed to be in doubt anyway. The English, after all, were sellers, not buyers these days.

Such financial tangles, coupled with the Rooney saga, not only left a sour taste among people feeling sullied by the greed and cynical double dealing of the modern era but also among those who saw that greed and the cynical double dealing of the modern era as par for the course. I even spoke to an agent who felt disgusted. That's how bad it got.

Publicly, United seemed to accept the behaviour of Rooney and his representatives as just business, though Ferguson was almost certainly harder in private, leaving Rooney out of the odd squad and sending him off to Nike's headquarters in Oregon for some fitness training on his own for a week. It could also have been to get him out of the spotlight ahead of a Manchester derby that would be a 0-0 damp squib and interrupt the debate. You hoped an element of it, in these days of player power, was punishment by Ferguson.

Rooney certainly wasn't going to get away with it that easily among United's fans, however. Their attitude was lukewarm towards him at best. He may have scored 34 goals in 44 games the previous season, adding a powerful heading ability to his repertoire to fill the void left by Ronaldo's exit to Madrid, but he had a long way to go still to rehabilitate himself with the faithful as a legend to match the likes of Best and Cantona.

Neither was he having a good season on the pitch as he struggled for goals despite United going on a long unbeaten run in the League and qualifying comfortably for the second phase of the Champions League. What was that the chairman of Barnet, Tony Kleanthous, said about players not being any better if they are getting £1 million or £2 million?

Some of us wondered why the fuss, as Rooney certainly did not possess the talent of Best or Meredith of fable. He was strong, that was true, had a fierce shot and worked hard for the team but the World Cup had shown him to be short of the real artistry of such as Ronaldo and the sumptuously skilled Lionel Messi of Barcelona.

It was doubtful that Rooney would ever be as loved, or make as much of a contribution, as Giggs, his pace waning but his left foot still incisive. Neither was the now 37-year-old's appetite for the game diminished despite, remarkably, having played in every Premier League season. Details to astonish would emerge of a private life that belied his reputation as a family man, but Giggs remained a paragon when it came to talent and durability. The fuss was because Rooney was about the best England had to offer currently, some way short of Paul Gascoigne for talent but a reflection of a more athletic modern game.

Awesome is an overworked Americanism but it does truly describe United's history, tradition and place at the heart of the English game. The club looked unlikely to cede its position, on the field at least, or to end up any time soon as a crumbling edifice in a desert like Ozymandias, but there were warning signs. It was certainly in danger of betraying the many who have felt a reverence for the club.

There were fans of certain other clubs who despised United, probably out of some jealousy due to the swagger that came with being winners and the lack of grace, even in victory, that Ferguson could exhibit. (It didn't help when a United fan could hold up a banner that said: 'We are Man United, we do what we want'. Millwall's 'No one likes us, we don't care,' was defiance at what they perceived to be a misguided view of their hooligan, racist image. This was just arrogance.) But when even the owners rarely attended matches and treated Busby's institution as a commodity, then the goodwill elsewhere among generations who were never touched by the Babes or Munich's aftermath and legend, could well have dissipated. I didn't know if the Glazers had been through the Museum and Tour Experience but they should have taken it on every rare visit over from their Florida base. It was, after all, United's attempt to cling on to a soul that the Glazers would surely sell on when the time was right and the market had picked up.

As I drove up Sir Matt Busby Way and back on to the Chester Road, I felt ambivalent; sad that the Rooney saga at the time was overshadowing the uplifting museum memories. In the film *Field of Dreams*, James Earl Jones as Terence Mann talked of baseball and 'all that was good in the game and could be again'. I wanted to see that in football once more.

Chapter 9

BALE IS THE SPUR

It is a man's duty to take his son to football as a rite of passage; nay, it should be legally enforceable that dads should introduce lads to the game. As with the facts of life, what they do with the information after that is up to them. This season, though, I wondered whether fathers might be accused of child cruelty were they to take the boy to a match.

The Wayne Rooney episode had highlighted all that was wrong with the sport, from tainted talent to naked greed, to the extent that it might be better to tell a kid to find something else more honest and noble to occupy them. Like pimping on the streets of Soho. Besides, it took a day's takings from that to afford the tickets these days. In my own lad's case, though, the whore had already bolted.

Growing up in Dorset in the 1960s, my own father took me to see Weymouth, the only team for miles and then of the Southern League, and of whom I later became chairman. But I had a benign old Uncle George, who lived in Wood Green, North London. In the summer holidays, I would be sent to stay with George for a week in the big city – such are breaks for those from the seaside. Usually, he would take me to Tottenham Hotspur for a pre-season friendly.

The whole area to me then seemed metropolitan and glamorous, a real place to be for a kid from the backwaters of the sleepy South-West, where the 1960s would not arrive until they were over. The North Circular was like an American highway. Even in its suburbs, London seemed to be Swinging. My uncle's nextdoor neighbour was a lad called Dave Clark of the Dave Clark Five (a popular beat combo of the time, your lordship, whose *Glad All Over* is still played at Crystal Palace as the club anthem) and his best friend at school, the comic Mike Reid, who would go on to star in *EastEnders*. George would always refer to him as Micky Reid.

The evenings were long and the floodlights would not come on until the second half but still the White Hart Lane experience was magical. We would walk from his flat the long way up Risley Avenue, men leaving their front doors to join what they call these days a walking bus, when kids traipse to school in on-foot convoy. After Bruce Castle Park, it was down the alleyway by the church on to the buzzing Tottenham High Road. I remember once being star-struck walking behind Warren Mitchell, then a huge celebrity as the bigoted West Ham-supporting Alf Garnett in the seminal comedy series *Till Death Us Do Part* but in reality a Spurs fan.

My boy Jack was born in April 1990 and was six weeks old when I went off to the World Cup in Italy. When I got back, he had doubled his age and wondered who this strange man walking through the door was. Settled in Hertfordshire, I took him to the odd non-League match at St Albans City as a toddler. 'Look Dad,' I remember him saying with huge excitement, 'a header.' It mattered not to him that the centre forward concerned had missed a sitter by nodding over from just a few yards out.

So that we could share an interest and time, I was grateful that he took to the game, unlike his older sister Alex upon whom I had tried to inflict it. I did not want Jack, though, to be subjected, like his dad, to a lifetime of semi-professional piss-taking and piss-pottery and so Spurs seemed like the team for him. We even went with Uncle George a few times before he died. It seemed like a good idea at the time. It was the mid-1990s and Arsenal were in disgrace under George Graham after his bung-taking. Graham's teams had won trophies but dourly so, and this new Frenchman called Arsène Wenger was untried and mistrusted.

'Anyway,' I said sagely to Jack, 'Arsenal buy centre halves. Spurs buy centre forwards. That's all you need to know.' Thirteen years later under Wenger, Arsenal had won seven major trophies. Tottenham's attacking reputation had brought them just three League Cup final appearances. Arsenal played their youth team in that competition.

That's not to say Jack hadn't enjoyed some good times. He had seen Spurs take the League Cup by beating Leicester at Wembley in 1999, then win a memorable semi-final over Chelsea 5-1 at White Hart Lane but lose another final at Cardiff to Blackburn Rovers in 2002.

A 2-1 win over Chelsea in the final of 2008 meant that Jack was also 2-1 up in finals attended. But the League Cup? For Wenger and Arsenal it was usually chewing gum on the shoe, an irritant that brought fixture congestion, even if this season they looked to be taking it a bit more seriously as desperation for a trophy increased. Perhaps, though, the worm was turning.

Jack had remained loyal to his team despite it all, even though most of Hertfordshire now had grown up supporting Wenger's purring, pass-and-move sides and even though he came under intense peer group pressure. Now Spurs had reached the Champions League for the first time by finishing fourth in the Premier League the previous season, a remarkable feat of leadership by Harry Redknapp, who had inherited a bottom-of-the-table team after arriving from Portsmouth. The last time Tottenham had been in the competition's previous guise, bearing the proper title of European Cup, was almost 50 years earlier in 1961. That year they had won the League and FA Cup Double when that achievement was genuinely rare and elusive. Indeed, they were the first winners of it in the 20th century, one of only three clubs to achieve the feat before the arrival of the Premier League. Since then, it had been won six times.

Now in the Champions League group stages, they were drawn against the holders, Internazionale of Milan, and I had procured two tickets for us. They were £76 each. Yes, £76 each. For those people under 25 who don't have their calculators with them, that is £152 the pair. Still, it's your son, isn't it? I just felt grateful to have got hold of them, to be taking my boy to football. Music, playing and recording it, was his thing these days but he retained an affection for football, even if meeting some only-too-human players as a result of what his father did for a living had taken much of its hero-worship mystique from him.

He was now 20 and at Brighton University but when I met him at our local station, his eyes looked like those of an excited five-year-old again, amazed at a header. I was worried about a tube strike due to start that night but the traffic was light as we navigated North London and found a parking place at the end of Risley Avenue. I wanted us to walk through Bruce Castle Park, down the alleyway by the side of the church and on to buzzing Tottenham High Road. Jack liked the walk as well. It reminded him of being younger too.

Instead of turning left for the stadium, we went right for the cafe on the corner, La Barca, with its A-board outside offering: 'Attractive Garden, Dessert, Jacket Potatoes, Daily Specials, Party Reservations'. Often a pub with a blackboard outside advertising food in coloured chalks quickens the urge to move on but this was clearly the best place for several hundred yards amid the kebab shops and burger takeaways. It was cheap and cheerful and busy with both Spurs and Inter fans, the latter the ones drinking beer. They didn't seem to draw the distinction made by British football fans between places to eat and places to drink.

We found a table just before the crowds began queuing through the door. 'You're getting your reward now for forward planning and getting here early,' Jack said, I don't think sarcastically. It worried me that I was making him old before his time. Still we arrived inside the ground too early, around 45 minutes before kick off. But then there was so much more to occupy a fan of a big club these days, including TVs in the concourses, with the club's own in-house station offering previews and chat.

Our seats were in a corner of the West Stand – goodness knows how much they cost on the halfway line – offering a decent enough view. The big screens at either end were showing great moments from Spurs' European history, including winning the UEFA Cup in 1984. The screens were a boon to fans, except during games when clubs were forbidden to replay controversial incidents. They also became extremely annoying when showing pictures of players and managers looking up at themselves. In some cases, it was because they too wanted to see what had happened in an incident; in others it was sheer vanity.

There was also the routine of players warming up now for at least half an hour, going through intricate drills and five-a-side games. How they weren't knackered when kick off finally arrived, I wasn't quite sure. In the old days here, Jimmy Greaves would run out five minutes before the appointed time, extinguishing his fag in the tunnel as he went.

By 7.45 p.m. (standard time for the start of night matches now, the change from 7.30 p.m. to give more time for fans to negotiate the increased traffic), the atmosphere was energising. Breath – and not cigarette smoke; another change for the better for those of us who had finally managed to give it up – hung in the night air.

In the lit arena the grass was pristine as the players emerged to fulfil the gauche Champions League ritual of standing to attention, not to national anthems but to UEFA's tune, that seems to sing 'lasagna'. Somebody once joked that the words, in deference to the governing body's Swiss location, were actually 'Lausanne, ja!' but more boringly they were meant to be 'the champions'.

Anyway, roars greeted its conclusion and the referee's opening whistle, with Tottenham immediately working the ball to Gareth Bale on the left wing. It was a signal of intent, and a warning to Inter. A fortnight earlier in the first leg, Spurs had been trailing 4-0 to them in the Giuseppe Meazza stadium in the San Siro district of Milan when the 21-year-old Welshman suddenly announced himself to Europe with a stunning hat-trick of drilled left-footed shots.

The Italians were patently scared stiff of him and soon their Brazilian right back Maicon, one of the world's finest, was suffering from the condition that Sir Matt Busby used to ascribe to opponents of George Best: twisted blood. Soon Bale was emulating the performances of another Manchester United player at his peak, fellow Welshman Ryan Giggs.

I looked to Jack, and he smiled back. We both knew that Spurs were 'at it' tonight. Soon came an opening goal, the skilful little Croat Luka Modric slipping a through ball to the signing of the season so far, Rafael van der Vaart – pinched on transfer deadline day for £8 million from Real Madrid – and he tucked the ball home. A bit of a fancy dan, he was clearly not the cup of cha of Real's new manager, the Portuguese Jose Mourinho, once so controversially, but successfully, of Chelsea and of Inter, under whom they had won this competition. At Spurs, though, they had always preferred fine art to painting by numbers and van der Vaart was a veritable Dutch master.

The game developed into titanic, top-class stuff. Inter were a slight disappointment, more attacking under the former Liverpool manager Rafael Benitez than Mourinho, but looking age-weary in places, notably the holding midfield player Javier Zanetti, especially when compared to the youthful, zippy Bale.

On the hour, Bale outpaced Maicon – 'taxi for Maicon' the Spurs fans were soon singing – and crossed for Peter Crouch to grab a second. Jack leapt up; I smiled and applauded. White Hart Lane was in rapture.

Except for one or two. Inter, as to be expected, began to work their way back into the game. Now it was a case of whether Spurs could also show resilience to go with their ambition. They began to wobble, as only to be expected at some point against such a side in such a game. 'Fucking hell, Spurs. That's fucking rubbish. Wake up,' shouted someone nearby as Samuel Eto'o, oozing class, went close. Jack turned to me and smiled. I no longer worried about the language as I did when he was a youngster. Football fans, eh? Give 'em caviar and they want Beluga.

Only a tannoy announcement interrupted the tension: despite the tube strike, the Victoria Line would be running after the game. Cue cheers. Normally people grumble at the walk to the nearest underground station at Seven Sisters, some 20 minutes away. But then came groans. The Cameroonian Eto'o, who looked far from the spent force you suspected when sold by Barcelona the previous season, pulled back a goal and the 'effing bloke was apoplectic. The rest of us were enthralled. This was some match.

As the game entered added time, Spurs gave the ball wide to Bale again on the halfway line. He knocked it into the space behind the covering defender, Lucio. Giving the Brazilian 10 yards start, Bale outpaced him by 10 yards and sent in another inviting low cross to the far post where the tall Russian Roman Pavlyuchenko arrived to slide the ball home. Even I, as a neutral, leapt up at this one. Jack hugged me. Spurs had won 3-1 and we had witnessed one of the great White Hart Lane nights.

Tottenham were talking of trying to move to the Olympic stadium five miles east in Stratford after London's Games of 2012 in an initiative that would prompt a national debate. They planned to demolish the £500 million arena, build one more suitable for football without a running track and refurbish Crystal Palace National Sports Centre for athletics. They reckoned that would cost

£100 million less than plans to redevelop the White Hart Lane site into a 60,000-seater stadium.

London rivals West Ham United, in their bid to take over the Stratford site, meanwhile, would retain the Olympic stadium and the running track, though would need £40 million of public money. Even then their long-term business plan was less robust than Spurs'. The head may have said Tottenham for the stadium – though not those of the poor traders and businesses of the area, like La Barca – but the heart said West Ham. And no matter that football at elite level is about the head and money, nights like tonight reasserted that it also had to be about the heart and glory. Wherever Spurs ended up, they would struggle to recreate this atmosphere.

In years to come, when Jack and I spoke of Spurs v. Inter Milan, we would not remember the £76 each. We would not remember that it was around that time when Wayne Rooney disgusted us. We would remember the walk to the ground, the meal together. We would also remember a famous Spurs victory and the night Gareth Bale became a superstar.

For over the next few days, every cough and spit of his life would come under scrutiny: how he was just a simple lad who went home to mum in Cardiff when given some time off, to remind me of that line from David Bowie's *Space Oddity*: 'And the papers want to know whose shirts you wear.'

Two weeks later, I found myself at a function where Bale was one of the guests, revealing himself to be a simple, straightforward lad. His girlfriend had described them as being the Gavin and Stacey of football, after the sitcom couple of the same name.

'Football can be gone in the blink of an eye,' he told a group of businessmen/football fans at a dinner at the BT Tower in London. 'One bad tackle and it can be gone. That's why I don't take it for granted. That's why I want to savour every moment.' He would, he said, love to play for Great Britain at London 2012, if the four home nations could sort out their political wrangling. He would remember forever that night against Inter Milan.

Afterwards, I approached him. He looked smaller in a grey suit and fancy pink shirt with oversized collar. Footballers are often less impressive and imposing off the field than on it. I told him of taking my son to Spurs that night and thanked him for the memory. 'That's nice,' he said with a smile that made him look a bit like Alfred E. Newman of the *Mad* comic (who once opined that sports people mind their builds, instead of the other way round). Had he heard the 'taxi for Maicon' chant? 'Yes,' Bale replied. 'I was trying not to smile.'

Jack and I would smile a lot at the pleasure and recall of it. Above all, after the gloom of England's summer and Rooney's autumn, we would remember why we still loved this game and were drawn back to it. The timeless pleasure of seeing a great performance or a great match survived any amount of change and the moneymaking attempts of those who would cling to its coat-tails.

As we drove home, the traffic lighter than expected after we had made a swift, satisfying exit via the park, Jack worked his way through the £5 souvenir programme. 'Who was Spurs' greatest player?' he asked me. Glenn Hoddle perhaps, I ventured. Maybe Danny Blanchflower, the Double-winning captain, who insisted that the game must be about glory above anything else. Jack found a feature on him in the programme and began reading. Maybe he would come to see Gareth Bale as his own favourite.

I also thought of Paul Gascoigne, though he had been at Spurs for only two seasons, one injured due to his reckless FA Cup final of 1991 after a sensational Wembley free-kick in the semi-final against Arsenal had got them there. Another such strike against Chelsea, a few months on from those tears of Italia '90 when Jack was doubling his age, had inspired me into writing my first book. Now there were more tears from, and for, Gazza.

Chapter 10

A GAME OF CHANCE

GAZZA HAD GONE and done it again. He had been arrested for drink-driving in the Jesmond district of Newcastle while four times over the limit and was up in court. He was pictured grinning as he entered, probably as a way of dealing with his nerves, but the smile soon disappeared when a district judge went further than the driving ban he expected. Paul Gascoigne, Stephen Earl said, could be facing 12 weeks in jail pending a probation report.

That prospect, along with returning for sentencing in a month's time, sent Gazza over the edge again. Twenty-four hours later, he collapsed at a cottage in Burradon, North Tyneside and a worried friend phoned the police. An ambulance crew revived Gascoigne, who was promptly arrested by police on suspicion of possessing cocaine, which had allegedly been supplied by a friend.

Sympathy for Gascoigne was waning. This was just the latest episode in a growing list of alcohol-related incidents and no one would have been surprised to turn on the news one day to find that he had died at an early age like that other icon of the 1990s, Princess Diana. There was indeed little sympathy for footballers in general any more. After the World Cup, after Rooney's antics, and in the middle of a recession, they were just cocky young blokes who had more money than sense or sensibility.

Take Jermaine Pennant. As a teenager playing for Notts County in his native city of Nottingham, he was signed by Arsène Wenger for Arsenal but deemed after a few years not to have the necessary dedication and was moved on. He had since made a living moving from club to club and you would have wanted to be his agent considering the transfer commission; Pennant was good enough for some big clubs to want to sign but not good enough for them to want to keep.

He was now at Stoke City, having joined them from Real Zaragoza, and a story emerged that he had left his Porsche at the railway station in the Spanish city, forgetting it was there. Rail staff, alerted by the number of parking tickets stuck to the windscreen, contacted Stoke, but Pennant at first denied the car was his. Until, that was, they pointed out that the number plate was P33 NNT. He simply got a pal to pick up the motor. He transferred the personalised plate to his Ferrari.

Then, this season of 2010/11, there was Ryan Babel, Liverpool's Dutch striker, becoming the first player to be punished by the FA for bringing the game into disrepute via the internet. After Liverpool had controversially lost to Manchester United in an FA Cup tie, Babel posted a doctored picture of the referee Howard Webb in a United shirt on Twitter. It was a piece of artwork that cost him a £10,000 fine.

These were among the more frivolous stories that give you a laugh at the modern footballer's expense. There were also the downright nasty and tacky, though, as the Premier League had become ever bigger business and players' wealth and celebrity increased. Players had been making the journey from back page of the newspapers to front, and thus on to national television news, and the pictures were often not pretty.

Back in 2000, the Leeds United pair Lee Bowyer and Jonathan Woodgate were charged with attacking a young student of Asian origin outside a nightclub in the city. The case turned into a debate about the modern game and its values. In the end, Bowyer was cleared of grievous bodily harm while Woodgate was convicted of affray and sentenced to 100 hours of community service. But, like a storyline in a soap opera, once it had played out, everybody just carried on.

The behavioural debate did intensify, however, after four Chelsea players – John Terry, Frank Lampard, Jody Morris and Eidur Gudjohnsen – were fined by the club for drunkenness at a Heathrow hotel in 2001. It was the day after the 9/11 suicide bombing of the Twin Towers in New York and their crassness took place amid Americans waiting to fly again and get home.

Stories of sexual infidelity and orgiastic episodes seemed to increase, too. Lampard, Rio Ferdinand and Keiron Dyer were involved in a taped session in the downmarket Greek resort of Ayia Napa that shamed them, and probably served as an alarm call to them to change their ways if they were to go on to good careers and to other young players not to do what they had done.

Was there really more bad behaviour than ever, sexual or otherwise, going on? Footballers had always behaved badly but nowadays they were just able to find new, luxury ways of doing it. Since the Premier League had taken off, since more attention had been trained upon them, it just felt as if there was more of it about.

Though less being reported during the 2010/11 season, it seemed; at least publicly. These days, players had recourse to 'super injunctions' that they could take out to prevent press coverage of their sexual indiscretions, granted often so as not to hurt their families but often requested by the players, or their agents, so as not to damage their commercial prospects. At one point, there were supposedly six top players trying to keep a lid on their activities, though the internet could still speculate and expose. Still, at a trifling £50,000 a pop, these super injunctions were value for money.

For some, the money was easy come, easy go. This season, there would be cases of bankruptcy involving two former high-profile players in Keith Gillespie and Carl Cort. Gillespie had been a young

Manchester United player – burdened by unflattering comparisons with his fellow Ulsterman George Best – who had gone on to play for Newcastle, as had Cort. Both had had plenty of seasons earning at least £1 million a year. Bankruptcy had befallen even bigger names the year before, too, in John Barnes, once of Liverpool and England, and Colin Hendry, of Blackburn and Scotland. Again, there was little sympathy from the public. It was, as one financial adviser with more than 40 players on his books, told me, the 'tip of the iceberg'.

The chief executive of the Professional Footballers' Association, Gordon Taylor, was worried about players throwing their money at unsound investments, rather than investing them in pensions. In 2006, the then Labour government had changed legislation that allowed sportsmen and women, and certain sections of the entertainment industry, to take a percentage of their pension pot at the age of 35. Now they had to wait until 55 like the rest of us. Taylor had approached the new coalition government in an attempt to overturn the legislation. 'It was a hammer blow to us when the last government stopped players' pensions beginning at 35,' he told me. 'Changing that back is high on our agenda and we have broached the subject already. We think there should be a concession for all sportsmen and women because they are dedicated to reaching the top and it can be a short career, especially if they are hit by injury.

'They used to put a lot into their pensions but now that they can't get at the money sooner, they are looking at other schemes, which can go wrong. We are seeing many cases of players who have been badly advised by agents and others, and who we are trying to help through debt counselling and re-organising their finances. These days, it is assumed that footballers have a lot of money, and there are plenty of people out there prepared to pressure them into spending it. They can get caught up investing in property in Spain and the West Indies, which can crash, along with things like film schemes, which they are told are tax deductible but when the revenue calls in later years, it causes a lot of pain.'

The financial adviser to whom I spoke cited the example of an American company targeting players to invest in a coffee bean which they claimed would be worth fortunes because it helped prevent cancer and lower cholesterol. 'Many players invested but, of course, it turned out to be a load of rubbish,' he said.

Property was the most attractive investment, he added, largely due to the examples of two former Liverpool players in Robbie Fowler and Steve McManaman, who had had much success in the market. Fowler even owned streets of terraced houses in Oldham. 'That has led to the emergence of a whole host of property "experts" who are basically flogging off duff properties to unsuspecting footballers,' added the adviser, who cited one company who had been trying to sell luxury cars to players but changed to property when told that was what they wanted.

'Too many players, if they have a spare £20K, £30K or £50K, would be looking for some get-rich-quick, "exclusive-to-footballers" scheme,' he said. 'They don't realise that the reason why some companies deal with footballers is because they perfectly fit their ideal client profile: young, loaded and not the brightest. Some "superstars" want their investments to be exclusive but what they don't realise is that the investments only attract footballers because nobody else in their right minds would invest. There is a very good reason why the multi-millionaire fund managers from the City don't.

'I have also known players being charged 50 per cent of funds in costs. A decent adviser will charge two per cent, maybe up to five if they are running the players' entire affairs. When you add big charges to some of them wanting the latest Range Rover or Audi R8, as well as giving money to their families, you know that bankruptcies like Gillespie and Cort are just the tip of the iceberg.

'I could name five of my clients who will probably end up bankrupt because they won't listen to sound advice and have put all their eggs in one basket. It's so frustrating. One told me that he came into the game with nothing, so won't be too worried if he left it with nothing. Our job is made so hard by opportunistic sharks but the problem is that we can only offer financial advice, not financial dictation.'

Added Gordon Taylor: 'We still want players to make safe investments and take out pensions. We wish more would come to us before they sign up to schemes.' The task of persuading some of his members of that, however, was as difficult as getting the government to rethink footballers' pension arrangements in the prevailing climate. There may have been many players in the lower divisions on £500 a week and even less but special treatment for well-paid footballers at a time when many of the game's audience were facing hardship through cuts and pension changes, was understandably not high on the government's agenda.

Too many players, too, were victims of their own indulgences, it was often felt. Tony Adams would have agreed in some instances, though in other cases there was a genuinely different reason. For their money did not make footballers immune from the illnesses that beset all sections of society. When the then Arsenal captain and England centre back admitted in 1996 that he was an alcoholic, football was shocked. Most knew he was a bit of a drinker, as many players were in the 1990s when the motto seemed to be: win or lose, on the booze. The game had changed with the influx of managers such as Arsène Wenger, however, and overseas players who were fitter, stronger and more dedicated. The English players could no longer get away with it.

Adams set up his own charity, Sporting Chance, which took over premises near Liphook in Hampshire and established a treatment centre for players. At first it simply dealt with addictive illnesses such as alcoholism and drug use – cocaine having grown in popularity as a recreational tool for players – by offering counselling and group sessions to promote a programme of abstinence from their drug of choice. Alongside was a fitness regime that would mean they were ready to return to their clubs and play again at the end of their four-week stint.

Now it had expanded to include many other forms of self-defeating behaviour, including anger management. Among the Sporting Chance alumni was Clarke Carlisle, now of Burnley and chairman of the PFA, who was approaching five years of sobriety.

Today I had come not to a game, nor to a stadium or training ground, but to a venue for fishing and clay pigeon shooting deep in the Staffordshire countryside. Here, on a day organised by Sporting Chance, members of the public paid to mingle with players and managers in order to raise funds for those, unlike the wealthiest footballers, who could not afford the cost of treatment.

Among the high-profile cast was Joey Barton, Liverpool-born Newcastle United midfield player and recent graduate of Sporting Chance. During his career, Barton had been involved in many scrapes, starting with stubbing out a lit cigar in the face of a youth team player, Jamie Tandy, on a pre-season tour when the pair were at Manchester City. Barton had also assaulted a senior teammate, Ousmane Dabo, at training and been given a four-month suspended prison sentence, 200 hours of community service and ordered to pay £3,000 in compensation. Then, in 2007, he was found guilty of an assault on two people in his native Liverpool and was sentenced to six months in jail, of which he served 77 days.

Alcohol had been involved in the majority of the episodes, fuelling Barton's rage. Even when he wasn't drinking, it coloured his behaviour, as he was now admitting as he tried to remain abstinent. Too easily billed as a toerag, there was no doubt that Barton was dangerous and obnoxious when drunk. But today he would be engaging company, to illustrate the change that his illness brought about in him when he was drinking. He was also thoroughly aware of how he was perceived; when a photographer wanted a picture of him with a shotgun, he politely declined.

Drinking had always been the most visible of addictions down the years but now players were wise to being turned over when out partying, media-savvy punters always ready to take pictures on their mobiles and phone a newspaper. Players also knew that drugs stayed in their system and they could fail a test.

For many with too much time on their hands and too much money in their pockets, there were new ways of escapism in the search for a buzz. Peter Kay, the chief executive of Sporting Chance, was reporting more instances of players getting hooked on internet pornography. Gambling had become a bigger problem, however, perhaps not surprising given the competitive nature of footballers. Now the opportunities were widespread. Apart from the high street bookmakers, private, computerised accounts were more prevalent – you could hide on the web. Advertising was everywhere, clubs were sponsored by bookies. It was a growing culture and industry.

Also present here in Staffordshire was Matthew Etherington, a Cornish-born player who was now at Stoke City having been previously with Peterborough, Tottenham and West Ham. The story he told me, of how he lost £1.5 million, his debt reaching £800,000 at one point, was a graphic and salutary one that said much about attitudes and behaviour among modern players.

Etherington, sensitive and intelligent contrary to stereotype, spoke to me of his dark West Ham days with the rare candour that comes to a recovering addict grateful to be free of their addiction. He would, he said, board the team coach and by journey's end would have gambled away that week's £20,000 wages. He shook his head at the times when the first thing he would do after a post-match shower would be to turn on his phone to check how the horses he had backed had run. 'Looking back on it now, how can you prepare for a game when you are playing cards on the bus with lots of money changing hands?' he wondered. 'It was silly.' As for those match-day horses, 'I wasn't even watching them run. That's how stupid it was.'

Thankfully for him, he also remembered what he called his 'defining day'; the fateful moment for those addicts fortunate enough to stop drinking, using drugs or gambling before their illness plays out its sickening endgame and kills them, if not physically, then emotionally and spiritually. The date when he came to realise how much he had damaged himself, his family and his footballing career through betting was 27 September 2009, shortly after his 28th birthday.

As a child, Etherington had stood out very quickly in the sporting backwater of the Falmouth/Truro area and was picked up by a scout attached to Peterborough United. His parents moved the family to Cambridgeshire when their son was 12 to give him the best chance of making it.

He did. After a Football League debut at just 15 years and 262 days, he played in an outstanding team that reached the FA Youth Cup semi-finals, and the sharp-dealing Peterborough manager Barry Fry – in charge at Barnet that day of their elevation to the Football League – scented a good deal. Fry persuaded Tottenham's David Pleat, then the recruiting director of football, to pay what would add up to £2 million for Etherington and the other top kid at London Road, Simon Davies.

Soon the pair were billeted at a hotel just off the M25 at Waltham Abbey and Etherington, then just 18, traced back the roots of his gambling – the chase for the buzz, the freedom from tedium and loneliness that assails addicts more intensely than is the norm – back to that time. 'I was bored out of my mind,' he said. 'Simon and I were sick of the sight of each other. I remember one night looking in the *Evening Standard* and there was a dog card for Walthamstow. I had nothing to do. I thought I would go along. I didn't see any harm in it. I actually enjoyed it.'

At first he would lose only £30 or £40 and thought little of it. But from once a month, it became once a week. He even bought greyhounds, though it was still just a hobby. 'I enjoyed the sport, apart from the gambling on it, and I had a fondness for the dogs and cared about their welfare,' he said. 'If it had stayed at 30 or 40 quid, I wouldn't have bothered, just gone home and not chased it. You never like losing but I didn't have that compulsion then that I needed to win that money back. That came later on.'

His career at White Hart Lane stalled under the management of Glenn Hoddle and, after a move to newly relegated West Ham, he revelled in the Championship. He was quickly Hammer of the Year, and in his second season West Ham won the play-offs to return to the Premier League. He had another good year as the club reached the FA Cup final, losing to Liverpool, but the gambling had been getting worse. That heady mix of money and success, dangerous for a developing addict, was about to extract its toll. 'I was gambling in all forms, but it was basically the dogs and horses, going into betting shops, betting online. Not football, or any games I was involved in, because there are a lot of rules and it was becoming known that I had a problem and I didn't want to go down that road. If there was a European Championship or a World Cup on, I would do then.'

Indeed, the instances of players being caught gambling on the game were few, such as the four lower-division players who received varying bans and fines in 2008 for betting on the outcome of an end-of-season match between Bury and Accrington Stanley. But the infamous mid-1990s cases of Bruce Grobbelaar of Liverpool and Hans Segers and John Fashanu of Wimbledon – all found not guilty of match-fixing to benefit a betting ring, though Grobbelaar was deemed dishonest by the House of Lords – appeared to serve as a warning to would-be betters.

'It was reported there were card schools at West Ham, which there were,' Etherington continued of his own gambling, 'and it did get a little bit out of hand. People were taking three, four, five grand on the bus with them. When that was gone, you were borrowing more. You could win or lose 20 grand on a single journey, which is ludicrous. Then some would play in their rooms. It wouldn't just stop on the bus.

'It can't be good for team morale. Any normal human being, if you are losing a lot of money, you are not going to be happy about it and you are going to resent the person taking it off you. You could be going out on to a pitch knowing that your win bonus or appearance money that day is more or less down the drain because you have lost it already. Alan Pardew [West Ham manager at the time] stopped it, which he was right to do.'

It didn't stop Etherington, however. His playing form dipped, and his bets grew bigger, indulged by the bookies. 'There are certain bookmakers who will give you good credit knowing you earn a good wage. My wages were gone every month and I was on good money, about £20,000 a week. It was taking over my life.'

Match-day rituals became obsessive, starting at his home in Chigwell, Essex. 'I would place the bets in the morning. It was the first thing I would do, either on the internet or going into a bookies. Instead of getting my head right for the game, I was thinking, "Right, what horse am I going to back today?"

'There would be afternoons when I would go into a bookies with a couple of grand and I would lose it and be gutted. I was full of shame and guilt and would hate myself. Within five minutes, that had gone and I would think, "Right, where am I going to get the money for the next bet?" I knew it was going to spiral out of control but I was still doing it.'

Issues were surfacing in his marriage to wife Claire, made worse by the gambling she knew about, and when they had a daughter

Seani, he tried to do the right thing. He went to Sporting Chance in February 2007, but he was not ready. 'I had a great week and came out thinking I was fixed and didn't need anything else. I didn't continue therapy and within six to nine months I was gambling again. They always say that when you relapse it gets worse and it did. I was in a bar with friends watching football. I still had debts and I was getting phone calls regarding them. I was getting pressure from people I owed money to, on to me all the time. I was thinking, "I am not getting anywhere here. What is this all about?" I just walked round the corner to a bookies and had a bet.'

West Ham loaned him £300,000 to pay off his debts on the understanding that he would get help. But he didn't and, with his marriage now over, he agreed with the club that he needed a fresh start. He also needed a signing-on fee. Stoke City obliged. 'It helped me pay off some debt but there was still some left to pay,' he said, a shame showing in his face as his voice quietened. How much? 'About £800,000. But I lost more than that in all. About £1.5 million. Definitely.'

Etherington did well enough in his early days at Stoke, laying on and scoring a couple of goals, but he knew himself that he was capable of so much more. There was still the odd bet but by now he was close to rock bottom. 'The damage was done. I was drowning but no longer had the money to gamble. It was all gone. I had gone through a divorce and was left with nothing every month. It got to the point where I didn't want to bet any more. I was sick to the teeth of it. It had got the better of me. It chewed me up and spat me out. I was in a bad, bad way.'

Then, that September day, he arrived home from training with Stoke to find his mum and dad at his kitchen table, along with his sister Hayley and partner Stephanie. Worry was etched on their faces. Remorse was etched on his now as he replayed the scene in his mind's eye. They had known for a long time about his gambling but not the extent. 'They asked me to lay everything on the table and I did,' he said. 'They were all crying and I was emotional as well. They said, "We want to help you." I had become very withdrawn, not the person my family knew. When you are a gambler, you are in another world, not really listening to them. You are thinking about your next bet.

'It does go on in football but it is hard to tell with some people. With an alcoholic or drug addict you can look at them and say, "you are not well," but with a gambler it is harder. I was a loner. Didn't tell anyone my business. Most people didn't have a clue about the sums and debt I was in. That day it hit home how much I had upset them. I realised what I had done to everyone in life I love the most. I realised this had to be it. If it wasn't, then the next step for me was a gutter somewhere.'

Etherington's family were stunned by the details, unlike Peter Kay and his staff at the Sporting Chance centre situated in the grounds of a health spa, where he went secretly a few weeks later. They had seen and heard it all before, after all. He took to the treatment this time and returned to Stoke to find the form of his life flying down the left wing, to the point where he was being talked about as a potential England player.

These days, his mum took care of his accounts while he concentrated on earning the money to pay off the gas, electricity and tax bills that once piled up unopened. 'It's a bit degrading for a 28-year-old but that's what it's come to,' he said, though it had left him free to do what he did best. 'Since I have stopped, my form has got better and better and I don't think it's a coincidence,' he said. 'I don't have a burden on my shoulders. I am not thinking about gambling every day. I am feeling as fit and as strong as I have ever felt. I have had negative press in the last few years so for people to be talking about my football and me having a chance of getting in the England squad is very pleasing.'

Most important, he recaptured the freedom of just wanting to play football. 'I genuinely do feel that something just clicked. I understand the illness now and have to go to Gamblers Anonymous meetings, which I do twice a week in Birmingham. The illness will always be there. And I know it is waiting for me to get sloppy or complacent and to be thinking "I am on top of this". Then it will come back and bite you on the backside again. If I have just one more bet, I could ruin the rest of my life. And I just don't want to do that.'

Etherington provided an example of how initial judgements could be wrong, of how not all footballers were simply overpaid prima donnas, but just people who might have had issues and problems like the rest of us. It was for them that Sporting Chance, which was celebrating its tenth anniversary, existed. And more besides; they had recently signed a deal with the Premier League to go into all 20 clubs to train staff how to recognise and deal with problem players.

'The aim is preventive education,' said Peter Kay, as we sat in the Staffordshire countryside, shotguns going off around us. 'We talk about lifestyle and addiction, how it can lead to other things. The training is for coaches, managers and academy staff, anyone involved with young people at clubs, to spot warning signs.

'Sometimes if a player turns up late or dishevelled, maybe they think he doesn't care but we want them to look behind that, to see if people might be gambling or who has problems. We want them then to find ways of supporting them, and help them to have a career.

'Every Premier League club has an errant young man in the group. Maybe he doesn't turn up one day. But talent and skill precludes them taking action, or perhaps they do it through disciplining. But it doesn't address the problem. We do weekend workshops where they would come down, six people at a time, and undergo a training initiation with older players who would be sharing and mentoring them, such as Clarke Carlisle, Joey Barton and Matthew Etherington. We would teach them coping mechanisms, and hope to change behaviour through emotional articulacy by offering them mentoring. If they take it great, if not they will lose their career ultimately.

'We will support people like Matty Etherington in carrying the message. People talk about overpaid footballers but they don't know what some of these players do for the charity in time and money.' Barton, for example, had paid £20,000 out of his own pocket for a minibus to take in-patients at the Liphook treatment centre out to meetings of Alcoholics and Gamblers Anonymous in the surrounding area in the evenings.

Kay, flaxen-haired confidant to some high-profile clients, had worked with Paul Gascoigne at one point but Gazza had not been ready to quit drinking. Kay was only too aware of potential similarities with Wayne Rooney, stories about whose errant behavior had included him gambling. At one point, Rooney was said to have fallen out with fellow England striker Michael Owen after running up debts of £700,000 in five months by betting on horses, dogs and football with Stephen Smith, a business associate of Owen's.

'I have no idea if Wayne Rooney is an addict,' said Peter Kay. 'But if anyone has run up big gambling debts, that is a problem, no matter what label you want to put on it. In my experience, players at that level have very few avenues to seek support. They are always wary of the truth getting out, in case it is seen as a sign of weakness or they lose their place in the team.

'Often players can stop, say, gambling, if they get a shock of some sort but compulsive behaviour can then surface in other areas, including drinking or sex with prostitutes or internet pornography. There can also be an internal anger building up that can then manifest itself in play on the field. You can't just put sticking plaster on a gaping wound. If these core issues are not addressed, they are not going to go away.' Matthew Etherington had certainly discovered that – and elsewhere, his struggle still public and painful, Paul Gascoigne was finding it out too.

WINTER

Chapter 11

AT THE EYE OF THE STORM

TERRY WAITE HAD not long been released from five years of captivity in Beirut, and Liverpool were the reigning champions of the old First Division. Merchandise sellers at stalls near their Anfield home were quick to offer for sale T-shirts bearing a picture of the former hostage's laughing face, with a bubble that had him saying: 'And Manchester United still haven't won the title?'

They loved to gloat on the red half of Merseyside and had good reason back in 1991, with Liverpool having extended their record of titles to 18 the previous year. For it was then 24 years and counting since United had won their last title and United were more detested rivals even than neighbours Everton, for whom there was at least an affinity as Scousers, with all that meant.

The Blues, after all, were partners in ancestry and accent 'exceedingly rur' as the song about their Liverpool home had it. Also to illustrate the bond – the city having been harder hit than much of the rest of the country during the Thatcher years of the Conservative government – at their 1986 FA Cup final the two sets of supporters stood side by side, no segregation necessary, though they were hard times in another sense, too.

The 'Mancs' were another matter. Their travails were to be savoured. At the start of the 1990s, then plain Alex Ferguson had been United manager for five years and was struggling as his team sought to add an eighth League title – the last one secured by Sir Matt Busby's side in 1967, and still 11 behind Liverpool. Fast forward, and after winning the inaugural Premier League championship of 1992/93, Ferguson and United had gone on to record a remarkable haul of another 10 by 2010, equalling the record of Liverpool, who had yet to win a single Premier League title. With United threatening to overtake the tally this season, things were getting serious at Anfield.

'You don't think it will be another 20 years, do you?' said John Aldridge, a member of Liverpool's 1990 championship team, when we spoke at Anfield. 'At the time the squad was good. Everything was fine. It was rolling on smoothly as it was 20 years before.'

Now the T-shirts sold on the stalls down Sir Matt Busby Way on match day, some 35 miles away, told of United delighting in the gloating rights. 'Which ship has never docked at Liverpool?' one asked. 'The Premiership,' came the punchline. 'I'd rather walk alone,' said another. A third had a picture of Del Boy, Rodney and Uncle Albert and proclaimed that Only Fools and Scousers thought that 'this time next year we'll be champions'.

Liverpool had come close now and then over the two decades since Kenny Dalglish resigned in 1991, wearied by the emotional aftermath of the Hillsborough disaster. At one point, he attended four funerals in one day and it took its toll on him. His successor, the abrasive Graeme Souness, playing legend in the Dalglish teams of the 1980s assembled by the shrewd Bob Paisley, would do no better than sixth.

'It didn't work with Souey,' added Aldridge, who himself went into management with Tranmere Rovers and was now a local radio pundit. 'He tried to change things round too quickly. Everyone was looking to him as he had been such a great player for Liverpool and I would have loved him to be successful. It didn't work out.'

Then came Roy Evans, a quiet member of the fabled Anfield Boot Room, the cubbyhole under the main stand where the coaching staff would meet for tea and talks. It was begun by Liverpool's father figure and founder of their modern club, Bill Shankly, whose core working-class values of honest hard work and the human touch set standards in the English game. Evans' team did achieve a third place but, in 1998, the Anfield board decided that they needed new overseas expertise and methods.

Gerard Houllier had been the technical director for the Fédération Française de Football, a key figure in the nation winning the World Cup they hosted in 1998. Urbane and progressive, initially as joint manager with Evans, he set about rebuilding a team and a club in a city for which he had a huge affinity. In the late 1960s, he spent a year as a teaching assistant at Alsop High School in the Walton district of the city. (And among his pupils, in a small-world way, was one Jimmy Mulville, head of Hat Trick Productions, Everton fan, and the friend who had set me out on writing football books.) Houllier's formative footballing experiences came on atmospheric European nights on the then seething, standing Anfield Kop.

The partnership with Evans did not work, however, and Houllier soon took sole charge. By 2001, he had made his mark in winning the FA Cup, League Cup and UEFA Cup but it would take its toll; in October that year, he underwent 11 and a half hours of heart surgery and was away from the club for five months. He returned to take them to runners-up spot in the Premier League with 80 points, a total with which Manchester United had won the title the previous year.

It would be the closest Houllier came to the prize. His legacy would be a modernised club, having played a major role in designing and overseeing the rebuild of the Melwood training ground, but not the title Anfield craved. When Liverpool could only finish fourth in 2004, Houllier was replaced by Rafael Benitez.

The Spaniard had some immediate success with predominantly Houllier's team, winning the Champions League of 2005 in an astonishing final in Istanbul, when they were 3-0 down to AC Milan at half-time before squeezing out a 3-3 draw and winning on penalties. Benitez also emulated Houllier in finishing runners-up in the Premier League in 2009, with no fewer than 86 points, but was gone the following season after finishing seventh.

'Under Houllier and Benitez, there were a lot of bad signings over a 10-year period,' said John Aldridge. 'Rafa made some good ones, like Pepe Reina, Fernando Torres, Xavi Alonso and Javier Mascherano, but not enough and too many that weren't worthy of the shirt. Then when you think of some of the players that Houllier bought towards the end – Salif Diao, Bruno Cheyrou, Djibril Cissé – and the list of injuries to players on top money, it was worrying. They never kept regenerating the team.'

Like Houllier, Benitez was given six seasons, in keeping with the club's ethos down the years of staying loyal to their managers. Liverpool, after all, were a club of dignity and tradition, owned for generations by the patrician Moores family, who had been made wealthy by Littlewood's Pools, once the nation's favourite way of gambling but now a sideshow. Not for them crass modern ways. It was part of their problem; while United had embraced commercialism and reaped the rewards on the pitch, Liverpool had never really capitalised on their worldwide appeal of the 1980s, nor even their last European Cup in 2005. Still, it should have meant that their latest manager, the understated Englishman Roy Hodgson, was safe enough just a few months into the job.

Times, and things, were changing, however. As if now embracing the old adage that if you couldn't beat them you had to join them, like United, Liverpool had acquired American owners. David Moores had been chairman since 1991 but concluded that he no longer had the financial wherewithal to compete in the modern game. In the 2006/07 season, he agreed to sell his 51 per cent shareholding. The unlikely pairing of Tom Hicks, then owner of the Texas Rangers baseball franchise, and George Gillett, Montreal Canadiens ice hockey team owner, combined to take over Liverpool in a leveraged deal that priced the club and its debts at £219 million.

All sorts of grand plans were mooted, including a new stadium in nearby Stanley Park, the municipal green space established in 1870 which divided Liverpool's Anfield from Everton's Goodison Park. Not enough money materialised, however, even though planning permission was granted for a new stadium, and the pair grew more and more unpopular. They even began to bicker among themselves.

Along came another American company in New England Sports Ventures (NESV), headed by one John W. Henry, owner of the Boston Red Sox baseball team. In a bitter courtroom struggle, with Hicks and Gillett at odds and unable to find money to service loans, NESV gained control. Hicks and Gillett suddenly united to describe it as 'a swindle of epic proportions' but they had illustrated that co-owners, just like co-managers, did not work out.

In the way that football has of resembling an echo chamber, where the past impacts so frequently on the present, Houllier now found himself back in English football, and with an American owner. After leaving Liverpool, he returned to France with Olympique Lyonnais and guided them to two national championships in consecutive seasons, before returning to the French federation as technical director for the 2010 World Cup.

Now, unable to resist a return to the English game, Houllier had accepted the job at Aston Villa after Martin O'Neill's sudden resignation on the eve of the season as a result of disagreements with the American owner Randy Lerner over money for transfers. And now the fixture list was sending Houllier back to Anfield.

Ahead of the game, I travelled to Villa's training ground, Bodymoor Heath, to have lunch with Houllier in the players' restaurant before interviewing him in his office at the now opulent facilities that rivalled

Melwood. As we exited the canteen, Houllier could not resist the table football machine, *baby foot*, as they call it in France. 'Come on,' he said. 'Let's play.' Naturally he won. It was just that competitive streak that had brought him back to English football.

At the age of 63, Houllier could have remained as technical director of the French game for a while yet to work with the new head coach Laurent Blanc in rebuilding the national team and seeing the fruition of his training schemes. He could have rested peacefully on the laurels of those trophy-laden times with Liverpool and Lyon.

He had, after all, turned down jobs in Turkey with Fenerbahce and Germany with Wolfsburg in the previous year because his family circumstances were not then right. And, mindful of his family, he was even going to reject Villa, despite fruitful conversations and meetings with Randy Lerner after an initial phone call while on holiday in Corsica. 'One morning I woke up and said to Isabelle [his wife], "No, I am going to turn down the job. We have a quality of life here in Paris,"' he said. 'She got angry and said, "In my mind now I am in Birmingham." She knows that I am a competitor and I have a fire. She knows I need to live outside the comfort zone.' And this was England – not Turkey, not Germany – the land whose football had most influenced him.

'It will be interesting to see what the crowd is like,' he said with a smile as he contemplated the return to Liverpool. 'I trust them to be good. After all, I didn't go afterwards to Everton or Manchester United, did I?'

There would surely be much sympathy for him, indeed, having almost given his life in the Liverpool cause. At half-time during a match against Leeds United, he started feeling unwell while giving a team talk. The club doctor Mark Waller called an ambulance and within hours he was under the knife of Dr Abbas Rashid at the Royal Liverpool University Hospital to repair a dissected aorta.

After returning from the operation, he now candidly admitted that he had been unable to devote enough energy to recruiting players. 'After my illness, some of my signings were not good enough,' he said. 'I didn't have time to check.' If only he could have signed a player that Manchester United had recruited, it could have been so different; a kid by the name of Cristiano Ronaldo. 'I saw him in the Toulon Under-21 international tournament and we went for him but we had a wage scale and we weren't paying the sort of salary he wanted at that time,' Houllier recalled. 'Then Manchester United played a friendly in Portugal against Sporting Lisbon and all their boys said to Sir Alex Ferguson, "You have to sign him." But I agreed with not breaking the wage structure. I thought it would cause problems in our dressing room.

'Maybe we would have won the title with him but we had Harry Kewell, who was outstanding at the time and was very hungry but got a bad injury. After that, he never had the same confidence, the same appetite.'

As Houllier talked about returning to the Anfield dugout, he knew that he would recall the great games and trophies, and the night he returned after recuperating from the surgery, against Fabio Capello's Roma in the UEFA Cup. 'That was very emotional,' he said. But it would be an event outside of his reign that sat most prominently in his mind's eye: the night in 2005 when Liverpool won their fifth European Cup by beating AC Milan on penalties from 3-0 down and his successor Rafael Benitez graciously allowed him backstage afterwards to see the players. 'If I had 10 memories to keep when I am finished, one would be when I went into the dressing room in Istanbul,' he recalled. 'Normally, one or two of the players would be a bit shy but they all came over to hug me and say, "Boss, it's your team." That was something special. I didn't realise then that 12 of the 14 players came through under me. We won things, we had difficult moments but we were together and they were grateful for the times we had.'

He can't remember quite how the end came the previous year. 'When it's not nice, I try to forget,' he said. 'Probably Rick Parry [then chief executive] came to see me but the deal was already done with Rafael Benitez. A few things now add up. It's like when your wife is cheating, you are the last to know. I think they were a little embarrassed.

'But I don't consider that as a dark period. It had to happen at some stage and six years at a big club is sometimes enough. I wasn't going to sign a new contract anyway because from a health point of view, it was better to have a sabbatical. Now I feel better than I did in Lyon,' he added and that much was evident as he smiled his way through Villa's training ground.

Before he had taken the job, though, he had gone back to Liverpool to seek the advice of his old surgeon, Dr Rashid, who gave him the go-ahead. His condition, after all, was not stress-related. Besides, he had now recruited Mark Waller for Villa, the Liverpool doctor from that day when he was unwell at Anfield.

'I could feel the chemistry here, with Paul [Faulkner, chief executive] and the chairman,' said Houllier. 'He is a good person. It is very true what Sir Alex says for a manager: pick a chairman, not a club. He lives for the club. I very much like the project here. I like the fans, the history. It is a club who is eager to win things. It is a club making changes and deciding on a different way of thinking, who are giving me the freedom to establish something.

'I knew they had some good young players and I have a chance to instil a culture, to say, "This is how we play, this is what we want to achieve." I want the club and the players to improve and progress. You have to improve as players but also as men and I think some are doing that already.'

When Houllier arrived at Liverpool some 12 years earlier, he encountered what was known as the Spice Boys. With the likes of Steve McManaman and Robbie Fowler, they were a group of players with a cockiness of youth surpassing their achievements, summed up best by the wearing of cream Armani suits for the 1996 FA Cup final when Eric Cantona's late goal won the game for Manchester United. Thus did passion overcome fashion. Houllier successfully set about changing the image and mindset of the players, bringing more dedication and a team ethic.

It was what the powers-that-be at Villa had hired him for. The word was that O'Neill's attitude to training had been relaxed, that the first team often trained only twice a week. Players on fortunes were being allowed to live in London or the North West and travel down to training. It was thought within the hierarchy of the club to be contributing to a dipping in fitness and form late in the seasons. Villa had done well under O'Neill, finishing sixth three seasons in a row, but always subsiding when a Champions League place was there for the taking.

'Players like to know they have a strong, sure and reassuring leadership,' said Houllier, fixing me with the steely stare that was as much a part of his management as his smile. 'I believe at the top level that there are three Ps – passion, performance and progress. We are not at the level of the top four yet. We have a good 25 but they need to repeat consistency.'

Houllier's initial attempts to professionalise the club, with more intense training sessions, led to a split within the Villa camp. There were the young players who enjoyed the new regime, wanted to improve, like Ashley Young and Marc Albrighton. There were also some old lags who did not like any intrusion into their comfort zone. Houllier had already had run-ins with John Carew, the Norwegian striker unable to buy a goal, and Richard Dunne, veteran defender whose career O'Neill had rescued but who was now labouring. The divide was patent on the bitterly cold December night when Villa went to Anfield.

On the way to the ground, I checked out the stall that was selling those Terry Waite T-shirts all those years ago. The stall was still there but there was little fun at Manchester United's expense these days – it was Liverpool's house that was made of glass and stone-throwing was unwise. Just a forlorn scarf reminded people that The Reds clung on to their superiority in one way, as five times champions of Europe.

The chance to add to that number was looking distant, however. Now Liverpool found themselves in the Europa League, a competition rebranded in 2009 from the UEFA Cup, which had absorbed the old European Cup-Winners' Cup a decade earlier. It was an afterthought adjunct to the Champions League and was played on a Thursday night, previously a fallow day in the game whose only purpose, Graeme Souness had once said, was for taking the long-suffering wife out for dinner. When they sang 'Thursday I don't care about you,' The Cure might have had the tournament in mind.

England had three places in it, for FA and League Cup winners and fifth-placed in the Premier League. But while it may have been fun for such as Fulham, who had reached its first final in 2010, for bigger clubs it was really just a sideshow that did not yield the riches of the Champions League. Even if a club did make it through the 17 games to win it, the financial reward of around £6 million was about the same as for playing in the group stages of the Champions League. It had been designed to allow the smaller clubs of Europe to get something from the kitty of international competition but it lacked the charm and attraction of old UEFA and Cup-Winners' cups, which Liverpool did used to take seriously.

Further signs of changing times could be seen at the memorabilia stall where, as evidence of less hostility between fans and the 'bizzies', there was a Mersey Police Mounted Department calendar for sale. Later there would be an announcement over the tannoy in the stadium that a fanzine was on sale. Once upon a time, fanzines were subversive and clubs would have nothing to do with them; now they were mainstream.

The chill did not stop the stream of Premier League tourists to Anfield and there were many Oriental faces among those around the statute of Bill Shankly at the Anfield Road end with its wonderful inscription: 'He made the people happy'. Even if there was not quite the throng that frequented Old Trafford's forecourt day and night, plenty more stood around the Hillsborough Memorial at the side of the Shankly Gates, with its eternal flame and list of the dead.

Inside the ground, the approach of kick off had always brought a hushed anticipation as nowhere else. Perhaps it was the honeyed tones of the announcer George Sephton, his lilting Liverpudlian accent and understated address a welcome contrast to the estuary English and excitability of screaming microphone men elsewhere. Here, it was mere lull before the sensual storm created by the Anfield crowd during the club anthem – the most celebrated in football – that accompanied the arrival of the teams.

'You'll Never Walk Alone' is a ballad from the Rodgers and Hammerstein show *Carousel*, which Merseyside singer Gerry Marsden and his band The Pacemakers turned into a No. 1 pop record in 1963, eclipsing for a while Liverpool's finest, The Beatles. At the time it was the custom at Anfield to play the No. 1 record of the week just before kick-off. So many people kept requesting Marsden's song long after it was knocked off its perch, however, that the club played it every week and it stuck. Its rendition was always a time for reverence at the tradition and history of the club, a time to gaze around the ground and reflect on heritage.

When you walk through the storm
Hold your head up high
And don't be afraid of the dark
At the end of the storm
There's a golden sky. . .

As Houllier made his way out to the dugout, there was that look of quiet satisfaction on his face. He clearly loved being back and appreciated the applause that accompanied him and the affectionate banner reading 'Gerard's heart beats'.

Actually, the reality of the game for managers – even if they cared about their own more at Liverpool than most places – was that managers did walk alone. As the saying went, success had many fathers but failure was an orphan. Houllier had found it out when he was sacked from Liverpool. Tonight he would discover it anew. It should have been a good time to play Liverpool. The duo who formed their English core, Steven Gerrard and Jamie Carragher, were both absent injured, while their expensive Spanish striker Fernando Torres was attending to his wife, who had gone into labour.

But Villa were 3-0 down by half-time, through goals by David Ngog, Ryan Babel and Maxi, and were lucky that Liverpool then declared. All the match did for Houllier was to highlight the issues he had inherited and for which Randy Lerner had brought him in. Villa were in need of a rebuilding job. The manager's problem would be to carefully tread a line between the revolution his instincts told him to implement, and the softer approach of evolution that might be needed if he were to coax the best out of the squad and some miffed players before he could make changes.

The Villa fans knew little of that for now, nor that Houllier would be indulged by Lerner while he rebooted the squad, cut down the wage bill and improved the training; modernised and professionalised the club, in short. They were just seeing results deteriorate and Villa being sucked into relegation trouble. There would be sticks with which to beat Houllier. He seemed to love Liverpool more than them, they reckoned. They would not take kindly to seeing television pictures of him tonight touching the sacred 'This is Anfield' sign at the entrance to the pitch from the players' tunnel. When underachieving players such as Carew and Stephen Ireland were sent out on loan, it was supposedly a sign already that he was – as the vogue lazy catch-all phrase had it – losing the dressing room.

'We jumped on a moving train,' said Houllier. 'It took three years at a club with a lot of history in Liverpool to take a step up. In football you cannot programme success, you can just prepare and plan.' There had been talk that Lerner would let Houllier have £30 million to spend. 'I haven't heard that from him,' he said, grinning. 'But I would like to.'

For now, it was about winning over those in the West Midlands who saw his Liverpool as an unadventurous side, and proving that Villa would be an energetic attacking force. 'I always play with two strikers, always play to win,' was his response to the accusation. 'When you play at the top level, you have a responsibility to play winning football with an entertaining style. It's a spectacle.'

He was certainly taking the criticism better than he did at Liverpool when confronted by some 25 ex-players working in the media. Now he just shrugged. 'As you get older, you keep things simple, you prioritise things. I do think the top level is a job for an older man,' he said, with himself and Arsène Wenger, even Sir Alex Ferguson and Roy Hodgson in mind. Yet he added: 'We do seem to find it harder to take defeat on the chin.'

One man's meat is another man's *poisson*. Hodgson had come under fierce pressure early in his tenure as Liverpool struggled in mid-table. The fans were not warming to his signings, such as Paul Konchesky from Fulham and Christian Poulsen from Juventus. It did

202 | THERE'S A GOLDEN SKY

not help that old King Kenny, Dalglish himself, was back at the club as an ambassador and sitting in the directors' box at every home game, a focal point for fans wanting change already. He had offered himself as manager in the summer before Hodgson's appointment so was clearly a shadow for the new man.

Hodgson, who largely carried himself calmly but could be fierce too, was also vulnerable to new owners, and a verbal power struggle was going on through the press. He almost seemed to be pleading for the chance to build his team before they judged him. The new regime was muttering about players playing for their futures. The subtext was that the manager's future was also under consideration. Tonight's win would help but you sensed that it was just a respite in a gathering storm.

New owners naturally want change themselves. It is why they buy. Having turned around the fortunes of the Boston Red Sox baseball team, made them winners of the World Series, you wondered if John W. Henry might want to introduce some ideas from Fenway Park. Perhaps a 70-minute stretch – as opposed to seventh-innings – to the tune of 'Sweet Caroline' by Neil Diamond? New owners also prefer to appoint their own man. It makes new ones, naive ones, prey to fans' whims, wanting to be popular in giving them what they want. John W. Henry had the discontented look of a man who had bought a stately home only to find it had a leaky roof.

You wondered what their motives might be, as with all the modern owners who had no affinity for the city and the club. Perhaps they had seen that the Glazers could have doubled their money if they wanted to sell. Perhaps they saw big bucks to be made if the Premier League's collective agreement with television was broken and the big clubs could do individual pay-per-view deals for a few dollars more in the Asian markets. One of the new men, Tom Werner, was already reigniting the debate about a 39th game in a foreign city, and had not received the same criticism that the

Premier League had in floating the idea. The Liverpool people were enjoying a honeymoon period still.

'Liverpool as a brand worldwide is absolutely mega. It still is,' John Aldridge insisted. 'We have fallen behind for whatever reason but it is still there. When you have Chelsea winning titles and Arsenal doing well, it dilutes things maybe. When we won in Istanbul, that kept it up there and people jumped on Liverpool on the back of that. That gave us a huge lift but I don't think Liverpool capitalised on it that night.

'The longer that we are out of the Champions League, the more difficult it will become to get the best players. People want to play in the Champions League. It's back to the old drawing board in many ways, and it's going to take time to get us back up there. With the two other owners still here, it would have been absolutely unthinkable. At least we have got no debt. All the other top clubs have. At least we can start afresh now. I think we do need a new stadium. If Anfield gets regenerated, then that will be special but as a whole I think we need to move on now.'

At Villa, Houllier was trying to move on but it was proving difficult. He would encounter a game changed behind the scenes in so many ways; not least in dissatisfied players – unwilling to embrace change and wanting to get rid of the manager – being able to get their agents to place unattributed stories in the press. Newspapers had so much space to fill, and the subjects of stories were so much less inclined to complain, that press standards of standing up stories had slipped as gossip became gospel.

Player power had increased, meanwhile, since the explosion in wages and the freedom of movement created by the Bosman ruling. 'The problem as a manager now,' Alan Curbishley of Charlton once said, 'is that you are talking to a roomful of millionaires.'

What changes had Houllier initially noticed since coming back? 'Premier League teams are better prepared now. They all have the capacity to keep the game fast for 90 minutes, where before it was maybe 60 or 70. And the things around English football, which means media, fans and sponsors, have increased by five or 10 times since I first came here. It means that if you lose two or three games there is a crisis. Win three games and you are champions. There is no middle way. The coverage, the interest of people has increased. They pay for football before food here.'

And as clubs grew ever more voracious in their desire for money to finance wages and their growing empires, the ways of getting the public to pay for it had also increased.

Chapter 12

SKY'S THE LIMIT

CHRISTMAS FOOTBALL REMAINS a wonderful English tradition, one that foreign managers who come to the country at first fail to understand. They complain about the frequency of matches and demands on their players and plead for a winter break, but once they have been here a few seasons, they begin to comprehend that the intensity is part of the attraction. The frequency and the demands are the very essence.

Take Arsène Wenger. 'It is the charm and craziness of English football,' he said. 'I personally like it. I am vaccinated after all the years I have been here. It certainly contributes to the promotion of English football. The whole world doesn't work and is bored and watches English football, which is not boring.'

For fans, Boxing Day is the real celebration day. After all the visits from aunts and uncles, all the presents of jumpers and socks, and all the television that has never been the same since dear old Eric and Ernie died, it is a chance to get out of the house. The fact that your team may well be playing local rivals only adds to the spice. A week later comes the New Year fixture, which used to be the return derby, as the second half of a double bill of delight.

For clubs, the fixtures are financial manna from heaven, which is why foreign owners very soon grasp the importance of the festive programme. Quite often, the matches produce the best attendances of the season and so the most revenue. As the games come thick and fast, so does the money to pay the bills and provide a cushion for

January; even a transfer pot or a fund to add a bit to the wage bill for that promotion push or relegation battle.

The 2010/11 season offered a real windfall, too, given the fact that Christmas Day and New Year's Day fell on a Saturday, meaning there were bank holidays on the Mondays and the Tuesdays of the two weeks. That offered an opportunity to get in four games in 10 days: two lovely home paydays over the holiday. They didn't even have to be local derbies any more. Clubs actually preferred unattractive opponents, as they knew they were guaranteed good gates anyway. Best to save the derbies for dates that were difficult to sell, like two weeks before Christmas when shopping took over as the national sport.

The reality was turning out to be a huge disappointment, however, one to rival the legendary winter of 1962/63 when some clubs went eight weeks without playing due to snow and ice. Boxing Day was unremittingly gloomy for most. There were even matches called off in the Premier League at Blackpool, who had not considered undersoil heating when they were hastily upgrading in the summer, and Everton, where frozen pipes meant no water at all in the ground.

Still, with all the Premier League money, it was not a problem for them. The hardship came for clubs lower down, where cash flow was becoming an issue. Yes, they would get the money in when the games were eventually played (though probably with smaller crowds on rearranged midweek nights) but right now, the gate receipts already budgeted for were not arriving and players still had to be paid.

In League One, just a single game survived the weather, the same in League Two. All Conference and other non-League games were postponed. For those of us pining for a game, it meant a forlorn, fallow time, though nowhere near as bleak as '62/63. The reason was, bless its rounded little head, a thing on the side of the house facing south-east. It was called a satellite dish and it beamed live football into your living room.

On Boxing Day itself, there were televised games at Fulham, hosting West Ham in the Premier League at lunchtime, and at Aston Villa, playing Tottenham in the evening. The next day saw Arsenal v. Chelsea and on the Tuesday a veritable bonanza: Coventry City v. Queens Park Rangers in the Championship, to be followed by two Premier League games, West Ham v. Everton and Birmingham v. Manchester City. On the Wednesday? It was Liverpool v. Wolverhampton Wanderers. Oh, and the enduring stalwart of the schedules, *Match of the Day*, offered highlights on the BBC.

Ever since the arrival of Sky, television had been king, other media outlets its attendants. BBC Radio 5 live, with its mixture of sport and news, was established in 1994 to take advantage of the volume of football now available for broadcast, and talkSPORT – the capital letters in its official name being telling – arrived less to talk about it than shout. Coverage of the game on the internet had been phenomenal, from websites devoted to the game to message boards where fans could have their often vicious say – much to the chagrin of chairmen, managers and players.

Newspapers were using the internet as an outlet for their material, too, though had not yet worked out ways of making money from it. Instead, they were trying to retain brand loyalty. A colleague emailed me during the season after being sent to cover a Manchester United game on a Sunday by a Sunday paper; there was no publication to put his report in but it would make the website. 'Arrived at Old Trafford at 11 a.m.,' he wrote, 'departed 7 p.m. after one running report, one quotes piece, 25 words on every player plus something on the substitutes and a rewrite. And not a word of it appears it print. How our game has changed, eh?'

Newspapers had changed dramatically to reflect television's influence, brought about by the sheer capacity of satellite TV, which news and sports desks had on in the office all the time and felt the need to react to. Channel 4 arrived in 1982; in 2011, Ofcom expected to issue a licence to the 1,000th channel.

Among them were football clubs with their in-house channels. There was wisdom in them beyond merely selling something else to their supporters. For, as talking heads, they signed up ex-players to expound about the club. It meant they were onside, rather than spouting criticism on more mainstream outlets; inside the tent pissing out, rather than outside pissing in. The Bruce Springsteen line about life in a hotel room – 57 channels and nothing on – had long since been superseded.

These days, there was a list of people officially allowed into the referees' room before a Premier League game. It included the officials themselves, their assessors, and two representatives of the clubs to bring the team sheets. Oh, and one other person: the TV floor manager. He was the man you sometimes saw on the side of the pitch at the start of the game on a wide-angled shot. He signalled to the referee when the official may start the match, the advertisement having finished or the studio being ready for live coverage to begin. His position there told of the access and power now wielded by television. The press, which is still useful for selling tickets through its preview coverage, does not pay. TV does – and how. What time's kick off? What time would you like to kick off, Sir?

Sky, naturally, was largely responsible for the metamorphosis of the game and its coverage and within Sky there was one man more responsible than anyone else. In fact, he had been one of the English game's least known but most significant figures of the past two decades, even though he was not a player, a manager, owner, chairman or administrator. I drove down the B roads and lanes of Hampshire to see him at his house in the country, as far away from the cityscape of English football as it was possible to get. It was probably a bolt-hole that had kept him sane.

Vic Wakeling, a Geordie, was an old newspaperman, working in sports journalism in Birmingham before moving into independent television as editor of a local news programme in Southampton called *Coast to Coast*. In 1990, he got a call from the fledgling satellite company British Satellite Broadcasting, which wanted him to produce a sports news programme along the lines of the American network ESPN's *Sports Center*. He took a chance, mainly because one of his TV production heroes, Brian Cowgill, was involved. It didn't augur well when Cowgill quit amid rows over finance.

Soon came the merger between BSB and Sky, which was really a Sky takeover. Sky asked Wakeling to become head of football. He agreed, though Sky was still just a tinpot upstart. 'We had a deal to do some FA Cup ties, some internationals and a Scottish FA Cup deal, along with the Zenith Data Systems Trophy for the Football League,' said Wakeling. 'The first match I ever did live was Tranmere Rovers v. Newcastle United and it was my decision.' It was bitter-sweet for him. The game finished 6-6, his beloved Newcastle losing on penalties, but Sky thought him a genius to have picked such a goal glut.

Then he chose an FA Cup replay between Derby County and Sheffield Wednesday, to internal criticism given the state of the old Baseball Ground pitch. It finished 4-3. The Australians and Americans running Sky thought that this guy knew about football. 'You get lucky, don't you? They weren't all like that, mind.'

Those Australians and Americans, instructed by Rupert Murdoch, were determined to base their strategy of selling dishes and building subscriptions on football and Wakeling was still head of football when the first Premier League deal was signed for the 1992/93 season. 'There's a well-known story in TV,' he recalled, 'which goes that after losing the Premier League bid in 1992, Greg Dyke, who had had the rights to the old Football League, stood up in front of the sports troops at ITV and said that Sky had paid far too much, that they would have it back soon and we would go broke.'

Wakeling's career moved to another level the following year, in December 1993, after Sky's head of sport, David Hill, left to run Fox Sport in the United States. Sam Chisholm, the bluff chief executive of Sky, called Wakeling into his office and asked if he was going with Hill. Wakeling wasn't. He wasn't a great fan of American football, he said. Chisholm asked if Wakeling expected to get Hill's job. He replied that he would like it, but didn't expect it.

'He said,' Wakeling remembered, '"You are not fucking good enough. I will probably end up sacking you in about six months but I am pissing off to Oz for Christmas and I can't find anybody else right now so the job is yours." We had one sports channel at the time. Now you have all these channels, skysports.com, digital telly had not been thought of. It has all happened since.'

(It was David Hill, incidentally, who introduced in that season of 1992/93 the brilliantly simple idea of putting the score and the clock counting in the corner of the screen. It was soon imitated and is now taken for granted, but according to Wakeling: 'Our switchboards went into meltdown with protesters and he was sorely tempted to pull it after the first couple of weeks. Andy Melvin [executive producer] and myself persuaded him to let it run, the protests died down and the rest is history.')

I reminded Wakeling that I had interviewed him on becoming head of sport at the time and asked him what effect he thought Sky and satellite television might have on future generations. He thought for a while, puffed on a cigarette, and replied with a smile: 'Well, we can't have a controlled experiment, can we?'

Now I asked him what effect it had had on football – indeed on English culture. Bespectacled and bearded, Wakeling looked like one of those intellectuals you see on Parisian chat shows on French television. He described himself, however, as a simple football enthusiast and the culture question did not initially appeal to him. He no longer smoked, having decided to give up after heart surgery; and now simply stroked his beard. Perhaps in his answers about football were indications about English culture.

At 66, Wakeling decided on semi-retirement but remained a consultant for Sky. He had served six chief executives at the organisation and oversaw 350 staff, rising to 750 at weekends. He was responsible for the four sports channels as well as Sky News. No one was better placed to contemplate the changes. 'Nobody thought that the Premier League would be the huge worldwide success that it is,' he said. 'I hate to talk about sport as a product, but the Premier League in most territories is the overseas set of rights that they must have. I don't think anyone saw that. At Sky, we thought the League was going to be an exciting new development and we wanted to be part of it.

'It turned out to be a huge success for the 22 clubs, now 20, and for Sky. We were great partners. We have grown together. If you remember where football was, it needed something to shake it all up. We are old enough to remember these broken-down stadiums where you would never take your wife and daughter. The pitches were mudheaps a lot of the time. We were losing our footballers overseas, like Liam Brady and Paul Gascoigne.

'Now look at what's happened with our stadiums. We could stage a World Cup tomorrow. Pitches are immaculate. They are good to look at even in the lower leagues. The pitch at Aldershot was not as good 20 years ago as it is now. And look at the players who have graced our game – David Ginola, Eric Cantona, Gianfranco Zola.'

As he galloped on, it was clear that Wakeling was an enthusiast indeed but some reining in was needed, to chart the development of the game and the broadcaster, to glean responses to the many criticisms that Sky had attracted. Initially, it was its sheer lack of an audience.

'We were aware people would criticise us and say that nobody was watching, nobody had dishes,' he replied. 'That was up to marketing. My job was to make sure the football looked good. We got the contract on a Friday and worked the weekend, making two decisions. We had Martin Tyler on contract, who I still think is the best commentator. Andy Gray had gone back to be assistant manager to Ron Atkinson at Aston Villa but we got him back. And we hired the best event director in Tony Mills.'

Tyler and Gray, indeed, were soon a hit. Tyler's knowledge of the game was deep, his vocabulary wide and he had good range of light and shade, understatement and enthusiasm, in his commentaries. Gray's Scots brogue conveyed well the passion of the game. His honesty and analyses hit home and contrasted with much of the blandness of terrestrial stations that had lost their way since the panels of the 1970s and 1980s featuring such outspoken pundits as Jimmy Hill and Brian Clough.

'We said we were going to pour everything in, to look good and sound good,' added Wakeling. 'We looked at coverage of the NFL, rugby league in Australia, football in Germany, and at cameras and how we use them. From day one, it did look better. And from day one, I had the backing of Rupert Murdoch and Sam Chisholm. Knowing that Sky was using football to drive the business did bring pressure on us but I wanted that and it was an easy sell. The Americans thought that the Olympic Games were the peak of sport, but I told them that in England it was football, and you had to have top class, week in, week out.

'There was also huge marketing behind the movie channel, and Sky One was doing *The Simpsons* as well, but what made it easier for me to persuade them to push sport was the coverage of the England cricket tour of the West Indies in 1989/90. It was the first live overseas series and people loved the sun and the location in the winter. It was always why I insisted on having a studio set by the beach. The Premier League has been important, but cricket was significant as well.

'Before we came along, ITV covered 18 First Division matches. In season one, we did 60 and it has gradually gone up over the years. That is not Sky's doing, by the way. It was pressure from European governments to say that the game's authorities had to spread the games around to have packages for other broadcasters. But it needed satellite television to make it work, and a company who were going to take the risks.'

Since the days of the autocratic chairmen and administrators of the 1960s and 1970s, the game had resisted widespread live coverage due to concern about its potential effects on crowd numbers at every level of the game. Now a new strategy was needed. The Premier League's then chief executive Rick Parry, who would go on to be chief executive of Liverpool, insisted that there should be extensive support programming around live games to foster interest. 'They wanted nine hours of support every week in the contract,' Wakeling said. 'We exceeded it straight away. There were match previews and post-match shows. In season one, we were doing two hours before kick off. We did the *Footballers' Football Show, Hold the Back Page, Soccer Saturday, Soccer AM, Goals on Sunday*. We were talking to characters, going behind the scenes.

'Football, more than movies, theatre even, is drama because you can't tell the outcome. But it is important that you care who wins and loses. You want the floating voter to look in and get involved. You want them to be interested in this or that personality so that they want to see how he does.'

An early innovation was Monday Night Football, a direct and unabashed lift of the tradition in the United States for their NFL games. 'It was something we wanted to do but it was a huge problem,' said Wakeling. 'I stood up in front of the clubs early in 1992 and they were saying "No". I said that with all their European and FA Cup games, the maximum would be 25 out of their 460 and we pushed it over the line.'

It also helped that Sky were offering to cover the less fashionable clubs, such as Oldham and Norwich City, in these games. To attract attention, they did what Wakeling called 'the whole entertainment' with flypasts by aeroplanes trailing banners, bands and scantily clad pompom girls called the Sky Strikers. 'Traditionalists were appalled, but they liked it up in Oldham,' was Wakeling's assessment.

What about attendances? 'I checked every equivalent game from the previous season,' Wakeling insisted. 'All the gates were up. And one of our sponsors did a survey saying that 40 per cent of our audience were women. I'm not sure I believed them but even if it was 30 per cent, that's a lot of women being turned on to the game.'

And the shifting of game dates and kick-off times that became a major bone of contention? 'With the first 60 matches we were negotiating, we were aware we wouldn't have 3 p.m. Saturday games under UEFA articles,' Wakeling explained. 'Nobody wanted other times on a Saturday. Sunday football had already been around and we asked for 5 p.m. kick offs. ITV had done a match for 3 or 4 o'clock that had been delayed for some reason and got their biggest audience so we wanted that. The clubs said no, they would have all sorts of issues with the police. It was the clubs who wanted 4 p.m. After that, and now, it has little to do with TV and everything to do with the European Union telling the Premier League you must have 135 live games, offered in different packages to different broadcasters.'

But what about away supporters, forced to endure changes in their plans? 'We were aware of the travelling fan but quite often we would run into policing issues,' said Wakeling. 'For example, we wanted to do Leeds as champions in our first season in 1992 but there was another big event in the city that weekend and we had to do Nottingham Forest

v. Liverpool. The first Monday night was Manchester City v. Queens Park Rangers.

'The second week we wanted to do Everton but the Tall Ships Race was on in Liverpool. We also had problems with their Sunday games because of the church built into the ground at the Gwladys Street end. Newcastle weren't in the league in season one but even when they were promoted, we didn't do them against Southampton.'

All valid explanations, but the tales of clubs who went weeks without a Saturday 3 p.m. kick-off abounded, along with those of away supporters arriving home late on Sunday nights when they had to be at work early the next day. 'We were aware on some occasions that we were upsetting fans and we had meetings with them,' Wakeling countered. 'They thought people should play at 3 p.m. but we had to make them aware of contractual arrangements. It was easy enough in the first four seasons but when we went up to 66 games a season more problems arose. The worst we had was an FA Cup tie, Sunderland against West Ham, which was a Saturday lunchtime kick-off and there were people leaving London in the dark. The West Ham end was full though.'

What about the allegations of hyping up games? 'Every game that we go to we are enthusiastic about it like every paying spectator,' said Wakeling. 'You hope you are going to see a good game and get excited about it. I reject that we hype up games. Once a game starts, commentators and studio will say if it is a good or bad game but I still want to know why, so tell me why. You will always get your bad games. I remember going to see Wimbledon v. Ipswich in season one on a Monday night in the middle of winter and it was just awful. Leading up to a Manchester derby, we get excited about it, every section of the media does, but once the game starts, if it is a damp squib, we will call it straight.'

There was also a suggestion that TV companies with contracts did not want to upset the governing bodies, and so pulled their punches when it came to criticism of the game and its personnel. Naturally, TV would always deny it. Besides, in the end, such was the Premier League's attitude, that it would always be about money and the highest bid.

It had left newspapers grasping at the leftovers. At the time of the Munich air disaster in 1958, a BBC Radio voice talked gravely of the football journalists who had lost their lives, too: 'writers who made the sport live for millions at home'. It was television which largely did that now, national radio to some extent complementing it, mostly through what was now named Radio 5 live. Some of us remained fond of the radio, in line with the story its once doyen commentator Bryon Butler used to tell about the little boy who preferred the radio 'because the pictures were better'.

The press still worked manfully to get its transfer stories – TV and radio still not as good at that – and interviews with players, a harder task than ever with club press offices seeking to control their availability and oversee what they said. Instead, it was often a diet of staged press conferences and writing big previews, often hyping games and players more than television ever did. Match reports were hardly that any more. For Saturday games, Sunday papers were often writing the type of piece, packed with the manager's and players' quotes, which used to appear in the daily papers on a Monday. The dailies thus contained more comment and were forced to throw things forward more. There would surely come a time when the dailies no longer carried pieces about Saturday football.

Newspapers had also trained their attention – even the upmarket ones – on to the behaviour of footballers, with scandal involving those the public saw on television a good selling point. For the top Premier League footballers were now celebrities and to be treated as such, their private lives considered fair game if they were making fortunes. Sky would never say so, but it surely enjoyed such tabloid coverage of football, for it stoked interest in its 'product' among the satellite classes.

It was a two-way relationship, though. Wakeling believed that Sky breathed life into sports writing – its quantity if not always its quality – with the burgeoning of sports sections and a greater, if sometimes grudging, respect from editors for what they used to see as the toy department of the newspaper. Circulations had declined, in some cases to about half of what they were 20 years previously, but coverage of sport had probably slowed the decline. 'I think we did sports journalism a favour,' Wakeling insisted. 'When I was in Fleet Street, nobody took you seriously and sports editors were fighting for space. Nobody was doing football pull-outs. Sky was the first to exploit the huge interest in sport in this country. Editors and publishers suddenly thought there was something there.'

There was also the issue of Murdoch's papers – the *Sun, News of the World, The Times* and *Sunday Times* – using their pages to promote Sky's coverage of football and other organisations thus being forced to compete. 'Years ago at the *Birmingham Post and Mail*, we thought about doing a national sports paper like the French paper *L'Equipe* but there was no advertising for it,' added Wakeling. 'Sky found target advertisers and Ford has been with us all this time. Now, sports pages are far too good for anyone to do a national sports paper. When I took over, I thought it would be lovely to have more subscribers than the *Sun*. We passed it at four million within a few years.' In November 2010, Sky would pass 10 million subscriptions, which meant that one in three households in the British population of some 60 million was being supplied.

Clearly football had been good for Sky, but had Sky been good for football? There was irony for Wakeling, who said that he once wrote an article for the Birmingham *Sports Argus* propounding the line of the old Football League secretary Alan Hardaker and Burnley chairman Bob Lord that TV would be the death of the game. 'I didn't know what the hell I was talking about,' he said, smiling ruefully. 'A lot of Sky money has been spent on stadiums. There is a breed of businessmen running clubs now and running them well. You will always have disasters like Portsmouth and wonder what goes on but you hope that the money is spent wisely, on facilities, on things like pitch maintenance and academies.'

Didn't it just go, though, on players – and their agents – in ever increasing wages that alienated the supporters? 'I would also argue that players have short careers, are entertainers and should get whatever they can,' said Wakeling. 'Good luck to them. I have to be honest, mind, and say that there have been a couple recently where I have thought, "Let's be careful about this". I've just started to scratch my head about a couple of them.

'But I don't think fans care. When I was growing up watching Newcastle, most of them were local players and there for life. It doesn't happen now. How can fans have loyalty when players sign a contract and want a move? But the fans don't seem to mind. Being a certain age and knowing what player loyalty used to be, I was gutted when George Eastham left Newcastle. Now I would be thinking, "Good on you". Players in those days like Jackie Milburn, Jimmy Scoular and Bobby Mitchell were exploited terribly. Newcastle got crowds of 50,000 and they were being paid a pittance. It was awful what used to happen.'

Had it been good, though, for the clubs outside the Premier League? 'That's a big question,' Wakeling replied. 'If you look at the scale of football in this country, the 92 clubs and the Conference, it's amazing the strength of the game and the amount of people who turn out and pay to watch it every Saturday. I have talked to chairmen in Leagues One and Two about the wages they pay and asked them how they justify them on gates of 3 or 4,000. They say, "We have got to if we are going to compete." You can't go on like that. It's got to be a sport but you've got to try and run it as a business. There are a lot of problems caused by paying ridiculous wages at lower levels.'

He can see the carrot, though. 'There have been 44 clubs in the Premier League and I think that's brilliant. They all want to be there,' he said. In that was a problem inadvertently caused by Sky. So much money was there for simply being at the top level, that clubs were borrowing fortunes to try and reach it.

There were new challenges facing Sky, one of them being the case of the landlady of a Portsmouth pub who was arguing in court that it was her right to buy in coverage from overseas broadcasters in Europe at a cheaper subscription than Sky was offering. It was a test case that was running and running.

Otherwise, Sky was still seeing off rival broadcasters, including ITV Digital and Setanta, which had both gone bust this Millennium. New players like ESPN were offering a challenge, by buying a Premier League package of live games, and Channel 5 liked its football, though could only afford the Europa League. How did Wakeling see them, ITV and the BBC – whose belt-tightening would mean that they would soon cede their Football League coverage to Sky and carry only the cosy Billionaire Boys' Club that was Gary Lineker, Alan Hansen and Alan Shearer on *Match of the Day?* 'I will never criticise people at ITV and the BBC,' he replied. 'There may have been a bit of complacency at the BBC but I know ITV were desperate to get more airtime. They both had rights to certain events but only ever showed highlights of some. Sky had the time. Now in this multi-channel world, they are more equipped to cover sport but unfortunately for them all, Sky saw the opportunity 20 years ago. Sky is in a strong position long term because of the gambles Rupert Murdoch took 20 years ago.

'There is huge competition between us but we are all friends. We all want to be the best. When the BBC lost the contract for Test cricket and it went to Channel 4, they got an Australian director and moved ahead of us. We had to kick ourselves and step up our game. Things happen on a slow basis in the BBC but they are now doing more than ever because others came along.'

And the future? 'People will always want to watch their *Coronation Street* but they can watch it any time, thanks to Sky+. You can get the news any time, same with films. But people want live sport, with bigger and better pictures and sound. That's why the internet still has a way to go, even if it can deliver games to your laptops. People also want the shared experience and pubs with their big screens have become the new terraces.

'I still watch *Match of the Day*. There is still something about that time on a Saturday night. It's a great hour and a half and a way to round off your Saturday night, seeing every goal. I could do with more of the match and less of the chat, though. Then I Sky+ the Football League show and watch it the next morning.' Soon the BBC would ditch that, however, leaving Sky to pick up the contract.

There were signs that the new overseas owners coming into the Premier League saw the really big bucks to be made by pay-per-view abroad. 'It always worried me, there were certain American owners, some now gone from the game, who came in and I knew were stirring behind the scenes, putting the pressure on the Premier League, saying you should be getting more for your overseas rights,' said Wakeling. 'I think they were off target, listening to their NFL connections.

'We were worried they would try and break up the Premier League but Richard Scudamore [the chief executive] has done well to hold it all together. The strength is the collective. If you look at the Manchester United books – as Sky did when we owned 10 per cent – and look at the merchandising and everything else, compared to the Champions League, the Premier League is their bread and butter and is vital to them.'

What, I wondered, might be the great leap forward for TV technology? 'There will always be somewhere it will go because someone will invent new technology,' said Wakeling. 'When I started, no one had mentioned digital, high definition or 3D. In some years' time, I reckon that we will be watching a football match with holograms playing on a table in front of us. I would love to be alive to see it. I heard that someone in Japan was working on it.'

I ventured that it sounded a little frightening to someone who made his living from the printed word. 'It's exciting,' Wakeling replied. Just remember that you read it here first.

Chapter 13

THE MONEY SHOTS

THE FRESH-FACED 19-year-old bounded across the floor of the television studio, shook Terry Wogan's hand, sat down on the sofa and proceeded to charm the old charmer himself. Spencer Trethewy's plan to save Aldershot Football Club from extinction had captured the public imagination and the producers of 1990's most watched chat show wanted to hear all about it.

Trethewy himself revelled in the spotlight. At 6ft 3in with blond hair, he certainly had stage presence and that spotlight was why he was there, after all. At first it was all about securing some publicity for his business and thus increase his borrowing power but his teenaged ego was now running rampant. Andy Warhol may have said that everyone would be famous for 15 minutes but he never mentioned anything about the years of consequences.

Some 18 months after Trethewy's *Wogan* appearance, Aldershot went bust after all. After buying into the Fourth Division club, he soon became embroiled in boardroom wrangling, murky claim and counter-claim. He lasted just a few months, Aldershot went from bad to worse over the next season and the gates of their Recreation Ground were locked in March 1992. Trethewy was denounced as a charlatan. 'Soccer Saviour is a Fraud' declared a *News of the World* headline.

It proved to be a blessing in disguise for Aldershot, albeit a disguise they would wear for quite some time. I remembered standing on the terraces for their last game, a testimonial against fellow Hampshire club Southampton for the then manager Ian McDonald, who had gone without wages. The crowd cheered when the tannoy announced that a new club would be formed, called Aldershot Town, its emblem a phoenix. Groans, however, accompanied the information that they would be entering the Isthmian League at its lowest level but hoped to be back in the Football League in a decade. In the event, it took them 16 years as they made it through four promotions, eventually winning the Conference in 2008.

I wanted to return for a game to see how time had weathered the Rec, which seemed an appropriate sounding nickname for the ground when it all went belly up back in 1992. I also wanted to see if going out of business and reforming, as was becoming increasingly prevalent at lower levels, was really such a good thing. First, though, I wanted to take a detour to the mansion on the hill of the man who became such a celebrity for a while, and set in motion the train of events, to hear his rarely told version.

After Aldershot, Spencer Trethewy received death threats, even claimed to have had the brake lines of his Mercedes cut. All his credit lines were certainly slashed and he lost his house. He then continued trading with a company that had been wound up, running up £23,000 worth of debt, and served six weeks in Wandsworth prison and four months in Ford open prison for fraud in 1994, his sentence of two years reduced on appeal.

From there, like the Shots, he rose again, rebuilding his career as a businessman and venture capitalist, doing very nicely, thank you. After changing his name to Spencer Day – to preserve the name from his mother's side of the family, he insisted, rather than escape his past – he even bought himself a football club: Chertsey Town of the Combined Counties League. He did not appreciate it when I tracked him down but after a series of phone calls and emails, he gave in and granted me an interview, even inviting me to his most luxurious of homes in the Surrey hills, a manor house with a winding drive leading up from security gates.

The whole strange saga began when Trethewy saw a piece about the plight of Aldershot on *BBC Breakfast* TV presented by Bob Wilson, the former Arsenal goalkeeper who had moved into the media. They were in danger of going under, the then club chairman Colin Hancock told Wilson, for the sake of £70,000 worth of debt. They had five days to find the money.

Trethewy was intrigued – and he also thought that getting involved would raise the profile of his embryonic property investment business. He was at the time, he claimed, being offered a £3 million loan by a banking concern on a property in Surrey that had been valued at £3.8 million and he made contact with Hancock. In return for a majority shareholding in the club, he offered £200,000 to stave off a winding-up petition as a loan against the £800,000 he expected to make from the property transaction.

The deal dragged on, however, Aldershot grew desperate and Hancock arranged for a friend, a Dr Alan Gillespie, to advance the £200,000 on the basis that Trethewy would pay it back. Then came another twist. One director, John McGinty, now dead but who had gone on to become chairman of the reborn club, claimed he had loaned the club £65,000 and that since Trethewy was the new owner, he wanted it back or would petition for a winding-up order. Trethewy pacified McGinty by giving him a charge over his own £500,000 house in Addlestone, Surrey, to prevent him closing Aldershot down.

Now Dr Gillespie started agitating for his money. Trethewy and his father Derek confronted Hancock about the running of the club and found out there were no shares assigned to him. His directorship was suspended and when McGinty called in the charge on his house, Trethewy was declared bankrupt. When Aldershot went bust, the actual debt turned out to be £1.1 million. Dr Gillespie was left £200,000 worse off.

'I was 19 years old, wasn't I?' Trethewy, now Day, lamented to me. 'It's hard to believe it happened. I am not saying I was perfect, not by a long chalk, but I was badly advised, I was very naive, got used and abused and spat out when they felt like it. If you surveyed Aldershot supporters, 90 per cent of them would probably want to kill me and 10 per cent might have heard a few bits of the truth.'

Now 40, Spencer Day had little time for Aldershot's cast of characters of the early 1990s. He did not, though, wish to speak ill of the deceased McGinty, who claimed before his death that he did not remember putting a charge on Day's house. 'Reading County Court will confirm the facts,' Day countered. As for Hancock, 15 years later, he surfaced in the East Midlands as a potential owner for Notts County, then Mansfield Town. 'He got me suspended from the Aldershot board but how could he do that? I never got the 51 per cent shares I was promised,' said Day. 'He didn't want that club saved. He wanted it to be knocked down and turned into real estate. When I saw him appear as the saviour of Notts County, I pissed myself laughing.'

Others, equally naturally, have different versions of events. I put it to him that he was viewed as a Walter Mitty character who never had the money he claimed. 'I turned up in a £50,000 car. If I didn't have any money, how did I mortgage my house to the club?' he replied. 'I may not have had millions but I had a ton of flats in London at the time. My intention was always right. I was in a sharks' game where I was eaten alive.'

When it blew over, he went to Barbados and started in business again, borrowing money to buy a couple of holiday homes for rent. He hired two passenger jets to fly the London route, forming a company called Cunard Airways. The shipping company Cunard injuncted, however, and he was ordered to cease trading. He didn't and ran up that £23,000 worth of debt, mainly at London hotels.

'After Aldershot, I was approached by some even worse people than those at the football club and I did some stupid things,' Day admitted. 'Hands up. I did it. I got punished for it. I was a kid and I was in that place because of football. My lawyer said it would get thrown out but I got slaughtered in court because of Aldershot. The judge said that this was nothing to do with Aldershot but their lawyer was brilliant. Within 30 seconds he had brought it up and from the jury's faces I could see it was all over.'

After jail, Day started anew, making money from car finance. He then became a business 'dragon', borrowing money, investing in companies, selling them and taking the profit. 'I kept my head down,' he said. 'I used to get one or two journalists contacting me every two or three years but I declined any interviews.' In his daily life, the Aldershot episode never cropped up, he insisted. 'The Trethewy thing... it was yesterday's news. It wasn't a long thing that sticks in people's minds. Michael Knighton putting the ball in the net at the Stretford end might stick but not me, not to people outside football at least. Surrey isn't a football area anyway. It's a middle/upper class rugby area. It's not like I am in Liverpool or Manchester or the North East. It was rare that somebody brought it up, certainly not to my face.'

Day had always played football, from his teenage years when he was a decent enough midfield player to have trials with Nottingham Forest. After buying into the Holmes Place chain of health clubs, he formed a club bearing their name and they rose through the non-League pyramid, playing home matches on a pitch next to the ground shared by AFC Wimbledon and Kingstonian. When Holmes Place was sold to Virgin, they changed their name to Kingsmeadow.

Then, when they needed to arrange a new ground, Day went to Chertsey Town and paid them £25,000 up front for sharing their compact Alwyns Lane ground. 'I wish it had stopped then,' he said wistfully. Soon they were prevailing on him to invest in them. In 2007, with his own career as a player winding down and now manager of Kingsmeadow, 'they wore me down' and he bought Chertsey Town for £1.

'A typical little club with no money,' was his description. 'The clubhouse was falling down, the gas bill was coming in. People were stealing from the club. It was a fiasco. The first thing was to get the club on an even keel, renovate the club house, the pitch, get a structure in, get the bar going.'

He also gave the manager a decent wage budget, £1,000 a week, but, said Day, he simply increased the wages of existing players. Some 15 games into a new season, Day sacked the manager and took over himself. Since then, Chertsey had finished third, third and second and were tussling this season with Guildford City for the title and the only promotion place up to the Ryman League, having recently beaten them 3-0.

'At least we get attendances. We averaged 144 last season and had 220 for the Guildford game,' said Day, with some pride in his voice. He also pointed out that Chertsey had housed more than 700 for the semi-final of the FA Vase the previous season, when they lost out on a Wembley place to Whitley Bay. Gate revenue did not cover costs, however, and he bemoaned the lack of backing from the business community as well as the general support from the town. He was beginning to sound like every other owner and chairman.

It felt even more acute to him currently. At the height of his earning power around 2005, he claimed he was offered a Championship club to buy and 'could have afforded it. But the thought of going back into the public eye put me off.' Now, he admitted, he was struggling in the recession, not that it was immediately evident. We were sitting in an office the size of a semi-detached house's ground floor, at a polished mahogany table that seated eight. There was a marble floor, leather sofas, jukebox, rows of bookcases and two large plasma TV screens showing the BBC and Sky news channels. 'People see the guy who's got yachts and homes around the world and it's true, I do, but I have huge amounts of bank borrowings,' he confessed. 'I have masses of equity but no credit and the crunch is killing me, even with mortgages of only 20 per cent on my other homes. It is all well and good being worth 10, 20, 30 or 40 million pounds but if you can't pay the gas bill you have a problem.

'Sadly, I genuinely believe that Chertsey has hurt my business. Up to a few years ago I was borrowing money so fast and everyone saw me as a business/property person. All of a sudden I am back with that history. It worries me. I know a lot of property people who have gone bust. I am fighting tooth and nail to get the correct funding to do the things I want to do but banks are closing and calling in loans. I have borrowed £58 million in the last 10 years without a credit dent and perfectly paid back, but if they are not lending to me with my track record, who are they lending to? I have told the people at Chertsey not to get carried away and believe the hype.'

He contemplated the sums he had put into the club, reluctant to give them out but unable to resist when pressed. 'If I said how much it had cost me, my other half would shoot me,' he said. 'All I can say is that it is a lot less than Aldershot would have cost me. I have done £40,000 on the pitch in the last two years. Then there's a new dressing room with plasma TV, shower blocks.' It totalled £30,000 on the clubhouse and £25,000 on the dressing rooms, he said.

'I wish they could filter some of the money from the Premier down here,' he added. 'Fifty thousand does a lot at this level. But the Premier League is a different planet. In fact it's as different a sport as rugby union is to tennis.'

The money on the ground was quite apart from the players' wages that he funded. At one point, he admitted, it crept up to £2,000 a week, high for Combined Counties though about half of what AFC Wimbledon were paying when they passed through. All in all, over four seasons, his outlay had probably totalled some £400,000.

'Chertsey have no debt, other than to me, which is only put in the books as a nominal sum anyway for tax benefit purposes,' he said. 'I would never call in the loans. Only if my children's lives depended on it.'

He wanted to carry on, to get Chertsey up as far as was feasible, which was Conference South, he believed. He had, though, been considering a merger with a club already in that division and nearby, which given the location – an M25 junction or two past Heathrow and the M3 – must have been either Woking or Hampton and Richmond. He had also been frustrated by the local council in his attempts to sell the ground for housing. The sale would be to fund a community stadium and other pitches elsewhere in the town as a home to all the club's age group teams, in which his sons played, as well as the senior team.

'We need to get up. Quitting is not good,' he reflected. 'How would I leave all these nice people? But the club needs to move forward and an offer last year was tempting.' He had also been approached by clubs higher up the non-League pyramid wanting him to come in as their manager. They also wanted his access to finance – if the economy picked up, that was. It was a modern trend; some managers at lower levels got jobs because of the funds they could bring with them, either their own or those of business associates.

Day would not want to go full-time in the game, though. 'No club outside the Premier League could afford me,' he said. 'Though that is this afternoon. I hope it stays that way. I love football but it would have to be an exceptional challenge.' So no going back to Aldershot then? He laughed. 'If Aldershot came in, the attendances would go up twice and they would make a lot of money but there would probably be a riot.'

They could certainly do with attendances doubling. I took in a New Year's fixture against Hereford United, the Shots' first home game for six weeks due to the snow and ice, making them one of the clubs worst hit financially by the bitter winter. The Recreation Ground had hardly changed since that final match for the old club almost 20 years ago. Nor had the town, the smallest in England with a Football League club. Its population was just 33,840, though the local Rushmoor council claimed a catchment area of 243,000 from the surrounding towns. Today's attendance would be 2,767, including 216 brave souls from Hereford.

On the edge of Thomas Hardy's Wessex, in which it was known as Quartershot, the town some 35 miles south west of London was celebrated for little other than its hosting of the British Army. With the numbers of soldiers stationed there having dwindled from the 16,000 of its heyday to some 4,000 now, Aldershot was struggling to find income. Many of the barracks had been sold off for flats but they remained empty in the current climate. Even though a three-bedroomed semi would set you back only £200,000, ridiculously cheap for the south-east corner of the country, there were plenty for sale in estate agents' windows.

Victoria Road, leading up from the football ground in the High Street, told of a town down at heel. Past the National Caravan Council offices and the Wok Away Chinese take-away, the Precision Martial Arts Studio and Bellybusters fried chicken and ribs outlet, there was a British Heart Foundation furniture and electrical shop selling wardrobes for £25 and chests of drawers for a mere £5. Next door was a bookmakers offering 10-1 on Aldershot winning 3-1 today, with their leading striker Marvin Morgan opening the scoring.

And there on the corner of Perowne Street and Queen's Road was the old Palais Ballroom where, on Saturday 9 December 1961, a young band played an early gig to just 18 people. Their name was The

Beatles and they promptly sacked their agent, Sam Leach. A few weeks later they hired a manager by the name of Brian Epstein and the rest was hysteria.

Further on was the Galleries shopping mall, a monument to the moment. Half of its units were unoccupied, the other half housing the downmarket such as Wilkinson, Peacocks, Argos and Milletts. In New York Nails, a group of Orientals wearing facemasks were doing a reasonable trade in manicures. Elsewhere, 99p shops were undercutting Poundland. Aldershot supporters seemed in short supply, though there was a lad in a red-and-blue replica shirt, the tail outside trousers bearing the words 'Alive and Kicking'.

With kick off approaching, I headed back to the ground, which was easy to find due to the old-fashioned floodlight pylons that obviated the need for sat nav and provided a beacon to away fans coming by car. Entrance through the high street turnstiles still took you past a fallow end with neither terracing nor seats, though scaffolding had now been erected so that they could put adverts up and get some revenue. In the old days, I could have sworn there were floral gardens here.

In the bottom corner next to the pitch, a gate still bore the sign of that day of the last game against Southampton, though. 'No unauthorised ball games,' it said. The small club shop was still there, too. Just past it, I met Jack Rollin, wise and wizened Aldershot vice-president. The man who has edited all but three of the 41 editions of the *Rothmans/Sky Football Yearbook* – the game's equivalent of cricket's *Wisden* – had supported the Shots since 1942, when he was 10, having returned from evacuation in Devon. 'I have never lived in the area but Father was a regular in the Army and when not abroad was stationed in Aldershot,' he told me.

He recalled the war years, when Aldershot had the pick of players stationed in the town, such as Frank Swift, Stan Cullis, Tommy Lawton and Joe Mercer. Why go to London, he wondered, when teams there had far fewer top players? There were many memories, as of all football fans: of a League Cup tie against Manchester United here, won by George Best's magic; of beating Aston Villa – then managed by Joe Mercer – here in the FA Cup in 1964. 'Even in the season of the crash, Shots drew at West Ham in the Cup and switched the replay to Upton Park too,' said Rollin, going on to describe a footballing scene resembling the last helicopters out of Saigon. 'What happened to the money from those two matches is another mystery. At the time, those in charge were just grabbing what they could before the end came.

'I felt very sorry for the players in 1991/92, most of whom were playing for petrol money and were prepared to carry on until the end of the season. The council closed the ground and, though Swindon Town and Cardiff City had offered theirs for home games, the Football League pulled the plug. The man who did it was Arthur Sandford – Arthur who? In fact, Sandford was the then barely known chief executive of the League.

What of Spencer Trethewy? Rollin's version was that: 'He borrowed money from Dr Gillespie, who is still a regular supporter at the Rec. I think Trethewy was living in a little world of his own.'

The feeling when starting up the new club, Rollin added, was: 'excitement but uncertainty, but it went incredibly well. We had a bunch of players who basically wanted to play for the team and a management to back it up. Gates were surprisingly good and for cup ties with Farnborough Town there were close on 6,000 inside.'

Going to Isthmian League grounds was 'great fun' he said, and reminded him of his own amateur playing days. It was in 1995 that he was asked to become a vice-president. 'I just wished my dad had been around then,' he said.

'So many people have given so much of their time and expertise to getting Aldershot back into the Football League,' he added. He cited ex-chairmen in Terry Owens, the prime mover in the Save Our Shots campaign, Karl Prentice and John McGinty, the man whom Trethewy/ Day accused of fleecing him for £65,000. 'These were men dedicated to getting us back on a firm footing,' Rollin insisted. 'Of course mistakes were made along the way. The intention was not to go full-time until we actually made it back to the League. We did it before then and might have suffered for it. Finances are still a problem. My great fear is that if we were relegated, the future would be bleak indeed. We still have diehards who can recall the club from its earliest years in the Southern League back in 1927. There has been a new generation added since 1992 and the mixing of the old and the new has been great to see.'

No spin-offs from the Premier League here then? 'I was against the formation in 1992 because I knew it would be of no assistance to clubs like Aldershot,' said Rollin. 'We did gain something when we had Chelsea reserves playing at the Rec for a number of years. They were good to us, and the association was much appreciated, but there has been little else.'

It was too cold to talk for too much longer; there was snow still lying round the sides of the pitch. We both needed to keep moving or at least get into a stand to evade the wind. It was certainly not the sort of day that prompted John Betjeman to yearn after Miss Joan Hunter Dunn, 'furnished and burnished by Aldershot sun.'

The football was raw, too. Aldershot were struggling six places from the bottom of the table – which was being propped up by Hereford – and right from the outset, you knew it wouldn't take much for the raucous East Terrace to turn. When Hereford took the lead within two minutes through the lively Stuart Fleetwood, it turned. 'Get behind them,' one voice urged forlornly. Within 10 minutes, he was joining in the general criticism and the particular abuse directed at Marvin Morgan. 'Hit him with your handbag, Morgan,' he shouted. 'Cross the fucking thing,' he added, before turning to a mate and declaring that he wanted his money back.

They found something to applaud at half-time when Shaun May, who had played 57 games for the club in the first two Isthmian promotions in the early 1990s, drew the raffle. There was clearly a reservoir of respect for the Class of '92, who were featured in the match programme. There were also cheers for a lad who hit the crossbar with a shot as intended in a competition. 'You want our No. 10 shirt?' somebody shouted.

It was back to the grumbling, groaning and foul language for the second half. The day's match sponsors were Integrated Cleaning Management, their slogan 'Let's Keep it Clean'. Shots supporters took no heed. There was much 'for fuck's sake' and use of stronger language. Finally Morgan was substituted to more derision, he waving sarcastically to the fans as he departed.

By contrast, Hereford had a target man in the Frenchman Matthieu Manset who looked too good for the level, and would duly be signed in the transfer window for a fee said to be in excess of £400,000 by Championship club Reading, who must surely have been watching him today. Manset helped set up a second goal for Joe Colbeck, and although Shots pulled one back in added time through Luke Guttridge, the cries were ringing out for manager Kevin Dillon to go.

(In the angry aftermath that night, Morgan would inadvisedly tweet a message to the Aldershot fans who had applauded his withdrawal. 'I hope you all die,' it said. Morgan would soon be suspended and fined two weeks wages as the message board went into overdrive. It also speculated on a new manager, a lot being in favour of the former Wimbledon player Dean Holdsworth, now manager of Newport County. 'Knowing our luck, we'll probably get Reg Holdsworth,' someone posted.)

By now, snow flurries were falling in the dark as the car park at the side of the ground emptied. Another defeat, restless natives. But, perversely, all was well at Aldershot. For when they got home, had their tea, and pondered it all around the warmth of a fire, there would be one abiding consolation for those who thought these things through.

They could remember fondly 1992, and be grateful that they had their football club back and playing in the Football League; 20 years of vast changes in order to stand still was seen as a redemption here. Spencer Trethewy had misguidedly tried to save them and not pulled it off. One of the great truths about the game, though, was that there would always be someone willing and able to do it, to keep a club alive so that it may dream again.

Chapter 14

THE CLUB THAT JACK BUILT

IN AN INTERVIEW with Kenny Dalglish once, I asked him if he would ever take over a lower division club who had money to spend with a view to leading them to the top. 'It would have to a be a lot of money,' he replied with a twinkle in his eye and the mischievous smile that became familiar in football through his playing career with Liverpool before he went on to manage them.

At Blackburn Rovers in 1991, he found a man with a lot of money. Jack Walker was a local industrialist made good. Very good. Two years earlier, he had sold his company, Walker Steel, for £330 million. It was then the highest sum that had been paid for a British private concern and made him the 20th wealthiest person in the country.

As a lad, Walker had grown up supporting Rovers and now decided that as he entered his 60s, he wanted to buy and fund them. He soon sacked the manager Don Mackay and hired Dalglish in a recruitment that stunned the game. After Liverpool, Dalglish said he would be taking an extended break. But suddenly he was back, after a mere eight months away, accepting the challenge of taking Rovers from the old Second Division to the top flight, then seeing if he could achieve Walker's dream of winning the championship. During that time away, he had turned down the manager's job at Sheffield Wednesday because of memories of Hillsborough.

Dalglish was also more attracted by the Blackburn project and knew he had a good chance of success. Walker was investing serious money. A very private man, he was then living in tax exile in Jersey and granted me an unheard-of interview after I kept writing to him. After the taxi had delivered me down the snaking flower-bordered drive to his large refurbished farmhouse at Mont Cochon just outside St Helier, Walker ushered me into what felt like a storage room, with just a table and two chairs.

He was wary and defensive but gradually opened up about how as a boy he had taken supporters' coaches to away games, about how he wanted to give something back to the town that had been so good to him and why he wanted to enjoy Rovers – he would fly back for each home game to Blackpool airport – while he could. 'The way we're going,' I remember him saying, 'we'll make Manchester United look cheap.'

They did – and had to. For many players would not take Blackburn seriously, given their absence of a track record of trophies. The facilities were basic, too. Not only was the Ewood Park ground in need of rebuilding, the training pitch was on a public park next to a cemetery. One early signing, Graeme Le Saux, once told me how the dog muck had to be cleared from the pitch and how kids attending relatives' funerals would shout and wave at the players from the cars.

It didn't take long for Walker to deliver, however, for he was a local man who wanted to leave a legacy beyond just a few seasons of success. The stadium would be rebuilt and a new training ground purchased outside town. 'And was Juventus builded here?' the football writer John Roberts wondered memorably in the *Independent*.

Without this evidence and enticement initially, however, Roy Keane chose Manchester United above them – thus no Roy of the Rovers story – having looked likely to agree terms with Dalglish at one point. It meant that the club had to pay above the odds in both transfer fees and wages to players. The real coup came in 1992 with the signing of Alan Shearer for a British record of £3.3 million from Southampton.

It left Sir Alex Ferguson at United now spitting feathers, with the England striker then the hottest property in the game as England's most promising striker, one who would go on to be the most prolific of his generation.

Shearer's goals duly brought Blackburn the title in 1994/95, clinched by Dalglish's side at Liverpool even though they lost the game. Manchester United were unable to force the victory they needed at West Ham in an exciting title denouement that left Dalglish beaming and the proud-as-punch Jack Walker shedding a tear in the Anfield directors' box. Many around the country joined in the touching moment.

There have been many clubs down the years who have bought the title but this was probably the first occasion in English football when one man had bought it. It made Blackburn champions for the first time since the start of the Great War in 1914. Few envisaged it then, but over the first 20 years of the Premier League, they would be one of only four clubs to win the title, the others being big city clubs in Manchester United, Arsenal and Chelsea. The population of the town, 20 miles north of Manchester, was 110,000 at the time of becoming champions.

Not the least ironic aspect of the club's title win was that their erstwhile chairman Bill Fox was fiercely opposed to the Premier League as president of the Football League. Indeed, he was saddened by its formation. I was once invited into the Rovers' boardroom for a cup of tea by a man who was viewed an as old buffer and a barrier to progress. 'Finest of the 92,' he said of our oak-panelled, coal-fired surroundings. Fox died in 1992, just before Rovers won promotion to the new league. He may have been a throwback to patrician mill-owner times (he was actually a potato merchant) but his heart was in his club as much as Jack Walker's.

I went again to Rovers' Ewood Park home early in Dalglish's reign to see what all the fuss was about. The ground was then still

THE CLUB THAT JACK BUILT | 239

in development, as were team and club. The sums being bandied around at the time were £12 million to fund the stadium, maybe £30 million for the whole project. Football was staggered. These were then astronomical numbers.

The game was an FA Cup tie against Kettering Town of the Conference; a compare-and-contrast exercise. Rovers had it all, the Poppies were a then huge £250,000 in debt and would suffer a fall due to that burden in years to come. King Kenny's team prevailed comfortably by 4-1, as most often happens in the Cup. We just forget those results and choose to remember the rare giant-killing upsets.

Now I returned to Ewood for another FA Cup third round match, against the West London club Queens Park Rangers, the leaders of the Championship and heavily favoured to return to the Premier League. They were haves, rather than have-nots, too, these days. After a period in administration, they were bought in 2007 by the Formula 1 tycoons Bernie Ecclestone and Flavio Briatore for £14 million. Their shareholders also included the ridiculously wealthy Lakshmi Mittal, a steel industrialist as coincidence would have it.

So much had changed at Blackburn, starting with the building of the M65 motorway across from the M6 through to Burnley. The junction delivering you to Blackburn was just a couple of miles away from Ewood on the Darwen side and cut out the old tortuous journey through the town centre from the motorway to the north. There was the usual sprouting of McDonald's and other fast food outlets around the ground but the patch of wasteland for car parking next to a travellers' site remained. The Ewood Arms had shut down, though.

These days the stadium stood out amid the surrounding streets as testament to Walker's legacy, the club having purchased many terraced houses back in the 1990s to effect its expansion. When Walker died in August 2000, aged 71, his obituary in the *Daily Telegraph* contained the following: 'Perhaps those whose homes were overshadowed by the vast new stadium grumbled a little, but elsewhere builders, shopkeepers, publicans and hotel owners were grateful for the business that the side's revitalisation had put their way and on the streets of Blackburn, the townspeople walked with a little more pride. In 1993, Walker was overwhelmingly voted man of the year by listeners to BBC Radio Lancashire.'

The ground was then a giant response to the Taylor Report, its 30,000 capacity seemingly oversized for such a town, but now Ewood was simply par for the course, the least that would be expected of a Premier League club. Rovers had certainly established themselves as that, their achievements of the League win and a League Cup victory over the two decades more than many bigger clubs had managed.

After Walker, a trust was set up to hold his shares and administer the club, as well as provide some income from his estate, which was believed to be worth £600 million at his death. His aim, though, had been for Rovers to be self-supporting and any funding had dried up midway through the new Millennium's first decade. Thus when the new money men came into the game and the bigger city clubs built up their financial reserves with revenue from the Champions League, Rovers could no longer compete at the very top. Survival in the Premier League was the simple aim, with the odd cup run and maybe a challenge for a Europa League place thrown in now and then. If they were to ensure that survival and return to the days of top-half finishes – sixth place their highest since 1995 – and possible European campaigns, new owners would be needed.

They arrived in the autumn of 2010. From Pune, 70 miles south-east of Mumbai, came an Indian company called the VH Group, and it paid £23 million to the Jack Walker Trust for the club, also taking on £20 million worth of debt, via a subsidiary company called Venky's London Ltd. Their core business was poultry supply to major companies such as Kentucky Fried Chicken. In the press room for the QPR game, chicken curry would fittingly be served.

The takeover was a shock to a sceptical Blackburn public, except perhaps the 20 per cent from ethnic minorities, who did not, however – as at Luton – attend Rovers' matches in any great numbers. It was also a gift to headline writers with the potential for puns relating to chicken feed, chickens coming home to roost, crying fowl and poultry returns. Some suggested that Rovers might change their name to Blackburn Roosters or Blackburn Rovers KFC.

The new owners seemed serious, however. The head of Venky's, Anuradha Desai, insisted that the company was prepared to spend a lot of money over time to make Blackburn a force again. It certainly had the resources, it seemed. It was reported that the owners' 28 companies were worth a combined £1.5 billion. Desai's two brothers, Venkatesh and the pony-tailed Balaji Rao, would be largely responsible for the club and they would devolve the day-to-day running to the existing chairman John Williams, leaving him to work with the manager Sam Allardyce.

Allardyce had been interviewed for the job in the summer of 2008 but Williams had gone instead for Paul Ince, the former Manchester United, Liverpool and England captain, after his impressive first steps in management with Macclesfield and MK Dons. It made Ince, then 40, the first black manager in the Premier League, which was a curious statistic given the barriers of blind prejudice that black players had broken down and with the aid of various 'Kick Out Racism' campaigns.

Sadly, after a decent start under Ince, Rovers endured a bad run and come December he had been sacked. It was sad, too, during this 2010/11 season, when he parted company with Notts County. Black youngsters had had plenty of playing heroes they could aspire to be, but not managers. It shouldn't have been needed for one to succeed at the highest level but it probably was, for both chairmen to open their minds and aspiring black managers to feel encouraged. After 20 years of development to the point where most spectators – beyond the rabid element among the national team's followers – never even considered the colour composition of teams, it would probably need another 20 before anyone even remarked on the colour of the manager's skin.

After Ince, Allardyce guided Rovers away from relegation to an admirable 10th in 2010. Now, with the arrival of the new owners, he was making noises about looking forward to discussions with them about their plans and how he might help them develop the club. They were ready, they said, to spend £20 million on players very quickly and were looking to be finishing in the top six in a couple of seasons.

There were stirrings of unease, however. Allardyce had known that Rovers were looking for new owners, with the consequences that can mean for a manager in situ, but that had been the case for a few seasons and the desire to buy English clubs seemed to have waned in the recession. It was more the involvement of others that may have been the problem.

It became clear that a Swiss-based sports rights agency (another modern phenomenon; among their activities was buying and selling games for TV screening) called Kentaro and its partners, the Sport Entertainment and Media Group run by the English agent Jerome Anderson, were friendly with the Venky's people and advising them on players. It was mooted that the fading Brazilian superstar Ronaldinho of AC Milan might be signed. David Beckham's name cropped up. The leaking of targets was the kid-in-a-sweetshop excitement of star-struck new owners.

Then, a fortnight before Christmas, with Rovers 13th in the table and five points above the relegation zone, Allardyce was sacked. The owners declared it to be part of a wider strategy but word leaked out also that they were not happy with the brand of football being played.

There were suggestions that Allardyce had objected to some of the players being suggested to him by Jerome Anderson when he himself as manager should have been in sole charge of recruitment.

There was bemusement, even outrage, in the game. Allardyce's old friend Sir Alex Ferguson described the dismissal as 'absolutely ridiculous'. Blackburn's beanpole defender Christopher Samba immediately put in a transfer request. Alan Shearer was mooted as the new manager. It was the usual kind of reaction, gossip and speculation that regularly accompanied a managerial sacking in the Premier League.

And this was becoming more regular. A week previously, the Newcastle owner Mike Ashley had sacked Chris Hughton not because of results – Newcastle were 11th, having been newly promoted after winning the Championship – but because he said he wanted a more experienced manager. Something similar had happened to Allardyce in being sacked by Ashley just eight months after taking over at Newcastle, his job prior to Blackburn. He had been hired at St James' Park by the chairman Freddie Shepherd, who promptly saw the club sold by the majority shareholder Sir John Hall to Ashley. At Blackburn, Allardyce had discovered that in football, lightning could strike twice.

'For most people under new ownership, no matter what kind of job you are doing, you get moved on,' Allardyce said when we met later at a hotel in Bolton near his home after the dust had settled on his departure. 'It had happened twice to me now in succession. I had fallen foul of new ownership.'

Allardyce, an old-school manager but who placed great faith in the methods of modern sports science, recalled the takeover, his brief meetings with the owners and how his sacking was conducted, after a 2-1 derby loss to Bolton Wanderers. It proved to be an ironic defeat. Allardyce had also managed Wanderers for close to a decade very successfully, establishing them as the Premier League's over-achievers with a Carling Cup final, two European campaigns and a lowest finish of eighth. That record made him a short-listed candidate for the England manager's job before it went to Fabio Capello. 'I met the two brothers twice, once when they were introduced on the pitch after taking the club over,' he said. 'They were only brief encounters, just five or 10 minutes before a game. The word was they were going to leave the club running as it was. My first conversation would have been about what their vision was, and me telling them what it would take to realise that vision, but we never had that conversation.

'I wanted to get a face-to-face meeting to consider what we were all going to do going forward, to see what their hopes and plans were, and I was willing to go out to India. I don't like all this email rubbish. I like to see the whites of people's eyes and let them see yours. I have never signed a player in my life without sitting down with him and having a proper conversation for a couple of hours, not just about football. Then he would know whether he wanted to come to work for me and I would know whether I wanted him to work for me. Running into December the game schedule was so ferocious that it was difficult. I never did get to meet Mrs Desai.'

He had grown uneasy, he said, by the owners talking openly about wanting more entertaining football. 'You think, "Who has been in their ear? Who's been advising them we are not playing entertaining football?" Somebody made the judgement for them because they don't know anything about football.' It irked Allardyce. He reckoned that at Bolton his teams had outpassed and outplayed most teams but had, he admitted, sought to outmuscle superior footballing sides such as Arsenal and Liverpool and it was that reputation which stuck.

After Newcastle, he also reckoned he could handle the expectation of Blackburn's support. As his nickname of Big Sam, acquired when a centre half at Blackpool and Bolton, suggested, he certainly had presence though in the way the physique of the game has also developed, at 6ft 3in he was nowhere near as big as some of the modern defenders. And despite Blackburn being seen as small town, and people accepting that Jack Walker's money no longer financed the club, there was still expectation. 'You have to remember that Blackburn fans are blessed with the memory of winning the Premier League in 1995, so not one Rovers fan goes there and can't remember,' said Allardyce. 'They have grown up with that. Apart from Manchester United, Arsenal and Chelsea, fans of other clubs haven't.'

John Williams, Allardyce recalled, phoned him the day after the Bolton defeat and asked him to come in to see him. 'I knew from the tone of his voice that I was going to get sacked,' Allardyce said. It clearly pained Williams, who considered his own position and would soon be gone. The pair had worked well on looking to increase crowds through price offers – though they disagreed on the wage bill. Williams reckoned Blackburn had the 12th highest budget in the League; Allardyce that they were much lower than that when all staff costs were considered, not just players' wages.

'In many ways I am glad that they got rid of me so quickly because if I wasn't the one they wanted, at least they had done it without stringing me along,' added Allardyce. 'As disappointed as I was, it was best that it happened like that. I am not knocking Venky's. I just think it was unfortunate naivety.

'The only thing that concerns you is the knock on your reputation. It takes you an age in this game to build your reputation and other circumstances can knock that down in a day. "Why is he really being sacked?" Because they couldn't sack me on results, or what we were doing, or buying bad players. For what we were paying the players, it was miraculous what we were doing.'

The owners came up with a name as his replacement that surprised everyone: Steve Kean, who had been a first-team coach under Allardyce and his assistant, Neil McDonald, who had also departed. The owners apparently liked the 44-year-old Scot's fresh thinking, they said; more probably his malleability. The home support had a different view. At the Boxing Day game against Stoke, which Rovers lost 2-0, there were demonstrations of disaffection. They included the letting loose of live chickens, one of them in a Blackburn scarf, before the game. Another was confiscated by a turnstile operator. In a statement, Lancashire police intoned in all seriousness: 'A cockerel and a hen were released in the concourse in the Darwen End Stand. The chickens were then put in a police cell until they were collected after the game.' Fans also chanted 'Venky's out' and sang Jack Walker's name.

Walker still had a presence but not everyone was so reverent towards him. By the club shop, the Roverstore – which still bore a picture of Dalglish and the title-winning team in the window – there was a statue of him with an inscription telling of 'Rovers' Greatest Supporter'. With a little bit of snow still on the ground this January FA Cup day, some kids were grabbing handfuls and using Jack as target practice.

Though the FA Cup produced splendid moments for non-League clubs through the first and second rounds before Christmas, it was its third-round day on the first Saturday of the New Year which gave new impetus to the season, with the Premier and Championship clubs entering the competition. At least that was the theory. The poor old Cup, though, was enduring hard times, a gradual decline having set in after Manchester United were allowed to pull out to play in the Club World Championship in 1999/2000, which was being held in midwinter that year as FIFA's latest brainwave. It was part of a deal where England thought they were in with a chance of getting the World Cup of 2006, though it would go to Germany. United's absence had been bad enough but this year was developing into the worst ever for the grand old competition.

Today at Blackburn would tell a tale, the crowd a mere 10,284, which was not even half of Rovers' average Premier League attendance.

It was not untypical of the rest of the country. Fans were sated from Christmas and New Year football. The competition was losing its allure, amid all the Champions League football, and this year the final would lack status, with Premier League games due to take place on the same Saturday as the May final. The FA Cup final had to be played that day because Wembley was also the venue for the Champions League final this year and UEFA had decreed that they needed the stadium to be unused for a fortnight preceding their occasion.

The Cup's sponsor E.ON was also about to withdraw, leaving the FA desperately trying to find new backers for the following season. There was, however, no queue of companies wanting to be associated with a lame duck, certainly not at £10 million a season in the current climate. The competition was becoming so diluted and overshadowed that it was in danger of having less appeal even than the Carling Cup. Even mid-table Championship clubs with half a chance of the play-offs were sending out weakened teams.

All sorts of remedies were being mooted. They included the scrapping of replays, changing kick-off times (as if there wasn't enough of that already) and even seeding, the worst idea of the lot. It would remove the very ethos of fate's fickle finger, one of the chief ingredients of what was once one of the greatest knockout tournaments in the world. What could be done, then?

For a start, the Cup needed to rediscover its status of being special, to the point where delaying its arrival might help. Many big clubs, and the national team managers, had been clamouring for a two-week winter break. Let them have it at the start of January. That way, when the second half of the season then kicked off with the third round, there was new impetus for clubs and fans who have had time to recover financially from forking out for so much Christmas football.

We could then have forgotten about all the gimmicky ideas and simply encouraged clubs to agree on cheaper ticket prices. At the moment the away clubs can veto discounts, the gate receipts being split 40 per cent each to the clubs and 20 per cent to the FA. The competition could also be compressed. Currently, we had a month between quarter and semi-finals, then another month until the final. If the final was played in April, it would have been removed from the crowded end-of-season schedule and given more care and attention. And with that, quite apart from it being more attractive to sponsors who would see the competition given more prominence again, it would return 'event' status to the game both for clubs and fans beyond those of just the two teams involved.

Today would be pretty much a non-event as a game, with Junior Hoilett's second-half goal for Blackburn the only one of the match to end Rangers' unbeaten run of 19 games. It was hardly surprising given that that their star player, the skilful but unpredictable Moroccan Adel Taarabt, was given the day off. It showed what Rangers thought of the competition in their scheme of things at the time.

All was overshadowed, however, by a sickening leg break for QPR's Jamie Mackie in a collision with Blackburn's Gael Givet. The Senegalese El Hadji Diouf, one of the Premier League's most controversial, snarling and spitting characters, was alleged to have stood over the Rangers striker saying 'fuck you and fuck your leg'. Diouf would later deny it but there seemed to be plenty of witnesses backing up Mackie's version of events, witnesses who had to be restrained from getting to Diouf in the tunnel after the game.

The Rangers manager Neil Warnock, one of the most outspoken managers in the English game, labelled Diouf as a 'sewer rat' and 'a gutter type'. His opposite number Steve Kean's refusal to be drawn on the matter spoke volumes. Soon, commendably, he had Diouf out of the club and on loan to Glasgow Rangers.

The previous week, Kean's team had beaten Liverpool 3-1, a result which prompted the sack at Anfield for Roy Hodgson. Kean, softly spoken but with a shaven head that hinted at hardness, was certainly enjoying beginners' luck. A relegation struggle was looking unlikely, with Allardyce having left them five points off sixth place, and Blackburn were exactly the sort of mid-table team who might just get to Wembley. That would certainly be quite an initial return for Venky's.

'People used to say you would be mad to get involved in football,' said Allardyce. 'Well, I disagree, given the global exposure. For Venky's, it is a wise investment for their business. We are insular in this country. We keep forgetting that this is the biggest game in the world and the Premier League is the most watched and best financially supported league in the world. If you are in a global market industry, then there couldn't be anything better for your business than you buying a club as one of your arms for as long as you run that club correctly and allow that to be successful.

'You can market your product on your club shirt and round the ground with advertising. That goes to 250-odd countries worldwide and an estimated 900 million viewers. That doesn't even count the internet hits when your picture comes up, or all the sporting magazines who plaster your name. For creating a more profitable industry, it is one of the best ways.

'Venky's are well aware of the heritage and history of Blackburn and they say they don't want to change that. It is very dangerous if you do. With a bit more financial support, Rovers could achieve. You can still enjoy being the underdog and the experience, and enjoy the journey. And once a new owner gets into it, it becomes part of your life and you can't do without it, like players and managers.'

That had certainly happened to Jack Walker those 20 years ago as he commuted to games from Jersey, rarely missing one. The problem for owners based abroad was that they just didn't get the same feeling and nor were they around the club to discover the nuances, the internal politics, on a daily basis. Thus was it too easy to make ruthless decisions in ignorance based on hearsay. And, should results turn bad, it was easy for absentee landlords to get out of the habit of coming to games, and so losing interest.

Some modern Christians wear wristbands with an acronym on them: WWJD – What Would Jesus Do? At Blackburn, it stood for What Would Jack Do? Allardyce believed that if Walker had been alive still, he would have been putting money into Blackburn. 'But it wouldn't be to the level where he could afford to win the Premier League.' What would Jack have thought of all that was happening at Ewood now? Not a lot, you suspected.

Inadvertent as it may have been from a man who simply wanted to see his home town club become champions of England, Jack Walker did begin the process of investing heavily to win a Premier League title. The bigger city clubs had followed the lead and been rewarded subsequently with all that Champions League revenue, which now meant that the likes of Blackburn needed more investment simply to take part in the same competition as them. Given that set of circumstances in the modern game, you hoped that clubs such as Rovers would again come to see the value of cup competitions, their silverware a potential salvation, and thus restore them to former glories.

Chapter 15

THE OLD-SCHOOL CUP TIE

THE FOOTBALL LEAGUE CUP is the least regarded of the English professional game's three major competitions, after League and FA Cup. It came into being for the 1960/61 season as a result of clubs wanting to make the most of midweek nights to increase their takings with the majority of them having by then installed floodlights. At first, many of the bigger clubs declined to enter, Aston Villa profiting by being the first winners, though that changed when a UEFA Cup place was offered to the winners in 1969/70.

Latterly, though, the perception of it had reverted to that of its early days since the bigger clubs already had plenty of opportunity to play in Europe, through the Champions and now Europa Leagues, and were concerned about fixture congestion. If even the FA Cup was fighting for its life, what chance the League Cup, which was now sponsored by Carling after previous deals with the Milk Marketing Board, Littlewoods, Rumbelows (yes, I had forgotten that one too), Coca-Cola and Worthington? During that era, it became known as the Worthless Cup. Now it was more commonly called the Mickey Mouse Trophy.

There were some of us, though, who still enjoyed it, perhaps due to our fascination with night football that stemmed from being taken as a kid when it was exciting and even a bit subversive if it was a school night. And while some may have bemoaned clubs fielding reserve and youth team players to fulfil the fixture, it was also fascinating to get glimpses of up-and-coming young players who may be playing in the Premier League in future years. Added to that was the chance for youngsters to get access to games, which could be scheduled for half-term nights, on cheaper tickets. Thus did it have the potential to offer something different and justify its place in the English scheme of things. A February final helped, too, by creating an event at a traditionally gloomy time of year.

For the medium-sized and smaller Premier League clubs it also offered a real chance of a trophy and a place in Europe, though it was getting harder for them; there were signs that some of the bigger clubs were starting to see it as a way to appease fans with the bigger prizes eluding them. The likes of Roberto Mancini at Manchester City and Arsène Wenger at Arsenal were falling into that category. They had reluctantly come to see that it could boost morale too. When at Chelsea, Jose Mourinho placed early store in the competition and winning it opened the way to more trophies. On top, the February lift provided a fillip for the run-in at the end of the season.

Then there were the Championship clubs, who were grateful for any bit of revenue and glory that came their way. One such was Ipswich Town, one of the most delightful clubs in England, their tradition for warmth, hospitality and good football nurtured by the Old Etonians John and Patrick Cobbold, benign brothers from a brewing family whose civilised approach to running a football club had all but disappeared elsewhere.

Promoted to the old First Division in 1961, Ipswich promptly went and won it in 1962 under Alf Ramsey – and the Dagenham-born Ramsey, who would go on to manage England and become Sir Alf, remained the last manager born in the south of England to have won the title. 'Never say never', they said in football, but from promotion to Premier League champions in 12 months was looking ever increasingly a leap too far.

It has always been a joy to visit their Portman Road ground, not just because of the adjoining, copious car park, which remains. In one corner the Ipswich Buddhist Centre told of modern times, along with the arrival of offices for Suffolk County Council and Ipswich Borough Council in the roads around the ground, but there is still a bus garage in an opposite corner. The huge training pitch behind the main stand is now artificial.

Under Bobby Robson's management of the late 1970s and early 1980s they played some beautiful, mesmeric football with two pioneer overseas players in the Dutch midfield pairing of Frans Thijssen and Arnold Muhren. As a Second Division club they won the 1978 FA Cup, beating Arsenal in the process. Forty years on, in that way football has of its past forever casting shafts of light on its present, I found myself in Robson's London home in Fulham interviewing the great man when he broke off, insisting that he had to make a phone call. It was to David Sheepshanks, the former Ipswich chairman, to thank him for the gift of a silver half-size replica of the Cup as a commemoration. Robson was touched to the point of tears. 'I don't know how much to insure it for,' he said to me, scratching his head.

In 1981, Robson's grand old team that also included such England regulars as Terry Butcher and Paul Mariner, won the UEFA Cup and finished runners-up in the old First Division, as they would also do in 1982 with probably the best side never to have won the title. Succeeding Ron Greenwood after the World Cup of 1982, Robson then went on to become the second manager from the club to be chosen for the England job. Ipswich went back down to the Second Division after his departure but rose again, promoted to the new Premier League in 1991/92. They lasted 10 seasons until relegation in 2002.

Administration followed, along with hard-luck stories in the play-offs. In 2007, they were taken over in a £44 million deal by Marcus

Evans, who was described by his friends as a broker of corporate hospitality – and by his enemies as a ticket tout. You wondered what the Cobbolds would have made of it and him. It was certainly a tale to tell of modern football, as at Arsenal, as at Blackburn. Old money looked to have had its day. Clubs were having to sniff out new money to turn their fortunes around.

If Evans did not seem terribly Ipswich Town, nor did the manager he appointed in Roy Keane. The Manchester United hard man had been one of the iconic figures of the first dozen years of the Premier League but, brash and forthright, just did not seem the right fit for a town in rural, laid-back East Anglia. Their badge still retained the Suffolk Punch horse. Their nickname these days was the Tractor Boys, though many disliked its yokel implication. Perhaps Evans thought that Ipswich needed dragging into a new, more clamorous era but he too came finally to realise that Keane was not a match. Having given the Irishman a decent transfer budget to try and return the club to the Premier League, Evans grew exasperated at a bad run of results that saw seven defeats in nine league games.

What made it worse was that East Anglian rivals Norwich City were enjoying a good season – threatening to win promotion to the Premier League – under a manager surely destined for great things in the Scot Paul Lambert. Lambert had been a Celtic player and brought the intensity of Glasgow derbies against Rangers to facing Ipswich in Norfolk and beat them 4-1; from Old Firm to Old Farm Derby. A few months on, between a defeat by Nottingham Forest and a 7-0 drubbing at Chelsea in an FA Cup tie, Evans and Keane agreed a deal for the manager to go. 'Some people think I am nasty but I think I am too nice sometimes,' Keane had said shortly before his dismissal. 'I have been too loyal to one or two players.' It echoed what Graham Taylor said once; that the trouble with players was that they got you the sack.

It was a shame in many ways that – for the moment at least – the game had lost Keane's presence and his outspoken Friday press conferences. His opinions hinted of 'in my day', notably when he would lambast a Manchester United v. Arsenal game for lacking intensity due to all the players looking like pals. The trouble was, thinking back to his duels with Patrick Vieira, you found yourself agreeing with him. 'English football is changing and not for the good,' Keane said mid-season. 'It's not the game we knew 15 or 20 years ago, the one I first got involved in. I don't think we love it the way we did years ago because of what we see every week. If I lost my job, there would be nobody complaining too much but top managers getting good results are being sacked.'

He was referring to those dismissals of Sam Allardyce by Venky's at Blackburn and Roy Hodgson by John W. Henry at Liverpool as victims of new owners, along with Chris Hughton, sacked at Newcastle United by Mike Ashley. All three clubs were then in mid-table. 'Owners are coming in from other countries and I don't know if they understand the game of football,' Keane added. 'It's an ego thing, like a toy they play with. They buy clubs, sack managers – it's crazy. And we see players wanting to leave a club after only being there two minutes because they are not happy with what's going on.'

He had no complaints about his own dismissal when it came, he would later say, as he had 'another life outside football'. The parting came even though Ipswich had reached the semi-final of the Carling Cup – in which they had been drawn against Arsenal, old foes of 1978. Similarly, they were a traditional club with an old Etonian as chairman in Peter Hill-Wood, who had followed in the footsteps of his father Dennis and grandfather Samuel.

The tie brought back marvellous memories for David Sheepshanks, who was still a non-executive director at the club. The role enabled him to retain his positions of influence within football's governing bodies, having been a chairman of the Football League in the late 1990s and even joint acting chairman of the FA after the resignation of Lord Triesman more recently. He was currently chairman of the National Football Centre being established at Burton.

Thus he was a good choice – well spoken and articulate – to consult over Ipswich Town, the birth and effect of the Premier League and its impact on the rest of the game, along with football's changes, politics and economics. It proved well worth the price of lunch at a hotel just outside the town.

Suffolk-raised, Sheepshanks was sent away to Eton. He loved football, played for the second XI and was captain of his house. He was taken to his first Ipswich Town game as an 11-year-old in the 1965/66 season by three men who worked on his father's farm, a 3-2 win over Leyton Orient. 'It only took one game and it got under my skin,' he said. 'It emphasises the power of taking a young boy to a game, and I always tried to stress this during my time as a director and chairman. We have to remember how to make the game accessible.'

After a spell working in New Zealand and Australia, still trying to follow the club's results, Sheepshanks worked in London through the 1970s and travelled the country following the team. 'I met my wife, who was Swedish, and she was amazed that I used to do that, often on my own.

'From 1973, we had this quite extraordinary success when we qualified for Europe nine years out of 10. Six of those years we would have been in the Champions League had it existed. I was in the crowd in 1980 when we beat Manchester United 6-0 and missed two penalties. Mind, I can't crow. I was also in the crowd at Old Trafford in 1995 when we lost 9-0.' It remained the heaviest margin of defeat in the Premier League.

'I also remember vividly winning the UEFA Cup in 1981 and being runners-up in the league in 1982. They were football delights,' added

Sheepshanks, beaming as he warmed to his memories. 'We were also knocked out of the FA Cup in 1981 in the semi-final by Manchester City when extra time was played for the first time. My poor wife sat in a car park outside Villa Park and I paid two boys to look after the car. She had food poisoning. Any decent man would have said, "Darling, we'll turn round and go back" but I wasn't missing it for anything. I feel a bit miserable about that.'

By 1986, all was in decline, however, and Sheepshanks wrote to Patrick Cobbold saying that the club's public relations were appalling. He offered his help. By now he was running a successful business, Starfish, that supplied seafood to Marks & Spencer and Tesco. This being Suffolk, it took six months for Cobbold to reply. Finally, out of the blue, Sheepshanks was invited to lunch with the directors and a match at Portman Road. He painted a picture that tallied with how the Ipswich boardroom was perceived from the outside at the time. 'It was a cold lunch and a very liquid affair with more bottles than you could imagine,' he recalled. 'There was brandy, port and cigars and I watched the game through a haze. Ten days later I was invited for coffee and was asked to be a director. I was 34 and they didn't ask for any money, just said it was about getting the right people. It was a really glorious moment. I was the young blood, going to supporters' club meetings, travelling with the team. I had Ipswich in every cell in my body.'

He saw in the late 1980s the storm clouds that told of the advent of the Premier League. 'We used to have an annual dinner for officials of clubs from the First and Second Divisions and you began to see the start of a breakdown in relationships. The big clubs were getting more disillusioned and didn't want to be part of the thing.'

Ipswich were part of the new league – just. They won promotion at Oxford United in 1992 to become founder members. 'Terribly exciting,' said Sheepshanks. However, the manager who had taken them up, John Lyall, was ageing and wearying. Within two years,

258 | THERE'S A GOLDEN SKY

he was gone. 'As happens at many football clubs but untypical of Ipswich, there were demonstrations against the board,' Sheepshanks recalled. 'We toed a collective line but the board was fractured. It felt like a terrible time.' So tricky were times, indeed, such the fission, that the demonstrations were led by one Ivan Paul, who was a nephew of Patrick Cobbold and had been at Eton with Sheepshanks.

To replace Lyall, the board appointed George Burley, former right back in the Robson era and a promising Scottish manager who had impressed at nearby Colchester. But things worsened and Ipswich were relegated in 1994/95. 'People were saying good riddance to Ipswich. We brought nothing to the League,' said Sheepshanks. 'They had forgotten about the Bobby Robson era and it wasn't the same. It was mortifying for all who loved the club. There was a huge job to be done with the fans, the media and the football world at large.'

There was a vote of no confidence in the board and, although the board won the day, the chairman John Kerr had had enough of the infighting. Sheepshanks was prevailed upon to replace him and took little persuading. 'I was keen to do it, in that I had a huge amount of passion and energy to put things right.'

He did. It took a while but Ipswich were promoted after several near misses under Burley. Yet, back in the Premier League, life had changed. The big city clubs were endowed with Champions League money by the mid-1990s and were way ahead of the likes of Ipswich. They would also suffer, along with many other clubs, from a decision in which Sheepshanks was directly involved and which has been largely forgotten. He maintained, however, that it was a turning point for the game in this country. 'When the Premier League was formed, a lot of people said that this is just the old First Division under a new name. A marketing gimmick,' he said. 'None of us could see what it would be today. But within two years, it was absolutely clear.' It was why the events of 1996 still continued to trouble him.

He was invited to a meeting, along with all Football League chairmen, at the Connaught Rooms in London – the venue where the formation of the Premier League had been ratified. There, the Premier League and the FA both made pitches to the clubs to run their broadcast and commercial deals for them. 'The FA's was just a land grab, really,' said Sheepshanks, 'but the Premier League made a remarkable offer.'

Three power brokers, in the form of chief executive Rick Parry, David Dein of Arsenal and Southampton's Keith Wiseman, offered the Football League 20 per cent of any combined TV deal between the Premier and the Football League. Other chairmen have since recalled it as less but Sheepshanks – who would certainly know as a key inside figure – insisted on the percentage. Furthermore, he reckoned from private talks with Parry that the figure could even go as high as 25 per cent. The Premier League clearly thought that the top two divisions would be stronger, and more valuable commercially, if back together.

'It was a defining moment,' said Sheepshanks. 'It was essentially a rejoining of the Premier and Football Leagues. Out of the 72 Football League clubs, 71 put up their hands for the deal. The only one who didn't was Barry Hearn of Leyton Orient.' Hearn, the entrepreneur responsible for the snooker boom of the 1980s on the back of his 'golden nugget' world champion Steve Davis, had little feeling for the Premier League as would come to be seen down the years, notably when West Ham and Tottenham would fight over the Olympic Stadium in Orient's catchment area.

Ten days after the vote, Sheepshanks was in his office at Portman Road. He saw a headline on teletext announcing that the Football League had done a £25 million deal with Sky. 'I thought, "That can't be right." But it was. The board had done a deal with Sky to move from ITV, and get £25 million instead of £7 million. Vic Wakeling and Trevor East at Sky had very cleverly divided and ruled.

'I am sure the board made the decision in good faith and did what they thought was right for the league but this was a repeat of the tail wagging the dog' added Sheepshanks, anger still in his voice. 'The lower division representatives took the view that this was an enormous deal, a bird in the hand, and they had to take it. They didn't get the significance of the deal with the Premier League.

'It was a dreadful turning point. Even at that time, with the £25 million from Sky, had we taken the 20 per cent deal from the Premier League it would have been £42 million. With 25 per cent it would have been £50 million so we would have doubled our money. More important, we would have been reconnected to the rocket ship. These days, it would be worth £300 million a season to the Championship instead of the £100 million we get. Think about all that over the years. All the overseas rights, the commercial rights.'

Now there was a wistfulness in his voice but he admitted that at the time, he went 'apeshit'. He rang like-minded chairmen. They demanded a meeting to move a vote of no confidence in the board and it was duly carried at the Landmark Hotel in London. Sheepshanks found himself thrust forward as chairman and had meetings with Sky but the deal was dead. The League had missed the biggest of tricks and the chance would not come back.

'I had a two-year mandate to change the Football League so that this could never be repeated,' said Sheepshanks. I found a new independent chairman and a new chief executive in Richard Scudamore, who came from Thomson Newspapers for the eastern and southern seaboard of the United States.' Scudamore would go on to the Premier League, vindicating Sheepshanks's eye for a talented figure.

'I have got a few scars on my back,' Sheepshanks added with a smile as he recalled his time as Football League chairman. 'I got the old League offices in Lytham closed down, established modern offices in London and Preston. We got the constitution changed so that the board comprised three from the Championship, two from League One and one from League Two. Sadly, the relationship with the Premier League was by then irreparably damaged.

'I was appalled not by the formation of the Premier League but by the weakness of those who sat around the table and agreed the terms. The Premier League had their way with us and the financial terms for partition were wholly inadequate. The Football League were impossibly weak. They had their tummies tickled by the Premier League then Sky a few years later.

'For example, there was a tripartite agreement for participation in the FA Cup with the FA still paying around £3 million to the Football League. The Premier League were on a formula to pay £5 million but had a five-year time limit. When the new board found out, we appealed to the Premier League about this clause but got short shrift.

'The Premier League has been great for elite club football in this country but I can't conclude that it has done anything other than damage international football,' Sheepshanks continued. 'It didn't set out to damage it but the effect has been to create this leviathan club success machine and now international football is the Champions League.'

One of Sheepshanks' problems was that he was chairman when Ipswich went into administration in 2003 following relegation from the Premier League, thus giving ammunition to those who would say that it undermined his credibility to talk on football finances. It wasn't stopping the new Football League chairman, Greg Clarke, however. His participation in Leicester City's controversial administration of 2002, which began a domino effect of clubs getting out of their debts the easy way and led to the League having to start deducting points to stem the practice, had not prevented him from getting the job in the first place either.

'Administration was the most painful thing that ever happened to me,' Sheepshanks recalled. 'We had our critics but we survived because we came clean and hadn't been negligent or extravagant. We finished fifth under George Burley but were relegated the next season.

'In the first year of the August transfer deadline, the Premier League were in some disarray. There was the European inquiry into TV rights and the banks were getting nervous with the collapse of ITV Digital. It spelt the perfect storm. We were relegated into quicksand. But I took responsibility for putting it right and we were close to being promoted with Joe Royle. Ultimately, we sold the club. I lost money in loans and in the recovery period but it was just a privilege to hold the office.'

He was still a SHIT, he said proudly. A shit? It was a term coined by the Cobbolds for the Shareholders of Ipswich Town. Indeed, Sheepshanks was the chairman, with a four per cent holding compared to Marcus Evans' 90 per cent. There were still 3,500 old shareholders and Evans had kept an agreement, Sheepshanks said, to have an annual meeting to lay out the financial position of the club, not the plc.

Very quickly after the Keane sacking, Evans moved to appoint Paul Jewell, a manager who had taken both Bradford City and Wigan Athletic into the Premier League and he would be introduced to the crowd this evening ahead of the Arsenal game.

Portman Road – watched over by the statues of two knights, Sir Alf and Sir Bobby – enjoyed one of those nights to evoke the European splendour under Robson and Burley. Arsenal were outplayed, left to admire the teenage Ipswich striker Connor Wickham, for whom they were contemplating paying £10 million. As Ipswich chased a first Wembley final since 1978, the Hungarian Tamas Priskin scored what proved to be the only goal of the game.

In the second leg at the Emirates Stadium however, Ipswich were well beaten by 3-0 and it was Arsenal – Wenger desperate now for the silverware that would ease the criticism of him and his team – who would go to a final against Birmingham City. Thrillingly, they had beaten West Ham 4-3 on aggregate in the other semi-final. Ipswich were left to hope that Jewell's arrival might provide inspiration and momentum for a late charge into the play-offs.

I asked David Sheepshanks if, as the club moved close to 2012 and the 50th anniversary of their only First Division title, whether he could ever see them being champions of England again. 'No,' he replied without hesitation. 'But I do believe it is realistic for a club of our size to get promoted. Then it becomes a question of hanging in there against all these clubs who have accumulated wealth. But I have to say that the economic model of the Championship today is absolutely bust. It's so bad that the majority, maybe 21 out of the 24 clubs, are losing money and a lot are losing between £5 and £10 million a year. You tell me how that is sustainable. It's chasing a dream.'

It was a gloomy assessment. The thought that a small town club would never again usurp a big city outfit as had happened for every decade at least once before the turn of the Millennium was indeed depressing. Sheepshanks, now 58 and potentially a future chairman of the FA, added that he still believed in miracles, however.

Such was football and the mixed emotions and mixed messages it gave out. No matter the changes and finances of the game, as the two legs of the Carling Cup had proved for poor Ipswich, it giveth dreams and it taketh them away.

Chapter 16

MARSH FEVER

THE TWO WORDS Hackney Marshes have become shorthand for the grassroots game in England. Whenever there is a debate about whether the same rules should apply at the top and bottom of the game – such as the introduction of video technology – or whenever anyone talks about the amateurs who paid to play, the Marshes are cited as the most representative place.

They comprise an area of public pitches in the East End of London in the middle of the support base for Tottenham, West Ham and Leyton Orient. Many famous players have graced the turf here amid the many more anonymous players who have not quite graced it. Local boys Bobby Moore, David Beckham and John Terry played here as kids. Another England captain and Essex boy in Tony Adams told me of his own memory of the Marshes as a kid when his father was playing there. Adams recalled being so frozen, that at the end of the game the men had to throw him into a hot shower to bring him back to life. The reality beneath the romance could be bleak.

Once, the Marshes featured 120 pitches, many with just a yard separating the touchlines between them. They were established in response to the post-war football boom, soil and grass laid on top of rubble deposited there after the Blitz, which explained their excellent drainage. The London Borough of Hackney still proudly announced that on the current 340 acres, the 88 pitches formed the largest single concentration of football fields in the world.

The acreage and the number of pitches were ever dwindling though. London was preparing to host the 2012 Olympic Games, to the pride, joy and anticipation of many sports enthusiasts and ordinary citizens just wanting to acquire once-in-a-lifetime tickets to watch Usain Bolt scorch through the 100 metres or Tom Daley dive and Sir Chris Hoy cycle to more gold medals. On the Marshes they were not quite so happy. Paradise was being paved. Pitches were being dug up to provide buildings and car parks for the Olympic Park.

The great arenas of English football had been rebuilt over the previous 20 years and now development had finally caught up with the public parks game. While it may have been with a bigger picture in mind and for the greater good, here in Hackney it was not necessarily with the agreement of the players and administrators, nor to their benefit, they would say. 'Don't talk to me about the Olympics,' Johnnie Walker, chairman of the Hackney and Leyton Sunday League (established 1947), told me. He, though, could hardly be stopped from talking about the Olympics.

Walker, now 77, diminutive, grey and wizened, was one of those stalwarts of the game without whom it would be unable to function. You saw them on touchlines coaching kids' teams or in committee rooms in clubhouses. In the early 1950s, he was an under-18 player in the embryonic league for a team called Islington Queens. 'A rather unfortunate name but teams named the Queens were common in those days and the word Queens didn't carry the same attachment as present times,' he pointed out.

After his national service in the Army, Walker had a spell playing for Holborn Central Working Men's Club, the Coach and Horses pub in Clerkenwell and MG Sports, a club formed by Italian immigrants. He had to pack up, though, at the age of 40 after a heart attack. It didn't stop him training with them, nor managing them successfully to Premier Division titles.

He finally became an administrator in 1980 by joining the league committee, and chairman in 2003. He was prevailed upon by a local legend named Jack Walpole, who was general secretary of the Hackney and Leyton for 25 years until his death in 2001 and has one of the cup competitions named after him. 'We used to called him "Tuna," Walker recalled. 'He used to walk so fast round the pitches that he would get caught in the nets.'

We met early on this February Sunday morning, too early even for the players who were probably still just getting up, bemoaning their late night and desperately trying to locate their kit. Indeed, we were among the first few in the new car park on East Marsh, created, he reckoned, as a sop to stop them complaining about all the Olympic development. It hasn't worked with Walker, though. 'It's been a huge disaster for us really,' he said. 'It made us take a step backwards. People shouldn't be doing this in this day and age.

'I am a sportsman. I love most sports. I am a huge cricket and boxing fan and I love horse racing, though I can't say I like athletics too much. I am not against the Olympics but if they were that interested in sport, the £9 billion would have been better spent on sport at grassroots level.'

Warming to his theme, Walker told of an encounter with Sir Trevor Brooking, the FA's director of development and well known in these parts, having played for West Ham. 'I had him thumping the table, saying, "Don't tell me I don't do anything for grassroots,"' Walker, who is also an FA councillor, recalled. 'I said he had forgotten where the Marshes were and he needed to get a sat nav.

'To be fair, he invited me up there but the FA seem toothless. Their powers have diminished. You think they would fight more for the national game and say, "All right, we will back the Olympics but hands off any football pitches." For too long they have sat back and let it happen. Sports fields over England have diminished by 50 per cent.'

It was true. Successive governments had allowed them to be sold off to supermarkets and the like and now they were wondering why the nation had an obesity epidemic on its hands.

We were gazing across the car park at a huge pile of soil surrounded by green wooden fencing bearing pictures of smiling children and the 2012 logo. 'One team, one project, one Games,' said a slogan. 'Demolish, Dig, Design,' said another for the contractors.

Among the first pitches to go were one cricket and two football fields on the Wick Arena, just across the A12 flyover that separated the Marshes from the main Olympic site. 'I used to be able to look out of my bedroom window and watch a game of cricket,' Walker lamented. 'I look out at the media centre now, which is one of the ugliest buildings you will ever see.'

Here on East Marsh, the main pitch and three neighbouring ones had already gone, the piled soil the basis for a walkway and wheelchair ramp from here to the Olympic Park. 'They took that main pitch at the end of last season without me knowing,' said Walker. 'I was sick. Someone rang me to tell me what was going on and I phoned right away but the bloke in charge of parks and green spaces said he didn't know either. They must have known. They seem to have unbelievable powers, don't they?' he said. 'It's a government thing.'

(It was a little harsh. One leading light in the 2012 bid told a story of how he met a Chinese official at the Beijing Games of 2008 and was asked how things were going in London. The Briton replied that they were having some delays on the site because they needed to go through channels to get Compulsory Purchase Orders – CPOs. 'We don't have those,' the Chinese replied. 'We have JCBs.')

Over the following season, another 11 pitches would be disappearing to provide car parking for disabled people at the Paralympics, Walker said. 'But there'll be VIP parking there, I bet,' he added.

The Football Foundation, Hackney Council and the Olympic Delivery Authority did have a replacement strategy, however. The League had lost its old changing rooms but a new block, with 26 rooms, had been built over at South Marsh at a cost of £1 million. Work was also going on to create 12 new pitches as compensation for the losses but still Walker was not appeased. It was a 20-minute walk to the new dressing rooms over the River Lea and down the path where tattooed men walked their bull terriers, and most people changed in their cars for games on East Marsh. The charming old stable block of dressing rooms in which Tony Adams had been brought back to life was a casualty of the Games, too.

'That new complex,' said Walker. 'You've got to take your boots off when you go in there. The old block over here had leaking roofs but nobody moaned. We've got nothing here now. We have to bring a table, a Thermos flask and biscuits.' As for the new pitches being created, 'It looks like the Somme. They won't have time to bed down.' With some needing to lie fallow, demand would outstrip supply. In some ways, though, that was a good thing, a sign that the game was still thriving.

On a visit to the Marshes 20 years earlier, I encountered 20 pitches out of use due to vandals having damaged the old changing rooms and dog muck abounding. This time, I came expecting more signs of decline – in standard of pitches, number of teams and player behaviour – due to my own anecdotal evidence down the years. Having watched my son's teams play on public parks, coached some of them too from under-8s through to under-18s, I had seen changing facilities and pitches decline due to council cutbacks on maintenance. It saddened me that we were expecting kids to learn the game on either mudheaps or with grass around their ankles. It was no wonder they were often encouraged by unenlightened Sunday morning managers to hoof the ball forward towards the fast kid up front rather than learn to pass the ball properly.

It did make you lament the 'them-and-us' nature of the game in this country. Money washed around the Premier League but still our facilities were way behind the manicured, community facilities you would see travelling through, say, the Netherlands and France. The Premier League insisted that it poured fortunes into the grassroots game but, as with David Sheepshanks and his assertion that the League had worked a flanker on the FA Cup funding to lower professional clubs, so there were those who believed that it had reneged on an agreement to give generously to the amateur game.

In 1999, following the Blair government's Football Task Force, the League was granted permission to sell its TV rights collectively in return for making 5 per cent of the deal available to the grass roots from 2001. The Football Foundation was created to administer the fund, which also included money from government and the FA.

At first, the Premier League paid £20 million a year, though that had now fallen to £12 million due to wrangling among the various bodies. There were those, such as the former sports minister Richard Caborn, now at the Football Foundation, who insisted that the original agreement was for five per cent of all TV money. The League said it did not include the overseas rights, which had by now almost doubled the money coming into the League from television. With local government cutbacks and the comparatively pathetic amounts spent on the grassroots – £34 million a year from the Premier League, government and FA, compared to £60 million 10 years earlier – the country's facilities were in a sorry state.

Despite all that, the Marshes today were still vibrant, as testament to the enduring appeal of playing the game no matter the unpromising circumstances. Kick offs at 10.30 a.m. were no less optimistic now than two decades ago but some even wanted to start before that. 'Sometimes teams want earlier kick offs because we have Manchester United supporters and these silly sods want to go up there and support them,' said Walker. 'We deny them, of course.'

The usual wonderful team names, and sights and sounds, remained. There were FC Polit and the Poet Bar, Wounded Knee and Bristow City. There was a team in Arsenal kit, another in Argentina's. Albion Manor played in West Bromwich Albion strip, 'because the sponsor at the pub was Albion mad,' the manager on the touchline broke off from haranguing his team to tell me.

On one pitch, a big defender went down with an injury and the manager turned to a substitute to inquire: 'You're not going to be sick if you play, are you?' Presumably he was the likely replacement as he seemed to be the only one not smoking a cigarette. On a neighbouring field, meanwhile, a striker sent in a shot that did not stretch the goalkeeper enough for one of his teammates. 'What's wrong with you?' he demanded to know. 'That was straight fucking at him.'

You could tell embryonic relationships, because the girlfriends had turned up to watch, the lust not yet having worn off. You could also tell the divorced dads as their poor kids had to amuse themselves on the touchline, this being their weekend with him.

The fields were in surprisingly good condition, though the goalposts had mostly seen better days. Metal, rounded, most were rusting, with strips of tatty tape hanging from the crossbars as the signs of a season hanging nets from them. Teams in the Hackney and Leyton paid £47 for a pitch and £35 for a referee, splitting the cost. 'They are marvellous in Hackney and have kept the prices down,' said Walker. 'And the staff and the Marsh rangers are magnificent, couldn't be more helpful. But in inner cities we are still finding out that teams haven't got the money. When they come and learn how much it is to start a team, a lot fall by the wayside. You have to pay for so many pitches up front, you see.' Around half a dozen teams withdrew at the end of each season due to lack of finances.

Then there were the fines. It was £10 for a booking and more, at the disciplinary committee's discretion, for a sending off. An assault on a referee could go up to £250. The money went to the FA, with the Sunday League receiving only the administrative fines, such as for late kick-offs and not filling in forms properly, up to £20.

'Discipline fluctuates,' said Walker. 'It's no worse than it was years ago. I don't like all these cautions. It was never the case in my day. You just got the foul given against you and you got on with it. That was the end of the story, you didn't get a card waved in your face. And some of those tackles with big heavy boots were far more damaging than they are today. The problem is the FA can't exist without fines these days.'

It sounded as if they had become to the game's governors what speed camera revenue was to the police or parking charges to local councils. 'That's about right,' said Walker, who added that there had been an increase in the availability of referees, when you thought there might be fewer given recently released figures that showed assaults on officials on public parks was up by 30 per cent. Pushing and shoving offences had gone up over the previous year from 205 to 276 though serious incidents – punching, for example – had gone down from eight to just three.

While serious, those figures had to be placed in the context of more referees being recruited over that year. There were now more than 26,000 men registered, up by 29 per cent, and 853 women, an increase of 31 per cent. How so? It may have had something to do with the FA's new campaign designed to improve standards of player behaviour entitled 'Respect' – a campaign Walker thought might have been better tried in the professional game first before they rolled it out at grassroots, such was the pros' need to get their act together, he reckoned. It might also have had much to do with the recession and it being a good way of earning some pin money for a couple of hours' work.

'We don't find it difficult to get referees,' said Walker. 'I can't say they are perfect but then they don't have linesmen. Teams can't afford them as well at £20 a time.' Usually, a substitute was prevailed upon to do the duty, the most onerous of the morning, but it frequently provoked argument over bias and so most teams preferred to do without.

Today's match between Independiente and Army and Navy needed nothing much to provoke it but the two teams were certainly a volatile mix. After a couple of bad fouls, and the teams squaring up to each other, the referee warned the two captains and managers that if it continued, he would abandon the game. It continued. He abandoned the game after just half an hour. The two teams, Walker informed me, would be fined £120 each.

They were part of an 11-team Premier Division, one of five divisions in the Hackney and Leyton League encompassing 50 teams. Once it comprised seven divisions but that was before teams were allowed to name five substitutes and send on three. These days, more people seemed to be playing in five-a-side teams, due to it demanding less time as a lunchtime or early evening activity. And your kit didn't get so filthy.

'I think the FA should do something to get those teams from offices or law firms playing proper football,' said Walker. 'But all they keep coming up with is bureaucratic nonsense like CRB [Criminal Records Bureau] checks. You've got mothers who can't give kiddies a lift after games now. They wanted us as FA councillors to be CRB-checked. I was most offended. At my age? After a lifetime in football?'

There had, Walker added, been many social changes that had affected the grassroots game. 'The pubs and clubs are closing at an enormous rate,' he added. 'People might not want to hear it, but it has escalated since the smoking ban. These boys used to get sponsorship from the pub and go back there after the game but it's not the same any more.' He had noticed it at the Mildmay Club in Stoke Newington, where the league had its headquarters. 'It might have created a healthy outlook in some aspects but in others it's denied sportsmen. They are talking about stopping sponsorship from alcohol and tobacco but these things keep clubs going.'

One huge, patent change was the number of players and teams from ethnic backgrounds. Today's match on the main pitch by the car park was a case in point. It featured blue-shirted Lapton, champions for the previous four seasons, against Black Meteors, a team of Ghanaian origin, who played in yellow shirts and whatever shorts and socks they could find. The match would feature just three white players and a white referee in Bob Bernini, another FA Councillor, who wore a green shirt with a logo of the FIA, the Italian football federation. It was given to him, he insisted, by Pierluigi Collina, the bald-headed Nosferatu lookalike whose fearsome eyes had calmed down some of the world game's most tempestuous players and who refereed the 2002 World Cup final between Brazil and Germany.

The game was surprisingly good, with some decent athletic talents on view, if not quite of the quality of the old days when semi-professionals would play. With Meteors 2-1 up in the second half, Bernini was called upon to make a big decision when one of their players burst through only to be halted unfairly by a Lapton defender. 'Last man, last man,' shouted one of the Meteors, urging a sending-off, though the referee opted for a yellow card.

'That's another change I don't like,' said Walker. 'Players trying to get the opposition booked. They see it on the telly and think it's all right here.' Presumably the player wearing a snood – a form of neck-warmer – had seen it on the telly too, though he would soon have to throw it away, like the professionals. FIFA had decided to ban them, decreeing them dangerous, with would-be pursuers of the wearer possibly tempted to grab hold of it.

In the end, Bernini's moment was not decisive. Meteors scored again and though they conceded another, held on for a 3-2 win that put them top of the league. At the end, most players were soon away in their cars. For most, the pub was not the destination as of yore, as Walker indicated. Sunday morning football in such a multi-cultural area was no longer just a pubs' league. Besides, many wanted to get home to watch the televised football that these days dominated a Sunday.

'Football is huge now,' said Walker, who saw it as a kid in the post-war years when it was huge, too, albeit in a different way without the TV. 'There's positives and negatives. It's attracting people to watch football and even play it. And the kids are out there buying the shirts. The only thing is that they don't support their local club like we did as kids. They latch on to the top of the league, encouraged by their fathers.' Actually, that probably always happened; plenty in the playground in the 1970s supported Leeds and Liverpool though living far away, just as they now followed Manchester United and Chelsea.

Superficially, so much had changed here on the Marshes, from its reconfiguration due to the Olympic Games and the building of the site, to the nature of the teams competing. Much of it had been for the better, too. It may not quite have been how it was in Johnnie Walker's day, nor as he now wanted it to be, but the football had been good.

It had been a day of new development and old pleasures; of vast sums of money knocking about in sport and a struggle to meet costs for many. The talk was often of the professional game setting an example to young and Sunday players. It might have been the other way round. There would always be conflicts on the Marshes but maybe those at the big-money professional clubs might have benefited from a trip to Hackney to see how the other half lived and how the majority of young and Sunday players conducted themselves.

SPRING

Chapter 17

WHAT ROMAN DID FOR US

WEST LONDON WAS BUSY, buzzy even three hours before kick off, with traffic crawling through Earl's Court due to FC Copenhagen fans spilling out of the pubs and blocking the main road down towards Chelsea. They were fond of a drink to go with their football in the other cold countries of Northern Europe too, and the Danes especially liked to sample the blond brew of their homeland. A bottleneck indeed.

Bruce Buck was gracious enough to accept my apology for being 10 minutes late as a result at our arranged meeting point on the Fulham Road near his home, even though as chairman of Chelsea he had duties to perform, people to see on match days. He had kindly invited me as his guest for the evening. We could talk on the way to the ground, he said.

And so, on the same stretch of street down to Stamford Bridge that I walked with my friend Jimmy as prelude to that first journey through English football 20 years earlier, I would hear the detail of the game-changing deal – a deal that, in hindsight, was a logical consequence of the formation of the Premier League.

It was a bizarre scene; me holding a tape recorder, Buck – the American lawyer who had been at Roman Abramovich's shoulder every step of the way since the Russian bought Chelsea in 2003 – talking into it as he strode out purposefully. Some of the Chelsea fans on their way to the Champions League match against Copenhagen said 'hello' to him, others 'all right, Bruce?' as he divulged the details of the transaction that altered the course of their football-watching lives. That altered the course of everybody's football-watching lives, come to think of it.

The deal for Chelsea was conceived, it emerged, not in London but in Manchester. At the time, the then-36-year-old Roman Arkadyevich Abramovich was largely unknown, despite his fortune – all £7 billion of it, putting him among the world's top 10 richest people. Thus was he able to watch the Champions League tie between United and Real Madrid at Old Trafford in April 2003 in anonymity and, without TV cameras capturing it, the bearded grin that would become familiar as he delighted in a game won 4-3 by the home side.

'He came back and said to his advisers, "I wouldn't mind buying a football team in England."' So began the account of Buck, a senior lawyer for an American practice with an office in Canary Wharf which had been advising Abramovich's companies for more than a decade, and so began the bit of business that would astonish the game. Buck made it sound as if it were just another deal for your average oligarch, one who had made his money in oil, gas and aluminium after the economic opening-up of Russia in the 1990s, and had just sold his stake in the national airline Aeroflot. And indeed it was.

'Roman is a businessman and his advisers were businessmen,' Buck continued, 'so they did what they would do if they were buying a steel company or cement company and hired an investment bank to tell them what was available in the market place at what price and what were the pros and cons.

'They hired UBS Warburg, who did a study and came back with a report. It said that Manchester United would be expensive and the fans would go crazy. Aston Villa was for sale but it was in Birmingham and the long-term opportunities were limited. Tottenham were on the list along with Chelsea. They were in London; they were in financial trouble. Roman's advisers tried to arrange meetings with Tottenham and Chelsea but for whatever reason, they couldn't set up a meeting with Tottenham, or Tottenham didn't want to meet.'

Chelsea bit, though; unsurprisingly with debts mounting to around £80 million. The chairman Ken Bates was coming under increasing pressure from the banks and other financial institutions which had been lending the club money, and this was an opportunity to solve all the problems.

Abramovich's advisers met with the then Chelsea chief executive Trevor Birch during the last week of June. A deal was struck in principle, obviously subject to Bates' approval. The debt would be covered, and to gain control of the club, Abramovich would pay around £60 million for an initial 51 per cent shareholding from Chelsea Village, the company which owned the club.

'Mr Bates was generally on board though obviously wanted to get a little more out of the deal than he was getting,' said Buck, who was delighted to be involved, having been a Chelsea season ticket holder since 1988. Abramovich, his advisers and Bates then met in the bar of the Dorchester Hotel on Park Lane, according to Buck. 'I think they drank Coca-Cola,' he said. 'The Russians don't drink. Or at least the ones I work with don't drink. They are not big socialisers. They like to do their business and get gone.'

It was far from a simple deal, however, despite being agreed very quickly. Who actually owned Chelsea and where the shares were registered had always been the subject of scrutiny but with little clarity. Bates had bought Chelsea for £1 in 1982, taking on £1.5 million worth of debt, but subsequent investment had clouded the picture. 'Chelsea had gone public in 1996 and there were thousands and thousands of shareholders,' Buck explained. 'Ken said he owned 18 or 19 per cent but the people he knew could get together 51 per cent to commit to the deal. I forget what it was, four, five or six major shareholders. And then we did a tender offer like you do for any deal.

'The big issue was that Roman wanted to buy the entire company and the only way to do that was a process in company law called squeeze-out provision. If we were able to get 90 per cent of the remaining 49 per cent, then we could force whatever little stuff was left to get on with the deal. That was what happened.

'The deal was done over four days. We did our due diligence over the weekend and made the offer public on the Monday night. That was to maintain the confidentiality. We had to act quickly. A lot of people were hovering around. There was a lot of interest in the club. We made the announcement on 1 July.

'It wasn't until September that Roman owned the company entirely, though. There were lots of other things going on. They had €75 million worth of Euro bonds outstanding that were in default. That was Chelsea Village plc, so we had to strike a deal with them.'

There was also a deal that had to be done to buy up the inherited shares of Ruth Harding, the widow of Matthew, a businessman who had been a rival to Bates for control of the club but who had died in a helicopter crash coming back from an away game at Bolton in 1996. 'Just to clean things up took the better part of six to nine months,' added Buck.

There were suggestions that Abramovich – then Governor of Chukotka, a bleak, remote Russian province three times the size of Great Britain near the Arctic Circle – had bought the club to increase his profile in the West. However, reclusive and unwilling to give interviews, Abramovich soon disabused us of that notion. 'None of us had the perception that he was going to be a public figure forever thereafter. We didn't realise it was going to be such a big deal in the press,' said Buck. 'We thought, "Yeah, it will be a decent story for a couple of weeks and then Roman will go back and have his private life." Because he is a very private guy. He clearly didn't do things for the notoriety or publicity because that is not him.'

Given the turbulent state of Russian politics, along with allegations from rivals of theft and fraud, and the view towards those who had made vast sums from the privatisation of national, natural assets, Chelsea seemed to offer Abramovich an insurance policy. No one would dare assassinate such a public figure in the West, went the theory. One anecdote had it that Abramovich was once being driven in London when the car backfired and he hit the floor, fearful that he was being shot at.

Buck contemplated the theory. 'That it would protect him? I have never asked him but to be honest, I just don't think that's the way he thinks. I just think he loves his football.' It was a simple explanation, one that would have been hard to embrace at the time when there was so little known about him and so much suspicion, but one that would gain credence.

If Jack Walker at Blackburn had made Manchester United look cheap, now Abramovich made English football look miserly. Very quickly, he changed the transfer market – distorted it, rival chairmen and owners would say – with dramatic effect. In the summer of 2003 alone, he spent £100 million on players, including £15 million for Juan Sebastian Veron from Manchester United, £16 million for Adrian Mutu from Parma and £17 million for Hernan Crespo from Inter Milan.

While other clubs may have questioned the arrival of a sugar daddy and its potential effect on competition, and while some Chelsea fans may have had their doubts, the majority of the club's supporters were delighted. The smell and the colour of money can do that for football fans, especially those tired of living in shadows.

Chelsea had always been London's showbusiness club, sited in its poshest borough of Kensington and Chelsea, and the nearest capital club to the nightlife of the West End. Its status was embodied by Sir Richard 'Dickie' Attenborough, film actor and director – the luvvie's luvvie – who was on the Chelsea board through the 1960s, and remained a life president as Lord Attenborough.

Through the swinging 60s, when the nearby King's Road was held up as the centre of the universe to us provincial kids looking on in envy as we seemed to be missing out on all the fun, Chelsea played football with a swagger. Even through the grim, grey 1970s they stood out, in the form of gifted attackers such as Charlie Cooke and Peter Osgood. Misty-eyed memory even lends a charm to Ron 'Chopper' Harris, among the hardest of men in an era when hard men got away with all but an amputation.

Bates furthered the club's glamorous reputation as the Premier League took off. When Glenn Hoddle arrived as manager in 1993, with his pedigree and knowledge of the overseas market, he was able to attract some decent foreign talent. The charming Italian Gianluca Vialli would succeed Hoddle as manager, the Dutchman Ruud Gullit following. The club's most endearing signing would be the little Italian maestro Gianfranco Zola.

As he allowed his managers to build teams, so Bates built up the stadium, with a hotel on site. It was conducted against a backdrop of outspoken comments that upset many, his match day programme notes aiming barbs at all manner of figures, though he was known to use the law if he felt himself maligned.

Debt mounted too as he sought to establish the club as a genuine competitor to those such as Manchester United and Arsenal. Chelsea did win the FA Cup in 1997 and 2000, with the League Cup coming in between in 1998, the same year they also won the old European Cup-Winners' Cup. But getting them into the top six of the Premier League had cost fortunes. It came mainly in managers and players' wages – Gullit famously asked for a then huge £2 million a year 'netto' – and the creditors were closing in.

'This is a great deal for Chelsea,' Bates insisted when Abramovich took over. It also seemed like a great deal for him, as he would soon depart with £18 million. The initial £140 million to cover shares and debt would prove to be almost piffling as Abramovich, after buying up the rest of the shares over the coming months and paying off Bates, would go on to spend £600 million on players over the next eight years. Losses, to the chagrin of other clubs trying to compete while staying out of the red, would come in each season at between £80 million and £140 million, all covered by Abramovich.

Bates' choice as manager, the upright Italian Claudio Ranieri, immediately became a dead man walking. Although he had Chelsea finishing as runners-up in the Premier League – their highest finish since the League was established – and reaching the semi-finals of the Champions League, he was a goner at the end of Abramovich's first season in charge. Abramovich wanted a hungry young figure who would instil a winning mentality into the club.

In came a man who would be one of the most divisive figures in the English game: the maverick, charismatic Portuguese Jose Mourinho, who had just won the Champions League with Porto and who declared himself 'The Special One'. He soon proved it in the eyes of the Chelsea fans, winning the club their first English championship in 50 years in 2005. Another followed, the next year, and Mourinho would also add an FA Cup and two League Cups.

Yet Mourinho's relationship with the owner deteriorated as he became unhappy at having the £30 million signing from Milan Andriy Shevchenko foisted upon him. The manager's judgement would prove the sounder as the Ukrainian flopped. Abramovich grew weary of Mourinho's carping about the club's internal politics, and of his criticism of referees, which made the club look bad.

The club's tough interior, of director of communications Simon Greenberg and chief executive Peter Kenyon, sought to keep a lid on the leaks but frequently failed. 'The softest thing about him,' someone in the game said to me of Kenyon after a meeting, 'is his teeth.'

Besides, Mourinho didn't win the Champions League, which Abramovich coveted – though he might have done, had he been left in situ. After Mourinho's sacking in 2008, the Israeli director of football Avram Grant took over the team and they reached the final in Moscow – a venue in which Abramovich was especially desperate to win – but Chelsea lost on penalties to Manchester United, the captain John Terry agonisingly hitting a post with his spot-kick when a successful conversion would have won the trophy.

After the mournful Grant came the bouncy Brazilian Luiz Felipe Scolari, winner of the World Cup with Brazil in 2002, but he did not gel with players still piqued by the departure of their guru Mourinho. The Dutch replacement Guus Hiddink did, but it could only be temporary, as he had a day job managing the Russian national team.

Now the Italian Carlo Ancelotti was in the revolving hotseat, largely because he had twice won the Champions League with AC Milan. This, after regaining the Premier League title in 2010 along with the FA Cup in his first season, was the year he might well be expected by the owner to win in Europe. After winning their first five games, however, it had been a patchy season for Chelsea thus far, with the departure of Ancelotti's assistant Ray Wilkins producing more soap opera turmoil in recent weeks. The recent 2-0 away win at Copenhagen in the first leg of this Champions League round of 16 had promised better days ahead in the run-in to the season.

Thus was the mood around the club lighter than it had been for weeks as Buck began his tour of duty now that we had reached Stamford Bridge. He shook hands with a couple of journalists in the press room and said hello to some club staff milling around the dressing room area, the players yet to arrive two hours before kick off.

We took a seat in the home dugout on a pleasant early spring evening to continue his assessment of the Abramovich years.

The owner asked Buck to become a director after the takeover and he was delighted to accept, though he had to convince his law firm it could be good for business. 'I really wanted to do it as a Chelsea fan,' said Buck. 'If he had taken over Tottenham, I wouldn't have wanted to do it.'

His first job was to iron out some issues with Ken Bates. 'Mr Abramovich was in his 30s at the time and everyone around him was 40 so I was the only one that seemed old enough to deal with Mr Bates,' said Buck, then 57, who veered between using Mr and Roman in referring to his boss, probably as reflection of a relationship that veered between the professional and the personal.

Bates had been asked to stay on as chairman but, the new regime believed, he continued to see his role as executive rather than titular. Abramovich, though, was determined to be the power broker – as would come to be seen in the sacking of managers – rather than any mere figurehead. Buck reached a financial settlement with Bates, who left in February 2004 and retired to Monaco, though would be tempted back from tax exile for his allotted time in England to take over Leeds United. Buck replaced him as chairman at Chelsea.

'Actually, I am an owner', said Buck, tongue in cheek. 'Did you know that? Roman owns, like, 83, 642,000 shares and I own one. So as far as I am concerned, we are co-owners. Partners. It's insulting to me when people say he owns the club. I say, "What about me?"'

'We were a bit naive about what was going to happen,' he went on. 'We knew Roman wanted to invest and create one of the better football clubs in the world but we just didn't have a comprehension of how important a football club like this is in the culture and daily lives of fans.'

Neither could they comprehend the debate they would provoke in English football between the haves of the Premier League and the have-nots lower down the scale. (Actually, Abramovich was a have-yacht; five of them, though they were more like luxury liners.) Even within the Premier League, argument raged. Suddenly an arms race of money began that forced Manchester United to rejoin the up-market place.

The money in the game had traditionally largely been in the north, provided by the big crowds of Manchester and Liverpool, but now the balance of power had shifted south. London, a Cool Britannia magnet of a city following the wealth creation of the prosperous late 1990s and early 2000s, was the attraction for overseas owners at the time, before they saw the potential further north. The enormous irony was that Abramovich had been brought up in a Communist system.

What were Buck's first impressions of Abramovich? 'At that time he spoke no English. My early impressions were that he was a straightforward guy, no ceremony, had some great friends from many years back and was sticking with them. Shy. But to those of us meeting him for the first time, he was outgoing and friendly. "Have a cup of tea," or if you were at his house, "Have something to eat." He wasn't cold at all; he was very warm. It wasn't like I was slapping him on the back or telling him dirty jokes, though.'

At first, Buck agreed, it was simply about buying a club and having some fun. It had looked at times, though, as if it was fun no longer for Abramovich, particularly during the latter days of the Mourinho era. In recent times, too, there were rumours that he was now saying that the club needed to start breaking even. A feeling was growing that he might be ready to pull the plug, certainly financially. Tonight's visit would be his first of the year to the ground he owned.

'I would say that his passion for Chelsea has increased, not decreased. His passion for football has increased, not decreased,' Buck countered when I put it to him. 'His knowledge of football has increased exponentially. I'm not talking about what goes on at the megastore, I'm talking about football. It would be pretty hard to name a current footballer that he couldn't give you the statistics for.

'In 2003/04, I think he saw every game but since then maybe there are times when he doesn't get to games but that's more a function of the business, and the financial worlds are not what they were. In 2003, everything was on an up escalator. He has to spend a lot more time with his business interests. He also has a new family, a new partner and that requires he gives them the right amount of attention. But he doesn't miss a game in the sense that wherever he is in the world, he watches the Chelsea game. He calls Eugene Tenenbaum [trusted club director and business associate] or whoever after the game and they talk about it. He is very much on top of things.'

Any doubt about the owner's commitment, indeed, had been dispelled in the January transfer window. It also helped that his finances seemed to be in better shape. The poor soul had seen his fortune struggle to stay at £7 billion during the recession, when it might have increased through interest alone during more normal times, but recent figures showed that he had made £400 million in the previous year as the recovery began.

Some £75 million of that went on the team as Abramovich moved to interrupt Chelsea's decline. In a deal that surprised the game, in came the Spanish striker Fernando Torres from Liverpool and defender David Luiz for £25 million from Benfica. It spoke volumes about Abramovich. If the fancy took him, if he tired of seeing his club ail, he simply ripped up the business plan and put in more money. With those new UEFA rules about financial fair play soon to come in – though there were ways round them, with such possible initiatives as getting in sponsors from among his own companies – he clearly wanted to buy while he could.

'Our perspective was what it's always been, even last summer,' Buck insisted. 'We didn't do a lot of investment in 2009 or 2010 but we didn't think there was no more money. We thought if something made sense, Mr Abramovich would help us do it. It's not like he said, "I am not investing any more." He just wants, fair enough, to understand why we should buy this player or that player and if it makes sense, we will do it.

'People say they were surprised about what we did in January but I guess I wasn't. I knew we had been following Torres for some time and I knew that if the right situation came along, he was going to support the club and he did. And it was a hell of a support for the club in the transfer window.'

Was it the case that Abramovich picked the players to buy? The Shevchenko case, and all that. . . 'The coaching staff makes suggestions, Roman makes suggestions,' said Buck. 'Everyone agrees. The board and Roman decide the price. The coaching staff don't negotiate salaries or decide what the transfer fees should be. If they want to fill a specific position, we have to agree a couple of suggestions because one or two or three might not work out because of the price. So it's a collective. It's actually a fun process.'

Time was pressing. Buck wanted to have fun elsewhere. Via the bars at the old Shed End – Frankie's Sports Bar and Grill; the celebrity chef Marco Pierre White's restaurant – past the hotel where Ken Bates retained a penthouse apartment with the only view out on to the stadium, we headed round to the directors' box on the opposite side of the stadium from the dressing rooms.

Up three flights of carpeted stairs, the room attached to the directors' box was more of a modern bar and bistro than the oak-panelled chamber of yore at Blackburn. There were blue velour banquettes, mirrors and glass tables – and an impressive guest list sampling the hospitality. The England manager Fabio Capello may have been baffled by a tasty, sizeable pre-match meal of cottage pie and two veg but it did nicely enough for two peers of the realm in Lord

Mawhinney, former chairman of the Football League, and Chelsea fan Lord Sebastian Coe, now chairman of London's 2012 Olympic Games.

The sports minister Hugh Robertson arrived five minutes into the game, as if to inform everyone that he was a busy man importantly employed on matters of state. He hadn't missed much. Actually, he wouldn't have missed much had he turned up five minutes from time. A dour game was enlivened only by Copenhagen fans going through a repertoire of chants in perfect English including 'You only sing when you're winning'. Still, it gave plenty of opportunity to gaze around the ground, at the banners for the Texas Blues, Boston Blues and German Blues. That was an awful lot of depressed people around the world.

It also afforded a chance to talk to the guest next to me: Terry Brown, manager of AFC Wimbledon. Crawley's money was telling now – and they had even more of it after a run to the fifth round of the FA Cup that had recently ended with a huge pay day at Manchester United – and they were starting to run away with the Conference, but the Dons were clinging on to a play-off place in the runners-up spot, just ahead of Luton.

The most entertaining moment of the evening came at half-time as Capello lingered over the tray containing the cakes in the directors' bistro. Which to choose? A flapjack, an éclair? In the end, as if they were Frank Lampard and Steven Gerrard, he went for them both, deciding that the two could complement each other and play on the tongue together.

There was no sign of Abramovich, who watched the game from his normal eyrie on the floor above. One of a number costing a cool £1 million a year (though not all could be sold), his box was next to the boardroom where, Buck said, meetings were held monthly, even though – Buck didn't say – what one man dictated would inevitably decide. Often the television cameras would focus on the owner as if on a Roman emperor, ready to give thumbs up or down to his manager.

TV pictures tonight would show him not looking too impressed at Torres being withdrawn from a goalless game and you wondered whether the Spaniard, yet to score in six weeks and misfiring again, might become Ancelotti's Shevchenko. Winning the Champions League looked to be the only thing that would salvage the job of the Italian, who was maintaining a dignified demeanour through it all. With a large pay-off on its way for the last year of his contract if he did go, he could afford to. Who would replace him? Hiddink, whom the owner liked but was now managing the Turkish national team? Even Mourinho – now at Real Madrid, having won the Champions League with Inter Milan after leaving Stamford Bridge?

Abramovich would need to swallow much pride if Mourinho were to return, but it depended how desperate he was for that European triumph. Though he came less with baggage than with a suite of Louis Vuitton, Mourinho was a proven winner, even if the owner had wanted more entertainment than Mourinho's often pragmatic teams sometimes offered. Abramovich wanted more bang for his buck.

Actually, the talk was of Mourinho maybe heading for Manchester City, who were in a similar situation to Chelsea when Abramovich had taken over and themselves needed a winning mentality. By coincidence, City would be at Stamford Bridge the following Sunday for a confrontation between what were now the world's two richest clubs. For the Abu Dhabi United Group, an investment arm of the Abu Dhabi royal family, had bought out the disgraced former Thai Prime Minister Thaksin Shinawatra and were investing mind-boggling sums in players, even by Abramovich's standards. They had spent £300 million since taking over in 2008, including British record fees of £32 million for the Brazilian Robinho, soon discarded, and £35 for the Argentinian Carlos Tevez. They had even been prepared to pay Milan £100 million for the Brazilian Kaka, though that deal fell through.

The Arab sheikhs had certainly shaken things up, if not quite doing what the City-supporting Noel Gallagher of the band Oasis said he might if ever he bought the club: 'I'd say, "You – fuck off, you – fuck off, you – fuck off. You – make me a cup of tea."'

Bruce Buck was philosophical about City's new challenge. 'Certainly some of the things we did have changed football forever,' he said. 'I can't argue against that. That's why we aren't complaining about some of the things Manchester City are doing. We started it after all but, having said that, it is a free world. Obviously what we have done has not pleased the fans of, I don't know, West Ham or Manchester United, but they sure have pleased the fans at Chelsea.

'There were fans unhappy for many, many years. I'm not saying we don't have our naysayers still but by and large we have fans who had had a hard struggle with Chelsea for 20, 30, or 40 years, who now can't believe their good fortune, and I am one of those fans.

'We have to be competitive. We can't be in a position where our fans want ticket prices to come down and "we want more seats for families but don't abandon the stadium or change our history". I think we could use a bigger stadium. If it was this one, that would be great. Anyone that has a site in West or South London, we talk to them. You see how Arsenal's revenues have improved and Tottenham and West Ham will both have new stadiums.'

Was it sustainable without the owner? 'I think it is. We will be able to comply with the financial fair play rules. We need some more revenues but we don't need a lot more. Mr Abramovich will still be able to fund the academy and stadium capital expenditure outside the financial fair play. We will still be able to buy some big players and comply. I think our really big expenses are behind us. We expect to get more out of our academy. So I think we are on a pretty stable platform.'

It was true that Chelsea had built a splendid new training ground at Cobham in Surrey and invested in an academy, but the management hardly seemed stable. 'We would prefer to have a more stable management structure,' Buck agreed. 'We envy what Arsenal have done with Arsène Wenger and Manchester United with Sir Alex Ferguson but you can't have longevity for longevity's sake. It's got to be longevity with the person that you think can do it in the long term. In football, for better or worse, it's all down to results.' It sounded a little ominous for Ancelotti.

'There's a lot more focus on us than other big clubs,' Buck continued, 'more than Manchester United, Manchester City and Liverpool, because we are a London club, a bit of an upstart.' He admitted that Chelsea grew weary of being painted as the bogeymen. 'Yes, but what are we going to do about it, other than be fed up with it?'

Their attitude remained a mixture of defiance and compliance. Chelsea were, Buck said, proud of being the club that changed English football. 'We have helped the Premier League be the best league in the world,' he insisted. 'We want to work with the league, work with the FA. We don't put our middle finger up at all.'

Good or bad for the game? Chelsea had certainly uncorked the champagne bottle and it looked impossible that the cork could be put back in. It was all for the better, their own support would surely say. And Buck's defence of them was always plausible. Though things may have changed somewhat since the departure of Peter Kenyon as chief executive, still you wanted to see a bit more class from them, however, instead of the arrogance of the moneyed, certainly from a section of their brasher fans. Too often with Chelsea, the words of Dolly Parton sprang to mind: 'Honey,' she drawled, 'It costs a lot of money to look this cheap.'

Buck knew, though, that his and the club's good fortune could change, football being cyclical, people and circumstances moving on. 'I've kept my season tickets,' he confided. 'You never know when the end might come.'

Chapter 18

RED HOT IN ALEX

I HAD WANDERED into the wrong part of the training ground, into the weights room, where a young lad was working out. I apologised and told him that I was looking for James Collins, joint academy director. The lad stopped what he was doing and said that James was in the office. He would take me there. Chatting about what a nice day it was and smiling, he duly led me to the right part of the building then returned to his weights. Immediately, you knew that they were bringing the kids up properly here.

Here was Crewe Alexandra, currently of League Two, but with a reputation for producing talented young footballers completely out of keeping with a small Cheshire club and town whose population was only around 70,000. Socially, the place had always been seen as little more than a railway junction between the big cities of Liverpool, Manchester, Stoke and Wolverhampton. These days, the football scouts from the clubs representing those cities regularly made the journey of an hour or less to view the talent.

On a beautiful, unseasonably hot spring weekend morning I came to join them at the training ground of the Alex – according to some histories, the club was named after Princess Alexandra but more probably a pub of that name in the town – on the edge of nearby Nantwich to take in an under-18 game between Crewe and Newcastle United and find out what all the fuss within the game was about.

We were certainly off to a decent start. Those who despaired of Saturday girls at the tills of supermarkets who 'dunno', or lads in shops who told you that if it wasn't on the shelf, they hadn't got it, would have enjoyed the politeness and respect of the young player who had shown me to Collins' office. Some of us believed that those qualities not only led to more rounded human beings able to cope with life's vagaries but also, as a consequence, better players if they did progress.

'It's instilled in the boys,' Collins would tell me. 'However well you coach them, they are not all going to make it. They have all got to go out into life and there is a responsibility to develop them properly.' And he would cite a recent experience to tell of the rewards of his job. 'I was invited by the head of football at my old school, Sandbach, an independent school, to do a presentation recently,' said Collins. 'His name is Craig Malbon and he was a boy I coached at Crewe. He did a speech and I thought how well he had grown up and what a good man he had become. I felt as much pride then as I do when I see one of my lads play in the first team.'

The issue of producing young players had been at the centre of English footballing debate for pretty much all of the Premier League era. The influx of foreign players as a result of European Union employment law, and the British system that granted work permits to full internationals outside the EU, had inevitably led to fewer places in first-team squads for young domestic talent.

No longer could you shout down a mine shaft in Newcastle and up would come half a dozen centre forwards; no longer, as their fervently patriotic former owner Jack Hayward once lamented, could you find 11 Black Countrymen to represent Wolverhampton Wanderers. No longer did every dressing room in the country comprise at least a couple of Liverpudlians.

Youngsters may have looked at the Premier League still wanting to be footballers and heroes, but few possessed the dedication needed in the modern era when teenaged social lives barely existed for budding professionals. Now home-grown kids were being overtaken by the hungry from overseas, notably from Africa, who saw moneyed English football as a way to new lives for them and their families. In addition, the children of the fast-food, PlayStation generation were going through a crisis of obesity. There was also the lack of resources at state schools, which meant less coaching and less time for games. In short, fewer kids were coming through and there were fewer places at the top clubs for them.

As foreign managers had arrived, they brought with them their knowledge of overseas club academies and even began to bring in kids for English academies to hothouse ready for the first team. During his tenure at Liverpool, Rafael Benitez grew disillusioned with the talent emerging on Merseyside and imported a host of Spanish kids. Spain, indeed, had become the new best producer of players, replacing France. Arsenal's Cesc Fabregas, prised from Barcelona when an unpolished 16-year-old gem, had been testimony to Iberian methods.

Figures showed that in Spain a top young player would spend 4,880 hours being coached by his club between the ages of nine and 21. Though the system was not quite as intense as Holland (5,940 hours) or France (5,740), it was far ahead of England, where young players received a mere 3,760 hours over the same period. Overseas results were naturally better.

One problem was the FA guideline established in 1997 which decreed that Premier League clubs were allowed just three hours a week with 9- to 11-year-olds and five with 12- to 16-year-olds. In the Netherlands, they were permitted double that. Part of the restriction was laudable, in not pushing kids too hard too soon, but it was clear that elite players were missing out on developmental time at key stages.

And such was the science of the sport these days that coaches in academies could tell you what a player should be learning at each yearly age group, starting with 'reciprosity' at the age of five – learning the concept of passing the ball and receiving it back, thus replacing a child's inherent reluctance to give anything away as they fear it will not be returned.

The Premier League was now trying to respond by implementing a new elitist system allowing clubs three times as many hours with young players. The fear was that it would place them at odds with Football League clubs and the FA again – the triangle of mistrust and conflict that continued to work against the greater good – by going their own way without proper consultation. It could also mean that the best young players would simply abandon the smaller clubs for the bigger ones earlier in their development and without any proper compensation for the clubs who had discovered them.

At Crewe, the simple aim was to provide an atmosphere of learning and coaching – and fun. Fledgling talents would develop their skills as players, and their worth as young men there, so that they were not prematurely lured away to Liverpool and Manchester, Stoke and Wolverhampton. Instead, they remained at Crewe until they had learned their trade properly, been seen in the first team by the club's fans, and were then ready to fly the nest.

'We are trying to create an environment,' said James Collins. 'We play a particular way, a passing way with skilful football, and we create a pathway through to the first team. Results are not necessarily important, although we don't like losing every week. Anyway, when you have got good players you don't lose every week.'

The strategy and the system had been down to one Dario Gradi MBE, a remarkable footballing visionary and one of the great institutions and quiet heroes of the English game. As a young man, he played non-League football with Sutton United and Tooting and Mitcham before going into coaching as an assistant at Chelsea at the age of 29. He became a manager in his own right when taking over at

Sutton, then led Wimbledon up from the old Fourth Division in the late 1970s. After an unhappy spell at Crystal Palace, his embryonic managerial career seemed to be on a downward curve when he took the Crewe job in 1983.

There, Gradi revealed himself a brilliant coach of young players and hit on a plan: if he put in place a coaching system that could produce players for the club, not only would they not have to buy them in, they could even sell them on to bigger clubs. The revenue would sustain the system and the organisation as a whole. Notable graduates had been David Platt of Aston Villa, Sampdoria and England, Dean Ashton of West Ham and England, and Danny Murphy of Liverpool and Fulham.

According to James Collins, Crewe even made a better player out of Robbie Savage – blond, brash and becoming better known these days as a loud-mouthed radio pundit – after he was rejected by Manchester United. They set him on the path to a good career, largely with Leicester City in the Premier League, Collins reckoned. 'He made the most of himself and was probably a better player than people think,' said Collins, less judgmental and more forgiving than many of us – probably why he was good at his job. 'Robbie would be the first to admit he overachieved. I use him as an example to say to kids, "You have got to show some drive and spirit." He did improve under Dario and in the end did well for himself.'

All the while, as well as overseeing the academy, Gradi was in charge of the first team until 2007, at the time making him the longest serving manager in the English game. He then became the club's technical director, ceding the reins to the academy director, Steve Holland, to whom Platt and Ashton accorded great credit for their development. Holland only lasted just over a year with the senior team, however, though his enduring coaching skills honed at Crewe would be recognised when Chelsea recruited him as their reserve team manager.

Neither did Holland's successor, Gudjon Thordarson, last long and Gradi returned to take on the first team. It meant that the old system worked again. Gradi had a place on the board and ensured that the academy was given its rightful prominence in the club. There had been times when he could have left, could even have gone to work for the FA as the national system's technical director, but he would not leave Crewe. He was now in his 28th year as their guru and would reach his 70th birthday in July 2011.

Never one to thrust himself forward, Gradi did not especially enjoy interviews and was happy to let Collins talk on his behalf. Collins certainly had some experience to share. He came to the club at the age of 10 and worked his way through to play some 30 games for the first team. Spotting teaching abilities in both of them, Gradi then asked him and Neil Critchley, now joint academy manager with Collins, to coach in the evenings and they progressed from there.

'Everything seeps down through Dario,' said Collins. 'A lot of clubs are trying to have a philosophy but the difficulty is always changes at the top. The manager changes and comes in with a new philosophy and it is difficult to have one for the first team and one for the academy.'

The training ground was a testament to Gradi's building up of the club and was beautifully appointed – well beyond League Two standards. It featured six manicured fields, an all-weather pitch, an indoor centre and a clubhouse for offices, dressing rooms, fitness centre and a canteen.

'Dario takes pride in it all,' said Collins. 'When you come here, the first thing he'll do is take you round the place. He'll tell you where David Platt used to change, that sort of thing. All the players come back as well because of their affiliation with the place.'

Around the canteen were framed pictures of the most celebrated alumni, from Platt, Ashton and Murphy to such as David Vaughan and Luke Varney, central figures in Blackpool's first Premier League season. There were more England players in Liverpool's Rob Jones and Seth Johnson of Leeds. In the corridor was a picture of Platt, who played 152 games for Crewe, in the act of scoring the goal that had seen his career take off. It came for England in the 1990 World Cup last 16 game against Belgium and underneath the photograph was a quote from him: 'People always mention that goal against Belgium at Italia '90 and it did change the course of my life,' he said. 'But it wasn't my best ever goal. Technically I scored a better one for Crewe against Stockport County in the old Fourth Division.' It served as message and inspiration to young players. The subtext was that seemingly lowly games could always be memorable and important for honing skills. They could lead to great deeds and careers.

Above the dressing-room area, meanwhile, ready to be read as the players arrived, was the exhortation: 'To give anything less than your best is to sacrifice the gift you have.'

The players were arriving now for matches between the under-16s and under-18s of Crewe and Newcastle. As the visitors stepped down from their coach, their complexions bore witness to the harsh climate and diet of the North East. There was just one black face. They were the usual mixture of young footballers: the cocky, the withdrawn, the ones covering up their nerves by being brash. A few showed their individuality with earrings and tattoos but all had short hair. They had the air of big club players; they looked very serious.

By contrast, the Crewe players appeared energised but at ease. They were clearly full of intent beyond simply being relaxed in their home environment. Such was Crewe's reputation, despite the lowly status of the first team, that they were allowed into the Premier League's youth divisions and were in a North West group of 10 teams – the other nine representing Premier League clubs.

'There is definitely a mood, a more relaxed way of doing things,' said James Collins. 'And it produces a freedom in the way they play.

The negative side of that is results. There have been times when our teams have capitulated because they haven't got that steel. But you can create that. It's easier to put that in later than it is the skill. You can develop being well organised at 17 and 18 but you can't suddenly introduce skill.'

Which ones of these would make it? You never could tell. Talent and quality were clearly and immediately evident to even the layman with young players but it was the mental side of being a professional that would eventually differentiate the best players. At Arsenal, Arsène Wenger had always said that the development of a player came in the stages of ability, physique and then, from 17 to 20, psychological toughness. Mind you, at Arsenal latterly that had seemed to be elusive.

On first sight, there certainly looked to be at least two Crewe players with the ability to progress to high levels in Nick Powell, just 17 and a regular in the England Under-17 side, and Max Clayton. Watching them against Newcastle was pure pleasure as they gave performances to restore faith and remind you how privileged you were to be in on the early days of a talent, as watching Michael Owen at the World Cup of 1998 or Lionel Messi at a youth tournament in Holland in 2005.

After 20 minutes, Powell sent the right-footed Sean Cooke away for a fierce left-footed drive into the corner of the Newcastle net to give Crewe the lead. It was a remarkable goal.

'That's not a coincidence,' James Collins would tell me later. 'At six, seven, eight we do 20 minutes of striking the ball, right foot, left foot. It's relatively boring for the kids but we work on footwork, dragging the ball, dodging and producing a skill off both feet. We do 90 per cent of that from 6 to 9, working on attacking-based skilful football.'

There was plenty of evidence of it. The Newcastle centre forward, Dan Taylor – too early to compare with other Geordie No. 9s like

Alan Shearer and Andy Carroll – stabbed home an equaliser from close range, but then Powell drilled home a stunning half-volley to give Crewe a 2-1 half-time lead. 'That was excellent,' I said, turning to a regular spectator, an old man who had seen it all but was clearly still touched by it, if in an understated way. 'Oh yes, he's very good is Nick,' he replied.

Powell was showing himself to be a leggy, elegant player in that modern position called the hole, the area behind a lead striker and between the opposition's defence and midfield. So many kids wanted to play there because it was the heartbeat of the team, the glamour position, but few possessed the footballing brain to do so. Many young players, when asked to operate there, simply plonked themselves in the hole. The brightest, like Powell, drifted in and out of the space, aware of when the right moment was to receive the ball and damage the opposition.

He also ran well with it, or rather glided over the surface with the ball, taking on opponents, having pinched possession like a basketball guard stealing the ball. Add a change of pace, and it was plain to see why Arsène Wenger was said to have been monitoring his progress and why Liverpool were believed to have put in an offer for him.

Within a few minutes of the restart, a workmanlike striker in Harry Clayton had tapped in to stretch Crewe's lead to 3-1 and, although the Newcastle left back Michael Riley pulled a goal back with a good left-footed drive, Max Clayton made it a final score of 4-2 with a neat piece of his trademark movement and canny finish to atone for an earlier missed penalty.

Crewe had been a joy to watch, having passed the ball neatly and all looking comfortable with it at their feet. When in possession, they were encouraged to do better than simply kick the ball forward if no immediate pass was on and instead, even if being policed by an opponent, be brave enough to turn into space and then look for a free teammate. There had been no fear in them.

These boys, this team, had not yet found out how difficult this game was. You hoped they never would, that they would always play with this freedom, but you suspected that all that went with the professional game would intrude one day – probably soon.

'We have found a niche in the market, almost,' Collins would say. 'We produce a particular type of player, a style of football. When you watch David Vaughan at Blackpool, you can see he is one of our players. He does certain things on the ball.'

By contrast, Newcastle had been a disappointment for a Premier League youth team. They were full of industrious footballers fulfilling roles competently, but not one player excited with a flash of skill, nor even seemed emboldened to attempt anything out of the ordinary. Their captain Patrick Nzuzi began by protecting the ball well in midfield but faded as Crewe dominated possession.

It had been a good tempered but competitive game, with respect for the referee and an abiding by his decisions. But these were, they hoped, professionals in the making with competitive natures, and there had been five bookings including one for diving that looked extremely harsh.

On an adjacent pitch, Crewe's under-16s, managed by Neil Critchley, had also beaten their Newcastle counterparts, by 3-1. It was remarkable to think that two teams of 11 lads (plus three substitutes on each) all from the Crewe district had beaten the cream of football-daft Tyneside's youth, even if some of Newcastle's better players were apparently being held back for a forthcoming cup game.

There was another way in which Crewe's system worked for them. For half a season, Collins would take the under-16s and Critchley the under-18s before swapping. It kept both the boys and coaches fresh. Besides, the two coaches knew every boy in the system anyway. The night before, Collins had been working with the under-8s.

Today's under-18 game against Newcastle had been Crewe's penultimate of the season. They would finish eighth of the ten teams in the North West, though just three points behind Manchester United in fifth. To place in context how tough their section was (there are four sections in the youth Premier League, involving 40 teams in all), Newcastle would finish fourth in their group. Not that these statistics were pored over at Crewe. 'When we come in on a Monday morning, Dario doesn't ask what the score was, he asks who has done well,' said Collins. 'I wonder if other academies rely too much on results, whether that's for coaches to save their jobs, I don't know. I have never felt a pressure here to win games, and that goes for when I was in the first team as well.

'Some would say that's a bit strange but it definitely relaxes you and allows you to perform. Dario is very strong on that. Nobody wants to win more than me but you have got to see the bigger picture. You might say, "Come on, we need to get going here," but as a coach and a team, if that's all you're doing, you will struggle.'

According to Collins, Crewe stole a march on youth development when, ahead of the bigger clubs in the North West, they spotted a gap in the market. Gradi reasoned, that if they could get kids at the ages of 6, 7 and 8 and bring them up with the right habits on and off the field, they could keep them through their teenaged years through loyalty. Perhaps Crewe could then even get a couple of seasons in the first team out of them before selling the best of them on to bigger clubs.

'We did get a head start at a time when other clubs used to start them at 9 and 10,' said Collins. 'We used to smash everybody at under-9, it was ridiculous. Now everybody is doing what we are doing at Crewe, which makes it harder, but getting them young is still the key.'

Collins's own son, Harrison, aged 7, was even in the Crewe system, his father trying to tell him not to get his head turned by the scouts from Liverpool, Everton and Manchester United who had apparently been approaching him. 'Young lads don't have to be superstars to get spotted these days,' said Collins. 'It means that people don't get missed like they used to, but are they getting taught the right things at the right time? It takes me to say to him, "Steady down." The best players we get are the ones at 6 and 7 because you get longer with them and they buy into the whole thing. We don't have a big scouting budget so we don't compete for 14- to 16-year-olds. We send the scouts to sixes, sevens and eights.'

Players could be signed only yearly from the age of 9. If other clubs then wanted a young player, they had to pay compensation, though it was comparatively small. In 2009, Crewe lost two midfield players, Matt Lund and Ben Marshall, to Stoke City for just £110,000. They were concerned now about their 15-year-old midfield player Dan Smith, who had recently scored a hat-trick against Liverpool and was being monitored by Manchester City.

Crewe believed, however, that they had points of attraction, for both players and enlightened parents: their track record, the relaxed atmosphere – 'which is difficult to recreate at a big club because there is a pressure,' said Collins – and their pathway to the first team.

At bigger clubs that was often a mirage. Top Premier League clubs with sugar-daddy ownership were often hoovering up talent but many young players stood little chance of making it into the senior team, however hard they worked to chase the dream. With their jobs on the line, some managers were too reluctant to blood them. Besides, if the first team's results did turn bad, at the whim of the owner they simply bought in big-money signings. The patience to build teams was gone. The fashion was to buy one quickly. The more fortunate discarded youngsters made it to Championship clubs.

They had had their own problems recently at Crewe under the previous manager before Gradi assumed control again, Collins said, and they went back to the basics of their own system. 'Gudjon

Thordarson was not interested in it and we had six to eight months of issues with parents coming in and saying it might be time for their boy to leave because they couldn't see the pathway. In the end, that's why the manager went. The chairman buys into the philosophy and once Dario took over as manager again, everything settled down in the academy again. Max and Nick signed new contracts when they could have gone, with Liverpool and other big clubs interested.

'Dario wants the fans to see them in the first team. We could sell them – and the club is not well off – but they have been here since they were 8. When a player goes is important and Dario knows when to let them go. At the big clubs, they get them at 16 and they are not playing games so they loan them out. Some do it well but here they get to play in the team. If Nick Powell goes when he is 19 or 20, he will have played 150 to 200 League games. Dean Ashton and Seth Johnson both said they improved by playing men's football early.'

Collins acknowledged that when Gradi was finally forced to require, the club could be facing something of a crisis. 'His drive is unbelievable. It can be a freezing cold night and if it's five minutes to eight, all the coaches are ready to wrap it up. Dario will go to ten past and tell everyone that the next goal is the winner. And he is 70 years old. The club will be in a much worse state when he is not here. He is the link with the boardroom, he has proven himself and doesn't have to defend the academy. If they say, "What about pulling the plug on this?" it is quickly quashed. That will be the difficulty. That is where we are spoilt.'

For now, it all looked and sounded simple with its ability to develop players and make them decent people too, as well as a sound commercial property for the club. You wondered why more did not follow what was surely a blueprint for all but the biggest clubs – maybe even some of those too. Everyone was a winner: coaches, players, fans – along with the chairman and his bean counter. Then you remembered the mentality of the game, with few boards of directors brave enough to take a long view and give a manager his head; or the commodity that the game always seemed to lack: the thief called time.

Perhaps I was getting carried away because it had been such an uplifting and sunny morning. 'Because of the small club aspect, there is a nice feel here,' said Collins. 'Manchester United do youth football very well but there is always going to be a pressure because that's the nature of Manchester United. Here, whoever comes has a positive feeling about the place. It is difficult to recreate what we have here at other places, due to the money in the game these days.'

Maybe it would take more clubs suffering greater financial hardship, particularly at the highest level, for them to look again within themselves for players and to invest properly in their development. There were signs in these more cash-strapped times of it happening but the real test of clubs' resolve would be whether it was sustained when the economy picked up. It had not been happening at Chelsea, where bright young things looked even further from being blooded each time Abramovich decided to buy again.

A few weeks on at the end of the season, I would go to the first leg of the FA Youth Cup final between Sheffield United and Manchester United and witness a wonderful 2-2 draw. Manchester's finest – with the help of several from overseas, including a fine French holding midfield player called Paul Pogba – were naturally the silkier but the young Blades had a touching camaraderie that counted for much. A remarkable crowd of 29,977 at Bramall Lane illustrated that fans loved to turn out and watch their own.

'What you have seen out there,' said James Collins of his Crewe under-18s, 'Well, there should be more of those players. We can learn off other clubs and we don't do it perfectly but we do find players. We are now playing against a lot of overseas players at other academies and it is good for us, because it means our boys get to compete and judge themselves against them. But it's not good for English football. People say that the best ones will come through but there are some missing out. How you solve that is the big question. We will keep plugging on and see what we can turn out.'

Not that they appeared to want too many to see what they turned out until they were ready, with huge leylandii surrounding the training ground. There were certainly some they wanted to keep out until the time was right for Crewe. 'Agents and scouts by appointment only,' said a sign at the entrance and there couldn't be many League Two clubs where they needed to say that.

Chapter 19

OFFICIAL SECRETS

THEN ENGLAND'S BEST REFEREE, Phil Don agreed to allow me to spend a day with him back in the early 1990s at an FA Cup quarter-final for an insight into the strains and stresses placed on a top official. Illuminating it was too, though 20 years on, my most vivid memory was of arriving with him at Liverpool's Anfield ground several hours before kick off to find two small boys kicking a ball up against a wall, Don asking them where the Stanley Park car park might be and receiving the answer, 'Fuck off.'

It prepared him well for the afternoon, an intense tie in which Aston Villa would lose to Liverpool. It was at a time when the chant of 'cheat' directed towards referees was gaining currency. That afternoon at Anfield, Don proved it had no foundation with a masterfully assertive performance as I witnessed him standing firm amid pressure in tunnel and dressing room from the rival managers, Graeme Souness of the home club and Ron Atkinson of Villa. Prone to human error like the rest of us they may have been, but English referees were no cheats.

Don went on to referee the Champions League final of 1994 and a World Cup quarter-final in the United States that same year. He also became head of refereeing at the FA in the late 1990s before becoming the first head of the select group of officials when they turned professional in 2001. A couple of years later, he allowed me to sit in on a brainstorming session at a hotel in the Midlands where the professional referees then met regularly for seminars to evaluate videotapes of good and bad decisions as they sought to improve their standards.

Now I wanted to spend a match day with a top-class referee again to find out how the job and the expectations of officials in the professional era had changed in the Premier League. I realised I could do this just by spending some time with a referee who had become a friend.

Mark Halsey's was a moving story of drive and determination through a frightening period of adversity. Hertfordshire-born, he played non-League football as a young man for clubs such as Barnet and St Albans City before taking up refereeing and progressing with it through the ranks to Football League then Premier League, in 1999.

These days, he lived near Bolton, with his second wife Michelle and their daughter Lucy. All was well until Michelle was diagnosed with myeloid leukaemia. Then, over the summer of 2009, around the time of his 48th birthday, Halsey began to suffer repeatedly from sore throats and ear infections. 'I felt tired a lot,' he told me. 'My teeth were a funny colour and I kept getting ulcers. All through the summer I found it difficult to eat. Antibiotics didn't seem to be working, though I still did my training and got through my fitness test ahead of the new season.'

On Thursday 13 August, Halsey's GP sent him for a scan at Beaumont Hospital in Bolton. The next day, he was told he had a cancerous tumour on his tonsils. It was an aggressive and rare form of B-cell lymphoma. The day after that, he took charge of Everton v. Arsenal on the season's opening weekend. 'I shouldn't have done it but I did,' he said, recalling the emotional and physical toll it took on him. They had told him at the hospital that they would book him in for the Monday to have the lymphoma removed but he thought it best to carry on rather than stew about it over the weekend.

The operation could not remove all of the cancer and by the following week the tumour had grown to the size of a golf ball. He was referred to the celebrated Christie's cancer hospital in Manchester, where he came under the care of Professor Tim Illidge. The professor began by jokingly telling Halsey that he was an Everton supporter and was not best pleased by Halsey's handling of his side's 6-1 defeat by Arsenal the previous week.

Halsey's thinking soon changed from when he might be back refereeing to whether he might not even survive this. 'I drove home numb,' he said. 'Straight away you think, "Oh my God, are you going to die?"' He wondered, he admitted, what he and Michelle had done to deserve this.

Within another day, he was enduring the first of six regular eight-hour chemotherapy sessions, where potent liquid drugs were administered through a vein in the wrist. The smell of the drugs alone made him sick. He could not eat for 48 hours around the treatment and grew so weary that he could not even make it home and would have to spend the night in the hospital. When he did recover between sessions, he tried to keep fit, even if just for two or three minutes. 'I was told that if you exercised, you had a greater chance of survival,' he explained.

He lost his hair through the chemo. 'Bald as a coot from top to bottom,' he could joke now as we spoke ahead of a charity dinner at Lancashire's Old Trafford Cricket Ground that would raise more than £50,000 for Christie's and which attracted the attendance of North-West managerial luminaries Sir Alex Ferguson, Roberto Mancini, David Moyes and Owen Coyle. At the time there was little else to laugh about. 'The taste in my mouth was terrible . . . My throat was so sore . . . I could feel the stuff going through my veins. . . It hurt that my little daughter was asking me to play with her and I just couldn't.'

He caught an infection and was bedridden for three weeks that November. They said he could postpone the 15 daily sessions of radiotherapy that were needed in an attempt to mop up the remaining cancer cells until the New Year but he wanted them over with. They finished on Christmas Eve. 'It was a good Christmas in the sense that the treatment was done but gloomy because I couldn't eat dinner with the family,' he said.

The goal became to referee again in 2010 but, still losing weight after all the steroids that had been pumped into him, he suffered a setback in February when he failed the fitness test for professional officials at Warwick University. 'I was so distraught, that I had to get someone to phone my wife,' he said. 'I could never see myself passing it.'

He and Michelle took off to Lanzarote for a week to recharge themselves – 'The cancer makes you stronger, and made us stronger as a couple,' he said – and Halsey came back to take the test again in the May of 2010. This time he managed the demanding six 40-metre sprints in under 6.2 seconds each and the 20 runs over 150 metres in 30 seconds each with just 35 seconds rest between each one. He fell weeping into the arms of fellow referee Stephen Bennett.

Halsey made it back into the game before the end of the season, first by taking charge of a Leicester City reserve team match, then being allocated a professional game in April between Rotherham United and Port Vale. There was an internet campaign to get him the FA Cup final but he knew at the time he wasn't ready. 'I want to get it on merit,' he told me at the time.

Six months on, with him back in the swing having started the season in the Premier League by taking Blackpool's opening game at Wigan, I sought to arrange to spend a day with him. As well as finding out how he was coping, I hoped he might be able to offer an account similar to Phil Don's, but updated, on the modern refereeing experience.

He was entirely willing and we fixed up a date. As a courtesy, I emailed Mike Riley, the general manager of the Premier Game

Match Officials Ltd (PGMOL) and a successor to Phil Don in the role, believing it to be a rubber-stamping exercise. How naive I was. I had forgotten that the PGMOL now existed due to the largesse of the Premier League, to the tune of £2.6 million a year. In effect, the wages of the referees – for the top men, around £70,000 a year on average to include basic salary and match fees – was paid by the Premier League. As such, they controlled everything.

I received an email in return not from the manager of the referees, but the Premier League press office: 'Having spoken to the PGMOL general manager Mike Riley, the idea of accompanying Mark for the day is, for the most part, not possible,' it said. 'Integrity issues mean that the only people that can travel to the ground together are the officiating party. The same goes for the officials' room where it's only players, managers, the match assessors and TV floor manager.

'Happy to accommodate an interview with yourself and Mark regarding his fightback from cancer. However, if the interview was to explore refereeing and look for insight into its changes over the last 10 or more years then the best person for that is Mike Riley.' I emailed back, copying in Mr Riley. He did not respond to this second communication either.

It was all very unsatisfactory when Mark Halsey was himself willing to allow it. Besides, later in the season I would hear a radio feature where the station was allowed access to a professional referee's dressing room, and to question the official about the game, from a match at Dagenham and Redbridge. Perhaps they had agreed to certain controls that I might not have consented to.

I let it go, not wishing to get Mark into trouble, but he still wanted to talk about his cancer, to help other people by demonstrating that it was possible to recover and to show how he did it. We met again on the South Coast where he would take charge of one of Brighton and Hove Albion's last games at their unloved Withdean Stadium, an athletics track around which they had erected temporary stands, before their move to a spanking new stadium on the outskirts of town at Falmer.

It was also a chance to visit a club on the up after a miserable two decades. To pay off debts and finance a new stadium, Brighton's then board of directors sold their old Goldstone Ground in the early 1990s, but they committed the cardinal sin: they did not have a new home to go to. From 1997 to 1999 they spent two seasons playing at Gillingham's Priestfield Stadium – a 140-mile round trip to Kent – before returning home to the Withdean, its capacity at first 6,000 but built up to 8,500 over the next decade.

It had its charms. You reached it up a hill off the main A23 London Road, through residential streets and under a railway arch. The ground itself was in a valley, surrounded by woods. You could see why the locals called it the Theatre of Trees, with affectionate irony in its comparison to Old Trafford.

Today it was teeming. Brighton were just a few wins away from promotion from League One, which they had led convincingly for most of the season, and the opposition was Swindon Town, looking likely to be relegated. It was another glorious spring day, a good-to-be-alive day. Mark Halsey had more reason than most to feel that way.

He invited me in to the Portakabin that housed the dressing rooms and we exchanged pleasantries and agreed to meet and speak soon in more detail. While he prepared for the game, I went to speak with the Brighton chairman, a remarkable character named Tony Bloom, who had agreed to see me. Nicknamed 'The Lizard' for his penetrating stare, Bloom had won more than £1 million as a professional poker player. He had made much more than that in property and investment, mind.

The diminutive 41-year-old Bloom was Albion through and through. His grandfather and uncle before him had been club directors and he himself had helped out financially when needed in the past, though he had preferred to remain in the background. After various planning hoops had been negotiated, when the club was finally ready to proceed with the new 22,500-capacity stadium in 2008, they found the credit crunch was biting and they couldn't raise the money. Bloom stepped in with £80 million of the £93 million needed, as loans convertible to equity. In return, he was now 95 per cent owner of the club.

He was clearly not just a money man, however. The manager Gus Poyet, Uruguayan international who had played for Chelsea and Tottenham, had been Bloom's inspired choice as manager. It was thought that Poyet was one of life's assistant managers, having worked under Dennis Wise at Leeds and Juande Ramos at Tottenham, but now he had proved himself as a No. 1. 'I spoke to people in the game,' said Bloom. 'I thought he would be just what we were looking for. He has modernised the club but not gone too fast, just at the right pace. He has an amazing eye for detail.' That detail had included flying out to Italy to meet with the club's kit manufacturers to discuss with them the precise properties of the material he wanted for the shirts.

Poyet had assembled a team without stars but with solidity at the back and fluidity going forward, a promotion potion that had been a class apart in League One. They were not at their best against an obdurate Swindon but took the lead when the lively left winger Craig Noone's run was halted unfairly by Andy Frampton and Gary Dicker stroked home the penalty.

A 30-yard swerving shot by the former Nottingham Forest midfield player David Prutton deceived Casper Ankergren in the home goal for a Swindon equaliser but, after Dicker had fluffed a second-half penalty, Glenn Murray eased the Brighton nerves by drilling home a low cross shot from 20 yards and securing a 2-1 win. It was Albion's seventh consecutive victory and in another couple of days, they would set a club record eighth by winning at Dagenham and Redbridge.

Indeed, it would not be long before they were up and preparing for life at a higher level, then going for the highest – the Premier League. 'That's absolutely the aim,' said Bloom. 'I know this city could support a Premier League club. I do think we will have a head start on other clubs in the Championship because of our new stadium. We have sold 14,000 season tickets already.'

'That is my aim,' said the chatty Poyet. 'But I don't want to be in a rush. I am not going to promise anything that is not possible or, as we say in Spanish, sell smoke – something that nobody wants to buy. I think we have got the potential and basis and in a few years we will have a new training ground, which is going to change everything. That means you are going places.'

Poyet was realistic about this side's potential at the next level. 'I think when you are on a good run, you take the momentum into the next season,' he said. 'But I think you always need a little bit of extra quality in the Championship.' It may have meant him going back to the owner for more investment, though Bloom thought the increased revenue from Falmer would cover the inevitable increase to the wage bill needed.

For now, it was about enjoying the sort of moment that does not come along too often in the game, promotion from a lower league always more pleasurable than a relegation struggle in one above. For Halsey, it was about simply savouring each moment of life.

'We wish Mark Halsey all the best and continuing good health,' said the tannoy announcer as the referee and his assistants walked out of the Portakabin and crossed the athletics track before the game. During it, he exchanged some banter with some Brighton fans who were contesting a foul by one of their own players. 'It was only a touch,' shouted one fan. 'A touch is enough,' Halsey shouted back, smiling, and they smiled back. 'After what he's been through, it's good to see him enjoying refereeing,' one said.

When I caught up again with Halsey ahead of him taking a match between Stoke and Arsenal, he looked tanned and well but confessed to tiredness after a long season that had tested his physical and mental condition. The legacy of the chemo would be there for some time, as shown by the fact that although his hair had grown back, it was now thinner.

His tolerance for the politics of refereeing also seemed to have been tried. He didn't want to say things directly, but there sounded like a subtext to his statements and things that had hurt him. 'The sports therapist at the Premier League told me he couldn't help me,' said Halsey, for example, of the time when he began his rehabilitation after his treatment. 'They feared that if something had happened to me, I would have had some comeback with them and maybe sued them, but I wouldn't have done that.' Instead, he was grateful to Bolton Wanderers for their help and facilities.

In hindsight, he added, he would not have worked so hard to pass a fitness test at the end of the previous season if the PGMOL had only told him that he was still wanted for the following campaign. 'I felt a pressure to get back to refereeing so that I could come back the next season,' he said.

'They have never had a ref that has come back from full cancer so I suppose this is new to them as well. How do they treat me, what do they do with me? The PGMOL as a business has been great with me. As a business. They have made sure I got everything I wanted.

'There was many a day I thought I would never come back, especially with what my body went through with the chemo, but I have to say I feel really proud of myself for what I have achieved. It's been quite tough, getting my fitness back. I think I have been under a lot more pressure than any other referee, having come back from the illness, and been judged harder from the assessors because of what's happened.

'I still get problems when I am refereeing. I've got no saliva, due to the chemo and the radiotherapy on both sides of my face and it's killed everything. It affects what I can and can't eat. Some things get stuck, like bread, potatoes, cheese. I used to love chocolate and red wine but wine tastes like diesel in my mouth now. I've got a big hole in my throat at the back. I can feel it when I drink hot tea or coffee because it's sensitive.'

When he refereed, he had continually to take water on board. 'I drink plenty in the dressing room before the game but 10 minutes later I am dry. I fill up at half-time and also if there is an injury during the play, I have a drink of the physio's water. I have water put by the goals so if I am there I can get a drink.'

Now he went back to Christie's every three months for check-ups. 'I just have to pray it doesn't come back again,' he said. 'You just don't know, do you?'

There had, during the season, been a source of sadness that emphasised his own good fortune. At the age of just 31, the Exeter City striker Adam Stansfield had died from cancer of the colon. Halsey, who continued to wear a wristband remembering Stansfield, had asked to officiate an Exeter home game so that he could take part in a 5-kilometre charity run in the Devon city in the player's name that weekend.

Less serious, but painful nonetheless, was him not being awarded the FA Cup final when he thought he had a good chance as his 50th birthday approached. On this issue, Halsey could not contain his true feelings. 'It was a massive disappointment,' he admitted. 'Someone of my ability should have refereed the Cup Final before now. But it is out of my control. I won't get it now. They've got young lads they will want to give it to.' He would carry on, he insisted, as he was able to now that the retirement age had been lifted and referees were assessed season by season. 'I'll keep on refereeing. I just want to go and referee a game and come out unscathed, with no controversy if I can help it. If I can keep my cards in my pocket I am happy. It's all about 22 players and the spectators and not about the referee. Too many referees look after themselves and that's not me. I'm just glad to be here and glad to be alive.'

We left it there, even if he had seen much and would have provided good testimony about the nature of the job these days. The Premier League and the PGMOL, it seemed, did not like referees who become personalities or who were well liked by managers. After that dinner at Lancashire Cricket Club, when the top managers in the north came to the aid of the cause of cancer, Halsey was not given any big games at United or City the next season. Also, Liverpool's Kenny Dalglish had recently used a newspaper column to praise Halsey and he sensed it had been frowned upon.

But then, I had no need really to ask Halsey about the development of officiating because the evidence was there in front of our eyes in the multitude of televised games available. Refereeing had changed immensely – and yet not at all.

The most obvious change was the visual element, referees no longer being the men in black but in yellow, green, blue or whatever colour didn't clash with the teams. There was then the introduction of the fourth official, who stood between the two dugouts at pitchside and whose role was nominally to keep order. Their main function, however, seemed to be to hold up the new digital boards showing substitutions and the number of minutes of added time there would be. Another element of the job was to take the pressure off the linesmen or women – now called assistant referees – by being the butt of the two teams' coaching staff's ire when they disagreed with a decision out on the pitch. Quite what the fourth official was expected to do about it, no one was quite sure.

Actually, in European matches there were now six officials, with one at either end behind the by-line apparently to watch for fouls at corners that the referee might miss, or the ball crossing the goal-line. They were, in effect, assistant assistants. It was hard to recall, however, a fifth or sixth official giving a decision and they looked largely redundant. It didn't help much when they were given a pointy stick to make them look more important.

The new officials were introduced by Michel Platini, president of UEFA, as a response to the debate about whether video technology should now be used to decide on matters of fact, such as the ball crossing the goal-line. There was no question yet that it might be used for matters of judgement, such as offside. That law had been modified several times over the past two decades, the main change being that an attacker level with the second-last defender was now onside rather than off. There had also been the introduction of sub-clauses so that players could be in offside positions but not penalised if they were not taking an active part in the scoring of a goal.

The problem for Platini was that referees now actually wanted video technology as help, as officials had in tennis, cricket and rugby league, to ensure correct decisions. Platini wanted to retain the human element, with its capacity to get things wrong, and thus challenge players to accept injustice and see how they responded to it – character building and all that.

The argument against technology was also that football's simplicity was its strength, that the game should be the same at Wembley as at Hackney Marshes. However, the game was clearly not the same at all levels these days, and UEFA – indeed all governing bodies – knew it. Why, then, would referees at the top level wear earpieces and microphones to enable them to communicate with their assistants and fourth officials? And why, during the 2006 World Cup final was the Frenchman Zinedine Zidane sent off for a headbutt into the chest of the Italian Marco Materazzi when the referee and his assistants looked to have missed the offence? It could only have been because the fourth official saw a television replay on the sideline and communicated his views to the referee.

Where officiating had not changed was in the abuse that referees received. Phil Don had been called a cheat; Halsey might be called worse nowadays. Yet he did not mind where others might – it meant that he was being treated as a normal referee rather than one with cancer.

Otherwise, the FA had begun a campaign billed as 'Respect' to get players to modify their behaviour towards officials. The age-old issue of swearing would probably never go away, such was the heat of the game, but some distasteful behaviour needed addressing, such as Wayne Rooney's persistent haranguing of referees, or the oafish swearing into a TV camera during a game at West Ham that would see him banned for two games.

More serious was the fact that referees still endured crowds of players around them. It might have been different had Andy D'Urso stood up to Manchester United's snarling shaven heads, including Roy Keane and Jaap Stam, in the 1990s as they advanced on him but you couldn't blame him for backing off.

Still, too, referees had only a split second to decide whether a player was diving or had genuinely been fouled, and still they had managers criticising them for decisions that, as they saw it, cost clubs points and millions of pounds. At such times, you couldn't help recalling the American basketball coach who ventured that: 'The trouble with referees is that they just don't care who wins.'

Neither were referees allowed to answer back when well-known critics of them, such as Jose Mourinho when at Chelsea and Steve Bruce at Sunderland, berated them for an error or a one-sided view of incidents. It would have been interesting to have heard a referee retaliate by saying that Mourinho or Bruce had got team selections wrong, or that one of their players had had a bad game.

Why did referees continue to want to do it? The answer perhaps lay in the story about the circus worker whose job it was to clean up the elephants' dung left in the ring after every performance: 'Don't you get sick of shovelling shit night after night?' he was asked. 'Don't you ever feel like packing it in?' 'What,' the worker replied, 'and quit showbusiness?'

We heard at Wembley FC from Brian Gumm that football had probably taken years off his life. And with all the grief and worry, you understood what he meant. In the case of Tony Bloom and all at Brighton, you knew that the grief and worry were worth the moments of joy and achievement the game could also bring.

As for the admirable Mark Halsey – his openness and desire to share his experiences to help others in stark contrast to a Premier League seeking to control and suppress – you couldn't help wondering if football might even have added some years to his life.

Chapter 20

NEW BELLES PLEASE

IT WAS TWO hours before kick off and already there were more than 1,000 people milling around outside the ground. Unfortunately, they were here at Doncaster's new Keepmoat Stadium for a Sunday market and seemed more interested in cheap underwear and garden tools, combat trousers and pet provisions, than the start of the new Women's Super League (WSL).

An hour later, an hour before the referee's opening blast of the whistle, just a few traders were left packing up. The queues of traffic and people were heading away from the stadium rather than towards it to witness Doncaster Rovers Belles take on Chelsea in their inaugural game. It was a delicate time; was this going to work or not?

The WSL represented the FA's attempt, after at least one false start, finally to establish the women's game in English professional football. For years it had soldiered on, and had its niche in the game. It had even developed a Women's Premier League with Arsenal Ladies doing well in Europe and Mohamed Al Fayed for a time putting money into Fulham to make them full-time and thus the best side in the country. It also unbalanced the league, with most teams still amateur, and made it uncompetitive.

The FA had sought to sanction a full-time professional league after the turn of the Millennium when it looked as if the game was taking off in the United States and it could work commercially in England too. The economic climate turned, however. The American

League went bust in 2005 and the FA backed off. The idea was too ambitious anyway: from crowds of a few hundred to full professional was too big a step.

Now the American League had reformed and the mood within the FA was to have a proper go. They had done their homework and worked out a strategy, allocating money to back a new semi-professional competition after examining best practice around the successful areas of the women's game – Germany, the Netherlands and the reviving United States. It was almost, too, as if they had examined the worst practices of men's professional football, with its debts and dysfunction, and sought to do the opposite.

The FA had decided on a league of eight teams: Arsenal and Chelsea, Liverpool and Everton, Birmingham and Bristol, Doncaster and Lincoln. All would be awarded franchises for two seasons. Each team would play each other home and away, meaning 14 games, and there would be a league cup competition on top as finale to the season. Radically, it would become a spring and summer league, though this season of 2011 there would be a mid-season break while the England national team competed in the Women's World Cup finals in Germany.

To get the ball rolling, the FA were investing £3 million. Some would go to the clubs – £70,000 each a season to help with running costs – but more on marketing and advertising. In return, clubs had to employ a UEFA A licence head coach and a qualified accountant. The FA would go into the clubs quarterly to check on their finances and ensure they were adhering to the terms of their licence.

Each club would also be allowed four players on salaries of a maximum £20,000 per annum so that no one club could spend more than another. It was an attempt to spread the talent around the leagues and Birmingham were one of the early beneficiaries, the England winger Karen Carney returning from playing in America to join her home town club. With £16,000 on top also available to England players from central contracts, it made coming home attractive.

The biggest innovation was the playing of the new league in spring and summer. The aim was not only to fill a gap in the game's market but also for the women to create a new one for themselves. They no longer had to compete for audiences with men's football, after all. There would be television coverage of five live matches on the ESPN satellite station and a weekly highlights programme.

At the WSL's Wembley launch, I spoke to Kelly Simmons, the FA's head of the national game – which meant all tiers, men's and women's, below the Premier and Football Leagues. 'We have been fortunate that we were starting with a blank sheet of paper and could look at lessons from both men's and women's football,' she told me. 'We have looked at what would be best practice in coaching, stadiums, finances and marketing, as well as a good match day experience, and wanted to come up with something sustainable. The set-up will mean that clubs can't have a single benefactor.'

Simmons was one of those unsung stalwarts of the game that existed without fanfare within the FA. Quietly spoken and understated, she was extremely capable and did much for the grassroots game, her work often going overlooked. It might have been because of noisier colleagues and bigger projects. It might also have been because she was a woman. Since Pat Smith had been in on the formation of the Premier League 20 years earlier as the FA's administration officer, no female had risen to a great height in the organisation, though the bright Janie Frampton had become the National Referees Manager. Mostly, the FA's executive positions and committees were still full of white, middle-aged males – possibly one reason for the governing body's waning effectiveness in the modern world.

But then, women had made surprisingly little headway over 20 years in general in what had traditionally been seen as a man's game. Having been managing director of Birmingham City and vice-chairman of West Ham, Karren Brady was always cited as a woman who had taken on men and succeeded, but in truth she was largely an enforcer for the owners of the clubs, David Sullivan and David Gold.

Within the media, there were scarcely many more women covering the game for newspapers than there had been 20 years earlier, despite the huge growth in women watching it, while the capable Radio 5 live football reporter Jacqui Oatley was quickly jettisoned after becoming *Match of the Day's* first female commentator in 2007. It is hard to imagine a man not being given more time to develop their style.

'I never really agreed that we should have more women officials and I don't think we should have female commentators,' said the former Sheffield United manager Dave Bassett at the time, reinforcing the laddishness of the game. 'And my wife agrees.' While Luton manager Mike Newell had once decried an assistant referee, Amy Rayner, for not awarding his side a penalty, saying: 'She should not be there. I know that sounds sexist, but I am sexist.' He was fined £6,500 by the FA. However, more than any fine or opprobrium, what undermined Newell's arguments against what he saw as political correctness and tokenism by appointing women officials came this season of 2010/11. It emerged the day after a game between Wolverhampton Wanderers and Liverpool – with the leaking of footage by a disgruntled employee – that the Sky Sports broadcasters Andy Gray and Richard Keys had been caught off camera decrying the appointment of a female assistant referee in Sian Massey and questioning her efficiency. Along with her looks.

They were made to look foolish when she correctly allowed a Liverpool goal despite intense scrutiny. Gray and Keys were then made to pay days later when Sky brusquely terminated careers that had spanned the whole of the Premier League era. Massey had shown that her status was due to merit and she was just as capable of making the right decision as any man. In the debate that accompanied the episode, it was remarkable, and encouraging, how many men in the game now decried the Bassett/Newell viewpoint and urged the inclusion of more women in the media and the game itself. The proof, though, would be when it actually came to employing them or promoting them.

Perhaps we would see more overt signs of equality when the first woman was appointed to referee a Premier League game. This season did see the first to take charge of a Football League game when assistant Amy Fearn – nee Amy Rayner – replaced the injured referee Tony Bates for the last 20 minutes of a match between Coventry City and Nottingham Forest.

In the WSL, sisters were seeking to do it for themselves in their attempts to implement new ways of doing things. 'The licence is the biggest difference,' said Kelly Simmons. 'There are minimum standards for clubs. Anyone can apply but you have to be up to a certain standard, from coaching right through to marketing. Boards have to work with our financial regulation teams. This is about the FA and clubs as a partnership and slowly building the league to be sustainable.'

The England women's team manager Hope Powell was equally optimistic but realistic. 'The idea is that our game becomes more competitive with a good geographical spread of teams and top players,' she said. 'The long-term aim is to have a better way through for young players and to improve standards. We know there will be teething problems but we think we can grow this league, with the clubs and the FA forming a partnership.'

Powell was another of those characters that the women's game – indeed, the game as a whole – was fortunate to have attracted. Studious and dignified, she had managed England to the final of the European Championship in 2009, in which they were beaten by Germany, and had even been linked to the men's game and a vacant managerial position at Grimsby Town, though it had sounded like a publicity stunt on the club's part.

'We have to do something different,' she added. 'We have to be innovative to make sure we keep pace with the rest of the world. I think summer football will be a great attraction to get families to games. I also think there will be a whole new audience of football fans who will be missing their football and will watch us on television and be surprised by the passion, the pace and the talent on display. And it's not like they are getting £250,000 a week.'

All that, at least, was the theory. I came to Doncaster to discover if the reality could match it. As Arsenal and Fulham had developed over the previous decade, Doncaster Belles became overshadowed. Twenty years ago, however, the dominant team in women's football was the Belles (so named because they started as a group of women selling raffle tickets on the terraces of the Doncaster Rovers' men's team's former ground at Belle Vue). Then, I went to see them play at the Armthorpe Welfare ground just outside town as they beat Wimbledon 3-0 to clinch the inaugural National League title, to add to the Women's FA Cup.

Over the following 17 years, they would win the Double once more. Their exploits became the basis for *Playing the Field,* the TV drama series by the gritty Yorkshire writer Kay Mellor about the lives and loves of a women's team. Their history and tradition combined for an undoubted reason why they were awarded a Super League franchise. That and their facilities, which officially opened in 2007. The Keepmoat was a tidy all-seater 15,000-capacity stadium next to an industrial estate and shopping outlet centre on the edge of Doncaster. The Belles, who had linked up with Rovers in 2005, played in the same red and white hoops and had taken the men's club's name in their title. Thus they had use of the community stadium. It would be the best venue in the league, although Everton would get to use Goodison Park every now and then.

The problem, however, was that the crowd was clearly going to rattle around inside the Keepmoat. On the main entrance side of the ground where the dressing rooms were situated, just six journalists occupied the press box as kick off approached. Four photographers were at pitchside when the teams took the field having been preceded by the strains of the Sugababes' song 'Here Come the Girls'.

Across the ground in the one seating area opened up, next to the *Doncaster Free Press* family stand, there looked to be just a few hundred spectators paying the £6 for adults and £3 for children and pensioners. The crowd would be announced, though, at 578, which took all by surprise. Perhaps that number contained all the players and officials, too. 'Due to the unprecedented demand, there are no more programmes on sale. Sorry for the inconvenience,' said the announcer. Unprecedented? This was their first home game.

It started well enough for the Belles, with their star player 'Tricky' Vicky Exley – winner of more than 50 England caps and still going strong at the age of 35 – heading home from a corner to give them the lead. A splendid long-range shot by Danny Buet made it 1-1 at half-time, however, a platform that Chelsea used the better after the interval. After a mix up between the Belles' goalkeeper Helen Alderson and defender Lyndsey Cunningham, Danni Bird gave Chelsea the lead. Ashlee Hincks then drove home Chelsea's third and substitute Emma Plewa demonstrated some neat footwork and an accurate shot to make the final score 4-1 to Chelsea.

The game had been decent, but not great, the standards acceptable though a little disappointing, to be honest. Perhaps we could put it down to early-season rustiness. As women players were getting stronger through new training methods, the temptation was clearly to kick the ball harder and further, rather than playing a passing game that required more thought and composure. That was surely more suited and truer to the women's particular physical attributes, though.

'To be successful in England, women's football has to emerge from the shadow of the men's game and establish its own identity,' was one of the stated aims of the WSL at its launch. Clearly it was not going to do that by seeking to emulate the way men played, but by offering an alternative.

It was also a personal bugbear of mine that the goals were the same size as in the men's game, when women goalkeepers were plainly not, on average, as tall as in men's football, leading to the concession of some daft goals as the ball went over their heads. It was the same in boys' and girls' youth football, where the players were also smaller but had to operate on the full-sized pitches with big goals simply because it was cheaper for clubs and local councils wanting one-size-fits-all fields.

Otherwise it was good to see elements of the men's testosterone-fuelled game being cut out. There was no arguing with referee, nor complaining at decisions. At the end of the game, the losers formed a guard of honour for the winners and applauded them off the pitch.

During the game, it clearly frustrated the Belles' manager John Buckley that his team did not appeal for a penalty they might have been awarded when one of their number went down under a challenge. The only ranting, meanwhile, came from the Chelsea manager Matt Beard, who prowled his dugout grouchily until his side got going.

'I don't think the quality's any better but they are a lot fitter,' observed the watching Gillian Coultard. 'They're lucky now that they have better training methods and facilities these days. The best thing for the Belles has been the link with the Rovers.'

Coultard was one of the true legends of Doncaster women's football in particular and English women's football in general. Now 47, she had played for the Belles for 25 years until 2001, for England for almost 20, winning a record 119 caps as a busy, tenacious midfield player and sweeper later in her career. She had lifted that league trophy at Armthorpe those two decades previously. She did all that, along with training at least two nights a week, while working on the production line of a factory in Castleford and using her holidays to play for England. Given her natural feistiness, it was not hard to see her as a character in *Playing the Field*. 'It was all right,' was her verdict of the series. 'It was a drama, wasn't it? It didn't have much to do with the football. They obviously dramatised it.'

Despite offers from semi-professional clubs in mainland Europe, where the women's game was more established, such as Germany and Italy, she remained a Yorkshire lass unwilling to move far from her beloved Belles. She might thus have been forgiven for looking on enviously at the WSL and the contracts available now to its top players. 'I'd be doing all right but I'm not jealous, no,' she insisted, however. 'I don't regret anything. I was lucky to play when I did and do everything I did. I saw a documentary recently with Ryan Giggs saying that Bobby Charlton would have been a great player in any era. I like to think I would have been too.'

Coultard had had surprisingly little to do with football since her retirement, though she did have a spell as manager of Hartlepool Ladies a couple of years after her retirement, taking them to an FA Cup tie against Fulham. A major reason had been the life-changing event for her of 2005 when she was diagnosed with breast cancer and underwent surgery. She was fortunate, she admitted, to have had the tumour removed successfully. Now she was in her sixth year of remission, having recently celebrated coming off medication. That medication was a drug called Tamoxifen, suppressant of oestrogen, which is the natural hormone in women on which breast cancer could thrive. Coultard now worked at a pharmaceutical company in Castleford which produced 1.6 million Tamoxifen pills a year. Life's little ironies, indeed.

Today's game had given her a craving for another drug, though, she conceded: football. 'Yes, I am feeling like I might want to get back into the game again,' she said wistfully as she gazed out from a lounge on to the Keepmoat pitch. She would, she said, liked to have joined Hope Powell's England set-up, having played with her in the national side. 'I am a bit disappointed not to have been asked,' Coultard admitted. 'I don't think there is enough creativity in the England side. I think they are too rigid.'

Perhaps there could have been a role for her with the Belles and you couldn't help thinking that they were missing a trick not having her involved in some capacity, given her status in the game. Doncaster certainly did not currently have a playing figure of the same quality and influence. Neither was the latest star striker, Precious Hamilton, in the same league as Karen Walker, prolific Belles and England striker of 20 years earlier.

Coultard was sceptical of the new league, based on today's events at the Keepmoat, even if the competition had begun promisingly the previous week. Then, a crowd of 2,510 had seen Arsenal – featuring the most skilful of English players in the left-footed Rachel Yankey, who was closing on Coultard's caps record – beat Chelsea 1-0 at Tooting and Mitcham FC. 'I don't like summer football, I'm afraid,' said Coultard. 'I like to go on my holidays then. For me, it's an autumn and winter game, with a bit of spring. You only really find out about players in the middle of winter. It's got some TV coverage but it's one man and his dog, isn't it? Stadiums are only going to be full for the FA Cup final or England games. If Arsenal can't fill a ground with all the resources they have put into it, then who will? But no, I don't think it's make or break for the women's game. The American League went bust and came back.'

For all Coultard's reasonable doubts, I left Doncaster wanting the WSL to succeed. For years, women in football and the women's game had endured jokes: about the difficulty of finding 11 women prepared to wear the same outfit; of them needing to have early kick offs to get home to cook tea for their husbands. And there were genuinely women football fans who did not like watching the women's game, preferring the power and faster pace of the men's game that was inevitable given the natural and incontrovertible greater physical strength of men.

The problem was that women's football was too often compared with the men's. It surely had to play to its own strengths, of grace and elegance. Hope Powell had, after all, brought it out in the England squad, which featured the talented Yankey, now back in the fold after being dropped for a loss of form, the elegant defender Faye White of Arsenal and sharp striker Kelly Smith, still playing in America with Boston Breakers. It remained disappointing, however, that all eight coaches in the WSL were men. More top-quality women were needed.

The FA, though, were admirably looking to structure the league properly and develop it gradually, keeping finances modest initially and preventing one-person ownership. It could always expand from eight teams if its model was working. In the short-term, they did need to start getting more people through the gate with marketing initiatives. Perhaps at Doncaster, they could start by trying to sell tickets to that Sunday market crowd.

'It could be the best thing or the worst thing,' Powell said to me of the new league. 'But we have to find out. Everyone else in the world is moving on so we have to as well.'

Before I left, I just wanted to revisit Armthorpe, birthplace of one of the English game's best players and managers in Kevin Keegan but also that previous home to the Belles. The Welfare ground on the main road through the village, Church Street, was also home to a men's North East Counties League team. I passed the Markham Main Sports and Social Club and turned down past the new Morrisons supermarket opening up in a week or two to find the football ground's gates locked. As I peered through a gap between them, memories of the Belles as title winners came readily back, though.

There were dandelions on the pitch, the floodlight pylons were rusty and clearly had broken bulbs. There had been stirring deeds done here, though, by the pioneers of the women's game as it entered the modern era with the formation of that National League, precursor to Premier and now Super League, 20 years earlier.

There was no comparison between Armthorpe Welfare and the Keepmoat. Facilities at the latter were clean and modern. It encouraged a family experience. I couldn't help wondering if it might not be too antiseptic, however; whether the modern Belles players might be having it a bit too good. Four of them, apparently, were being put up in a local hotel that was sponsoring the team. Now there was a chance to make a living from the game and no one would deny them the chance of that, but you hoped that professionalism did not lead to the grandiosity that bred excess in some male players.

Twenty years earlier, the experiences of Coultard and Co. were more earthy and ultimately more exciting for it. Judging by her words, more satisfying too. The challenge for the Belles now was to embrace that history and seek to emulate it in another new competition. The challenge for the game was to offer an altogether more pleasant watching experience of a good-quality match, but to retain the grit and spontaneity that football was also supposed to encompass.

Chapter 21

THE WHITE TIGER ECONOMY

THE CORNISH CITY of Truro is not quite the end of the world, but it feels as if you could see it from there. It is certainly the end of English football's world. At 275 miles from London and 35 from Land's End, it is home to the most westerly of the country's professional football clubs, one who were growing more professional by the year as each passing season brought promotion after promotion.

This season would see a fifth in six seasons – a British record they reckoned – as Truro City rose from Zamaretto Premier League (the old Southern League) to the Southern Section of the Conference, which was sponsored by the Blue Square online gambling company. It had given rise among their growing support to probably the naffest chant in football. 'We're gonna win the Zamaretto,' it went, to the tune of Tony Christie's 'Amarillo', 'And Blue Square South awaits for me.'

It continued the quest of their chairman Kevin Heaney, a high-achieving but controversial figure in the region, to build a Football League club for a county that loved its sport. The problem was, that sport was rugby union. 'I think that Cornwall is crying out for a professional football club, or at least a Conference National team,' he told me during the course of an interview that was reward for having made the journey down. It was epic enough for any visiting team but turn it around and imagine the away trips that Truro faced. This season alone, they had totalled 10,000 miles. That made them, they believed, the third most travelled team in the country behind Plymouth Argyle from neighbouring Devon and Cumbria's Carlisle United. Now there was a title for a book about their recent history: *The Road Most Travelled*.

'We've got nearly 600,000 people living within an hour of our ground,' added Heaney. 'Let's give it a go. A lot of people said to me that the travelling would be too much, that it would be difficult to get players. They are fair comments but, to me, life is about trying to achieve things and having a go. I like challenges.'

Heaney was clearly a determined man. He had certainly developed the asset that any football chairman needed: a thick skin. A Londoner born in Cricklewood and once a season ticket holder at Tottenham Hotspur, he decided to set up business in Cornwall, despite the initial coolness from locals towards all outsiders who come to live in the South West.

At first phenomenally successful, his housing development company had gone bust. He appeared to prompt mixed feelings among folk; some welcomed what he brought to the local economy, others wondered about his methods and motives. Through it all, he ploughed on, a man on a mission.

Heaney's fondness for a challenge was evident from the way his involvement with the club began. In March 2004, he was running one of the county's then most successful companies, Cornish Homes, when a man called Chris Webb, backbone of impoverished Truro City FC, knocked on his door seeking sponsorship. Heaney's house cleaner had told Webb, who was then in charge of youth development at the club and overseeing the age-groups teams in which the cleaner had a grandchild playing, that this bloke had a few bob.

Webb outlined to him the parlous state of the club, which was £300,000 in debt and averaging fewer than 100 through the gate. A half-hour meeting turned into a three-hour question-and-answer session, after which Heaney declared to Webb that he wanted to buy the club.

Truro had played in the South-West League for many a year, never crossing the River Tamar that separates Cornwall from Devon. Though the Cornish capital, the city was celebrated for little other than its pretty cathedral, which was bijou by the standards of such buildings. With a population of a mere 17,500, they weren't even the biggest town or football team in the area. That was Falmouth, 11 miles away, with a population of 21,000, having played in the further-reaching Western League for a while.

On a visit some years back I did notice that Truro had one of the last Woolworths to feature a parquet floor as some sort of point of distinction. The floor was long gone, however, but then so was Woolworths. With parking problems and modern retail chains, in fact, Truro looked a disappointingly unremarkable town save for its cathedral, confirming a description of the coastal county as an ordinary picture in a beautiful frame. Then again, perhaps my view was coloured for the worse by a huge seagull that swooped on me and sought to prise my cheese and tomato roll out of my hand.

'I won't go into the position of Truro out of respect for others,' said Heaney, dapper in club tie and matching TCFC cufflinks, as we sat in his office at the football ground – a Portakabin at one end. 'But it was pretty much on its knees, in Step Seven of the football pyramid, mid-table, holes in their socks.'

He got to thinking and believing that he could do something about it. It took Webb eight months to persuade the old guard at Truro that Heaney was for real and that they would be mad to turn him away. They were worried he might build houses on the ground. To allay their fears, Heaney said he would put the freehold of the ground in trust for the club.

The deal to buy the club was completed in the autumn of 2004. He introduced a new badge with an image of the city's cathedral on it. He changed the club colours from red and black to a main colour of white with a trim of Cornish gold, giving the Tinmen a new nickname of the White Tigers in the process. He then set about dragging them up by their bootstraps, with Webb his faithful lieutenant as director of football. 'I wanted to get two or three key young players in and show we were serious so that we could then attract other players,' Heaney explained. 'I went for first year pros who were going to have a good future.' The plan included a kid by the name of Stewart Yetton, who would become the signing from which others flowed.

Yetton had been a promising apprentice with Plymouth Argyle, coming back from a broken leg to score goals in the reserves. He grew frustrated at not getting his chance in the first team, however, and asked to be released from his contract. He then joined Tiverton Town of the Southern League, playing part-time and developing a career as an accountant. Heaney took note of the move to Tiverton and invited him up to a lunch in London. 'I told him my plan for Truro,' said Heaney. 'This was a young lad who should have been playing League football, was offered a good contract at Plymouth, but preferred part-time. I told him I wanted to build the team around him. I sold my vision. It's about how you portray yourself and how seriously people take you. We all know goalscorers win games and he was a natural.'

Yetton signed for an unheard sum of money in the South Western League, said to be £500 a week, but insisted there were other motivations. 'I never felt valued at Plymouth,' he said. 'It hurt because Argyle was my club but I was so unhappy there. Leaving made me into a man, though. I knew I'd get stick coming down to this level but I am here because of one man's ambition.'

He soon began banging in the goals and would go on to average almost a goal a game over the next six seasons. Truro took off, flying through the South Western and the two divisions of the Western League in successive seasons. Then it was straight through a regional division of the Southern League. Along the way, by beating AFC Totton of Hampshire 3-1, they won the 2007 FA Vase – a competition for the smaller non-League clubs, below the FA Trophy – at Wembley in the year the stadium re-opened, which undoubtedly contributed to the record gate for the competition of 36,232. That season, Yetton scored 72 goals.

Horror of horrors, Truro then failed to go up immediately from the Southern League's Premier Division, having to settle for 11th place. A mere blip. This season they had battled at the top with another cathedral city in Salisbury but had prevailed towards the end, clinching the title before their final home match, against Weymouth. That would now represent celebration day, when the championship shield would be presented.

Though it was a remarkable achievement, this was not quite the heart-warming tale of little club winning through that it might have seemed to those who did not follow the non-League game. Many among the fraternity resented Heaney spending freely to get Truro through the divisions, though they had postponed plans to go full-time. The gossip in the game was that Truro's wage bill had been some £500,000 for the season around the time of promotion to the Southern League. That budget in the current Southern League would still probably have been double that of the next best financed club.

'In terms of wages, we pay less than we did four years ago,' said Heaney. 'I learned a lot about being a chairman. Originally when I was new to the business, I was a little bit green but we were on a mission and I was trying to send a message to potential players that I was serious. I don't believe I paid over the top. I was just paying the going rate for a certain sort of player.'

There were also the local recriminations of him liquidating his Cornish Homes (UK) Ltd company in 2008, owing £4.5 million. This at a time when he was reported to be worth £145 million in the *Sunday Times* Rich List, which had him as one of the 500 wealthiest people in the country. After the company was wound up, with 38 staff losing their jobs, Heaney was confronted by representatives of some of the 162 creditors at a meeting in Exeter, including one Derek Giles, whose building company was owed £38,222 for work at Truro City's Treyew Road ground.

'You have to make decisions in life. I made a decision that the development market was gone,' Heaney explained to me. 'And if you look at the development world when I shut the company, it has got steadily worse. Cornish Homes was just one company in a group of companies and 96 per cent of the money owed was owed to me and my subsidiary companies.

'Banks pulled out from funding and I wasn't prepared to let people lend money to my company without getting the banks to lend me money to pay them. I did what any prudent director would do when faced with a situation where a company can't make money. Unfortunately I was in development. If I had been in insolvency, I would probably have been opening another three offices and made £50 million.'

Heaney stayed in land acquisition afterwards, though concentrating not on housing but retail development. He now had plans to move the club from its current ground high on a hill overlooking the cathedral on the A390 out of town to a new site nearby. There, he wanted to build a 10,000-capacity 'Stadium for Cornwall' that could be used by the community and shared with the Cornish Pirates rugby union club. It would enable the national championship team finally to meet ground criteria for the sport's Premiership.

He was quick to counter any suggestion that he, rather than Truro City FC, might personally profit from it. 'We've got the land, now it's about what it's going to cost to build,' he said. 'There is a willingness from the council to support that. The intention is to build on the current ground and create a regular income for the club. The club then becomes self-funding and takes me out of the equation. But we've got a bit of work to do before then. We need to build some training facilities. There is a lot of building to be done over the new few years and if we could get another promotion to the Conference National, that would be good.'

You hoped the new stadium might retain some of the features and charms of Treyew Road amid the rolling hills of Cornwall around it, not least the palm trees in front of the clubhouse behind one goal. Was there any other ground in the country that had palms inside? The boardroom, in another Portakabin, doubled as a learning centre for local kids.

The rest of the place had gradually been built up over the seven years of Heaney's tenure to meet the various ground requirements of each new league they entered. At the far end was a seated stand with marquee-tented roofing. Along one side was the old stand housing just a hundred or so as reminder of times past. Opposite, a symbol of progress, was a large temporary one housing several hundred. The capacity of the ground was now 3,000, adequate for Conference South. Clearly it was not worth doing much more ahead of a planned new stadium.

Today against Weymouth, Treyew Road would house the Zamaretto League's biggest gate of the season at 1,696. Indeed, kick off would have to be put back 15 minutes to allow the queues to get inside. While we waited, we were treated by the DJ to a selection of football's cheesiest championship songs. Was there a compilation CD on sale out there somewhere for such an occasion? For 'Heroes', 'Simply the Best' and 'We are the Champions', David Bowie, Tina Turner and Queen must have been coining in the royalties from football in April and May.

The reason for the throng was not just Truronians wanting to acclaim the local promoted heroes – actually, most of the players were ex-pros from Plymouth, Exeter and Torquay, though Truro boy Jake Ash had been through all the divisions with the club. Well-supported Weymouth had brought with them a few hundred anxious souls from 120 miles away seeking to urge their team not to get relegated for the third season in a row.

The Dorset club were fourth from bottom and three teams would go down. If they lost, they would need Didcot Town also to lose for them to stay up. Didcot had a more comfortable fixture on paper, at home to lowly but safe Oxford City, so Weymouth's best hope might lay in Truro having been on the razzle ever since clinching promotion.

Weymouth, dear reader, were your author's team. Having grown up in the town and supported them from boyhood, I had even had two spells as chairman. The first was a glorious period of 18 months from the spring of 2003 when I appointed Steve Claridge as manager and he had immediately led the club into Conference South as runners-up of the Southern League when it was a stronger competition. Before he came, Weymouth had finished 17th in front of average gates of 650. Claridge's team attracted an average of 1,490.

The creation of such a buzz around the seaside town and club had fired the interest of a local hotelier, one Martyn Harrison. He bought himself a majority shareholding and promptly threw money at the club in an attempt to reach the Football League. I was not chairman for much longer, and Claridge was soon sacked. Such is football. For a while none among the club's support cared, as Weymouth were promoted to the Conference and even reached the heady heights of third in the table around the New Year of 2007. The Football League was indeed in sight.

However, it came at a huge cost – another example of a club overstretching itself. Weymouth had gone full time and their wage bill, on crowds averaging fewer than 2,000 – though very healthy for a town with a catchment area of around 80,000 people – was a shocking £22,000 per week at one stage. When Harrison pulled the plug that January 2007, the club's accounts showed that he had put in £3 million – as loans. He expected it back from a prospective £11.5 million deal with the supermarket chain Asda, who wanted the site of the club's Wessex Stadium on which to build a new superstore in return for finding Weymouth a new home. But the deal fell through. Harrison could bear the costs no more and the gravy train hit the buffers.

Naturally no one would pay Harrison £3 million for a bankrupt club and he was forced to walk away with nothing, handing it over to a Bournemouth music promoter by the name of Mel Bush. He immediately saw what a money pit the club was, however, and quickly offloaded it in turn it to a local property developer by the name of Malcolm Curtis. Soon, Curtis had sold all the land around the stadium, car park and training ground, to himself for a mere £500,000 before walking away from a financial mess with the club on the slide.

I went in again as chairman in March 2009 at the request of a couple of local businessmen who were trying manfully to clean up the cesspit, but the state of the club was way beyond my ability to sort out and I had to resign after just six months. Relegation from the Conference was inevitable, then from Conference South.

A new owner named George Rolls, formerly chairman of Cambridge United, had arrived and put the club into administration after the previous board had desperately tried not to leave the club's creditors in the lurch. Rolls was now deeply mistrusted by a long-suffering fan base that could no longer discern who was a good guy and who bad, having seen so many administrators and board members. Managers kept coming and going, too. Now, new attempts locally were being made to oust Rolls.

It had all become sour and miserable, and depressing to those of us who retained a love for the club but for their own health and sanity could no longer be involved and had to watch from afar. My own sadness had increased during the season with the death of the club's genial president, Bob Lucas, aged 84, who had been a goalkeeper then physiotherapist with the club for 60 years, and a rock to me when I was chairman. He was, too, a beacon of probity. Now he was gone and with him went a big part of the club's conscience.

At least there was good grace shown by the dignified Martyn Rogers, the latest Weymouth manager – whom I had sought to get for the club from Tiverton in my first spell as chairman before Claridge had taken the job – as he instructed his team to form a guard of honour and applaud the Truro team out on to the pitch.

Weymouth offered largesse to Truro very quickly after the game had kicked off, too, their defence wide open as Marcus Martin raced through to put the home side ahead. A surprising equaliser came through Dan Smith, tapping in after a shot by Jamie Mudge had hit a post.

Again Truro took the lead, though, when Scott Walker scored for the home side from the penalty spot after Ben Gerring had brought down the lively former Exeter striker Les Afful. Weymouth were lucky to make it to the interval just a goal behind, with Barry Hayles, once of Fulham and who travelled down to the South West every other weekend from his South East base, hitting the crossbar with a fierce shot.

Weymouth surprised again with an equaliser early in the second half when Mudge's free-kick was deflected into his own net by Barry

McConnell and their safety was looking assured. Oh no. A late goal by Joe Broad, a former Weymouth player, made it 3-2 at the final whistle to the home side.

This being non-League football, there were no scenes of fans listening to radios for coverage of other games as championship and relegation issues unfolded in higher leagues. This was about trying to get texts from a mate who might be hearing from someone at another ground. Then the news filtered through and Weymouth could celebrate in their own relieved way, if not with Truro's gusto. Didcot had lost 3-0 at home, and Weymouth were safe to endure another season of potential ownership wrangles and politicking. They looked on enviously as Truro received the Southern League shield, which bore the name of Weymouth, twice, as champions in 1965 and 1966, along with those of Tottenham, Southampton and Watford from the early part of the 20th century.

'I am a very proud Cornishman today,' said the watching Chris Webb, now Truro vice-chairman and back in his property maintenance business after leaving his full-time position with the club following the cutbacks after Heaney's troubles of 2008. 'I suppose it does all go back to the day that I knocked on Kevin's door. It has all been down to his enthusiasm and passion. When Kevin says he is going to do something, he does it.'

Heaney had not always been as popular with everyone employed by the club, however, having parted company with, at last count, five managers during his tenure. 'The trying times have been with managers,' he confessed. 'I have found them more difficult to deal with than players. We are a progressive club that wants to go through the leagues and you have to have the right personnel. If a manager has never managed above a certain level, suddenly it's hit and miss. Has he got contacts? Is he up for the challenge? Does he have the commitment?'

The latest incumbent was a former Tottenham apprentice in Lee Hodges, also a player with Plymouth and Torquay, and who had taken to the position readily at the age of 36 the previous summer, having come to end his playing days at Truro. It seemed certain that he would get at least another year with a crack at Conference South. That league, Heaney said, would be an even bigger step up. 'We will have bigger sponsors coming on board, and gates will be bigger. Hopefully we will average 700 or 800. Eventually I think we would get 1,500 to 2,000 for the Conference National, maybe even 2,500 with away supporters who would come down for a weekend. It's about educating the community in Cornwall as to what's available here. They don't know enough about the club. I have got four new staff coming in next year to sort out branding and marketing.'

Heaney reckoned it would mean smaller, rather than bigger, losses at the club. I asked how much this had cost him. A loss of £100,000 a season, perhaps? 'No, much more than that,' he replied quickly. Indeed, some in non-League circles calculated that Heaney could be underwriting up to £500,000 some years, with all the wages and travelling. 'Travel costs are high but we are in a routine,' he said. 'All the players live in Devon and Cornwall and for away games we meet at Exeter and drop them back there. We do overnight stays if the journey is more than four hours. We have a nice luxury coach these days with beds and leather chairs on it. It's not like the old days where you feel every bump.'

Heaney cited a game at Cambridge City on a Tuesday night, where they left at 7 a.m. After a break at 11 a.m., they reached Cambridge at 3 p.m., ready for a pre-match meal at 4 p.m. They won the game and arrived back home at 6 a.m., 23 hours after setting off. There were League One teams who did not enjoy such treatment.

There had been a temptation this season for Heaney to get out of Truro, to circumvent promotions and get himself into the Football

League. He had been approached by a consortium looking to take over struggling Plymouth Argyle, who were in administration, had been docked 10 points and appeared likely to be relegated to League Two. They had even been unable to pay their players. The consortium had attempted to involve Heaney, possibly to develop the club's Home Park ground and release money that would eat into their £17 million debts.

'It's not rocket science to work out that I understand development,' said Heaney. 'And I suppose people would argue that I am not a bad chairman. That doesn't mean to say that I think I have made it. I haven't. But some would see me as an attractive package to take their club forward. But my loyalty and my love is towards Truro. It's my baby. I have taken this club from nothing. Why would I throw that away when we are in the most exciting time in the club's history? I am on a mission and that mission is to produce a stadium and a full-time professional team in the next three to five years.'

It was easy to be sceptical about Kevin Heaney – property developer, bringing those London ways down to the South West. I had seen it myself elsewhere. Ever since Roman Abramovich, there were plenty of businessmen who thought they rather liked the idea of stepping into the football arena. It brought publicity; it brought excitement. It brought a release from the anonymity of an office.

It was one way in which the Premier League had had a significant impact on the game at this level, even if the competition seemed distant – not just in miles – from backwaters such as Truro and Weymouth. In non-League football, indulgence was more affordable, even if many wealthy men still found themselves less wealthy.

The drawback was the criticism and the carping that took many owners by surprise. They expected fans to be mild and grateful at such levels. Not a bit of it. Actually, they could hear the criticism more loudly. In full stadiums and on well-visited websites, the noise was just a general din. At small grounds and on the less-trammelled message boards, the barbs were more audible and hurtful individually.

The test for Kevin Heaney would be if the club hit a glass ceiling, if the promotions dried up. Then, the idea of mediocrity for a man with such a winning mentality can pall. In fairness, he had already shown himself to be in it for the long haul, however. And to Truro and back, especially up from South West to North East, was quite some haul.

Chapter 22

FINDING PAUL GASCOIGNE

NEWCASTLE IS A CITY devoted to two great passions: football and partying. The 52,000-capacity St James' Park is one of the great modern day cathedrals of the game. Its black-and-white striped Magpies carry the hopes and dreams of the North East region – at least in the county of Northumberland, north of their fierce rivals Sunderland and Middlesbrough – in the same way that Barcelona do in Catalonia.

A few hundred yards away from one of the few big city centre stadiums remaining is the Bigg Market, a collection of bars and pubs devoted to post-match recreation before that gives way to the serious business of the hen and stag nights. The title of a book by one Billy Furious summed up neatly the combination of those twin interests of following Newcastle United and the seemingly inevitable drowning of sorrows that accompanied it: *And They Wonder Why We Drink?*

It was a club, a footballing city, like no other in England. With its surrounding districts, Newcastle embraced more than half a million people. Many similarly populous places, such as Sheffield and Bristol, had two clubs but here attention was firmly focused on one. Every cough and spit of the Mags were covered in voracious local media outlets – they still had morning and evening newspapers – and every move of the players recorded if they dared venture out into the fleshpots. Even if they didn't, word would quickly get round about anything untoward occurring behind their closed doors.

Because of the location 60 miles south of the Scottish border and the harshness of its winters, Newcastle felt a long way from anywhere, which appeared to deceive footballers into believing that they were well away from the bright lights and out of range of the prying press, the microphones and the cameras. How mistaken they would be.

Into this environment was born Paul Gascoigne on 27 May 1967. And in this environment, first growing up on the Gateshead side of the river Tyne, began his drinking as accompaniment to the sparkling footballing talent that would take him from his home town club to stages and stadiums in London, Rome, Glasgow and Liverpool. (Middlesbrough, they didn't like to talk about in these parts.)

To this environment he returned when it was all over, a sad and seemingly washed-up figure living in hotels. Not only the drinking had caught up with him. He had had obsessive compulsive disorder and bulimia; he had been diagnosed as bipolar – manic depression in old-speak – and also used cocaine. He was nursing all manner of psychological issues, from witnessing the accidental death of a close friend in childhood to the ending of his marriage. When he was sectioned on a local psychiatric ward, the half-time DJ at St James' played the Pink Floyd epic 'Shine On You Crazy Diamond'.

And from this environment, finally, Gazza knew he had to get away after that madcap lager, chicken and fishing rod excursion to the Raoul Moat siege in Rothbury. Within England, you couldn't get much further away than Bournemouth, 350 miles distant on the South Coast. He was an expert in treatment centres, having been in the Priory, the Sporting Chance clinic and Cottonwood de Tucson in Arizona – more than once at a couple of them. This time he opted to go to an organisation called the Providence Projects, run by a Tottenham fan and recovering alcoholic called Steve Spiegel.

Spiegel had always looked at Gazza's career and thought he might be able to help one day. He contacted him and offered him a place.

He believed that his establishment differed from others and might be more suited to Paul. It retained the same principle of recovery through abstinence, based on the twelve steps of Alcoholics Anonymous, but patients lived in flats in the community rather than behind the closeted walls of some retreat or country house. They would then come in daily to lectures and group sessions at a central house.

The idea was to integrate them immediately back into the community, to teach them to exist within it, with all its temptations; AA, after all, was supposed to be a bridge to normal living. They would have to pass pubs, off licences and even drug dealers on street corners. Bournemouth had plenty of temptations, too, like any seaside town.

Gazza had turned down Spiegel's offer at first, to be followed by a couple of abortive trips to Bournemouth. The time came for desperate measures, though; the problem with drowning sorrows for alcoholics like Gazza, after all, is that the sorrows learn how to swim. Finally he rang earnestly for help. Spiegel drove up to the North East to collect him.

I saw some pictures in the papers of Gazza out in the streets of Bournemouth and let some months pass. Then I contacted Steve Spiegel to see if Paul was staying sober and might be ready to talk. To my surprise, a message came back that he remembered me, remembered from 10 years earlier an in-depth interview we had done for my then employers, the *Observer*, after he had come back sober from Arizona when he was with Everton. Yes, he would be willing to see me, would even allow me to file some material for my current newspaper, the *Daily Express*.

And so I came to this rambling old house in a residential street in Boscombe, the suburb back from the seafront and which housed the town's football club that was now known as AFC Bournemouth, rather than Bournemouth and Boscombe FC, after becoming another bailed out by a supporters' trust. The house looked as if might have been an old-style hotel or boarding house in years gone by, with bathrooms along the corridor, of the sort in which Tess stabbed to death Alec D'Urberville, Bournemouth being Sandbourne in Thomas Hardy's Wessex.

I was led up several flights of stairs, through fire doors, past rooms where group sessions were going on. I could see a big poster saying 'Hope' through one small window to a room. In the converted attic were the offices where Steve Spiegel awaited. Paul, undoubtedly nervous about being interviewed when so often it had come out badly for him, wanted him to be present.

I sipped the coffee made for me for a few minutes and wondered and worried whether Paul would show. I needn't have. Soon he bounced in, wearing jeans, pristine trainers and white T-shirt, and trendy grey woollen cardigan. A smile appeared. It was toothy, indeed, but his dentures – the result of up to 30 cans a day of energy drink he had often consumed having rotted so many of his teeth – needed repairing.

There was a light back in the eyes of the man the nation had taken to its heart as he wept in that World Cup semi-final more than 20 years ago. Since then he had evoked in us a range of emotions from pleasure through sadness to sheer fear that we might suddenly learn of his premature death, if not through the drinking itself then as a result of an accident caused by it.

He looked gaunt and his hair was thinning as he approached his 44th birthday. He was coming back to physical health, though, with gym work. More important, he was discovering an emotional health. Most important of all, he was sober. I told him it was a relief to see him having pulled back from the brink and he thanked me. I told him that there was still a vast fund of goodwill out there for him. 'The country cares for me, I know that,' he said. 'And I take everything on board people say. But now I have to do everything for myself. I'm more at peace with everything and enjoying myself.'

It did begin to sound as if completing the three-month course at Providence had brought him to an understanding of the illness of addiction and how to arrest it, one day at a time. It had certainly brought him to his knees. Following the Rothbury excursion, came a car crash which hospitalised him. Then there was a court appearance for drink-driving before he finally surrendered.

Gascoigne insisted to me that he spent the first half of the year hardly drinking, his tolerance for alcohol of the old days when he could drink bottles of wine and spirits in a session now gone. Instead, he was a recluse, just leaving his flat in the upmarket Newcastle suburb of Jesmond to buy food or, once a month, a few cans of lager. 'The only way I stayed sober was to stay in the house,' he said.

Then, one June Sunday in the summer of 2010, he decided to go to a pub to watch a World Cup game. He was immediately harassed, he said, and called a friend to drive him home. The car arrived with the friend's girlfriend driving. Minutes later, the Vauxhall Astra ploughed into a lamp post and bollards at high speed in the city's Quayside district. 'I woke up the next day with a broken nose, a cut over my eye, a cut on my arms, broken ribs and a punctured lung,' he said. 'They told me I died in the ambulance twice. My dad and my sister were standing next to the bed and she took a photo of me that shocked me.'

It wouldn't have been Gazza, though, without an element of black humour. 'I went home 12 days later and didn't have my house keys so I got up on a ladder to get into the house, fell off and did another rib,' he added. 'I went back to the hospital and they put me on an oxygen machine to pump up the lung again. Then I accidentally switched it off and was turning blue.' Now Spiegel, smiling, slipped back into his office, clearly sensing that Paul was growing comfortable with his disclosures, a relaxing Gascoigne barely noticing him depart.

After coming out of hospital, the drinking took off again, the amounts small but the dependence still the same. 'Four cans was enough for a couple of weeks, because I hadn't been drinking for a while, but then it became six,' he said. 'Ask anyone, I could drink a bottle of whisky but give me six cans and I will be drunk. It was getting too much for me. I was trying to fill my days doing my dad's garden or things for my mum, playing football in the street with my nephews Cameron and Joe, trying to get through till 8 o'clock till I allowed myself a drink.'

Then, one night in July, he was watching the news and saw events unfolding in Rothbury. He jumped in a taxi. 'The driver was shaking like a leaf,' he recalled. 'He was saying, "Paul, don't go there." I told him just to keep driving. I wouldn't be long. I just thought Moat needed help, maybe someone to talk to. But because I was in a bad way myself, maybe I didn't realise how bad a way he was in. I thought I could take him fishing, because stuff like that has worked on me.

'But his situation was different from mine. I was oblivious that he shot a policeman. I feel guilty sometimes now looking back because he shot a copper in the face and killed someone else. But there's things I don't remember. I was in blackout. It was stupid of me but at that time, that was the place I was in. I would still try to help now that I am sober but not to that extent. Bloody hell – fishing rod, four cans, some bread and a bit of chicken?'

Gazza lasted five weeks at Providence the first time before heading back home, spooked by a newspaper report that people were buying him cans in treatment, which he vehemently denied to me. In his state of mind at the time, he wondered what the point of getting well was if people were still going to lie about him. He then came back to Bournemouth for another 11 days but was still thirsty for Newcastle.

There, one night he drank a quarter bottle of gin. The next afternoon, he was in Jesmond at a cashpoint when a woman – after getting a photo of him with her two sons – reported him to the police. He was unsteady, she claimed, as he was about to get back into his MG sports car. Police arrested him in the car, 142 mg of alcohol still in his system against the limit of 35mg.

At a court appearance, the judge told him he could expect to go to jail. The next day, he collapsed at the cottage he was now renting in Burradon, North Tyneside. Police were called and, it was reported, he was arrested on suspicion of possessing cocaine. 'I never was a drug taker,' he insisted. 'I have slipped up with cocaine a few times, I know that, when people have offered me a line in a pub toilet, but I have had to take some of the stories about me because I have done it before.'

Now Gazza knew he had to give Providence a proper try and again rang Spiegel, who agreed to fetch him. This time, Gascoigne lasted the course, the judge in the drink-driving case accepting in his absence that treatment was more beneficial than a prison cell. He was given an eight-week sentence suspended for a year on top of a three-year driving ban.

'When I was in the box at that appearance, I was scared of going to jail,' he admitted. 'But the judge was fair on me. Sometimes during the treatment, I thought it might be harder than jail, mind.' Providence, he added, had sorted him out like no other place had, though clearly all had played a part in helping him on his journey to recognition that he was finally ready to recover properly.

'I've been different places for different things,' he acknowledged. 'I went to Arizona once for Red Bull. I was drinking 30 cans a day.' He had also been hooked on the child's medicine Calpol, he said. 'After I was sectioned in 2008, the police sent me to the Priory and I sorted out my obsessive compulsive disorder (OCD), which I am 90 per cent cured of now,' he added. 'Moving the curtains, locking the door and touching it, having the coat hangers all the same way. I don't do any of that today. That other 10 per cent, well everyone has a bit of OCD.'

And his eating disorders? 'I did binge and vomit, yes, but I stopped all that in my 20s when I was worried about my weight. When I was drinking I never liked to eat. When I was drunk, I would eat then be sick and carry on drinking. I went to treatment centres for other people, for my family, for my managers, for the papers. This time I came back for myself.'

While at Providence, he made a deeper and more detailed attempt to deal with many of the demons that had assailed him down the years, not least the ruins of his relationship with ex-wife Sheryl, son Regan and stepchildren Mason and Bianca. A documentary about them had recently laid bare the pain all round. 'That was my programme but I realised I didn't want to be with her and decided not to do it any more,' he said. 'But I had signed a contract and she went ahead and did it and changed it to *Surviving Gazza*. I never got paid for it and I never watched it.'

Neither did he watch the ITV reality show *I'm a Celebrity Get Me Out of Here* when Sheryl was in the jungle while he was in treatment. 'The people in treatment with me refused to talk about it, which was good, the counsellors didn't mention it and the lads in the house turned the TV off when it came on.

'I would like one day to see the kids. I don't like it when they go to the papers and say "I don't want to see my dad" but I understand why they might say it. I can't let it ruin my sobriety. I am not being selfish. I would just rather the kids see me when I am better.'

What kept him going through the demanding daily regime of group sessions, workshops, one-to-one counselling and evening AA meetings was the thought of making it to the treatment centre's passing-out ritual in a green chair and receiving the commemorative coin awarded to those who have successfully completed the programme in front of up to 50 of his recovery peers. 'The buzz was unbelievable,' he said of the moment it finally happened after five months of treatment. 'Nothing is going to beat a World Cup semi-final or European Championship but it was a different buzz. The hairs on the back of my neck stood up.'

I asked him about how life changed for him after Italia '90. 'Twenty years ago? Life is kicking on,' he replied. 'Football went a bit mad, didn't it?' So, too, did he at the 1991 FA Cup final when he emerged for Tottenham against Nottingham Forest in a hyperactive state and quickly damaged cruciate knee ligaments with a reckless hack at Gary Charles that delayed his move to Lazio of Rome by a year. Surely he was on something, as rumour had it? 'I had Valium the night before to calm me down,' he admitted. 'But on the day it was just adrenalin. I came out so hyper.'

Gazza also broke his leg while at Lazio and in all his absences from the game totalled four years. Some of the injuries were clearly down to alcohol, if not directly from being drunk then as a result of his dulled reaction and physical condition due to the drinking and its effect on mind and muscle. He could defend his career with some justification, however. 'I achieved more than enough,' he insisted. 'I played in a World Cup semi-final and a European Championship semi. I always went for record transfer fees, from Newcastle to Tottenham to Lazio to Rangers. All you have to do is look at my trophies. I won six awards in two years in Glasgow and an FA Cup with Spurs.'

There had been one thing he wished he had done, however: played for Manchester United under Sir Alex Ferguson, who initially wanted to sign Gascoigne from Newcastle. Gazza instead chose Tottenham but, when he was leaving Lazio, phoned Ferguson to ask if he could now come to Old Trafford. That ship had sailed, however. 'The only regret is that I didn't get to work with Sir Alex,' said Gascoigne. 'It's a massive regret. I worked with some great managers in Bobby Robson, Terry Venables and Walter Smith but I would have loved to have been managed by him. He talked to me but he wouldn't sign me. He was deciding whether Eric Cantona was staying at the time. Cantona stayed, so fair enough.

'But I just knew I wasn't going there, even if Cantona went. You only mess with Sir Alex once. I have been to the training ground since and he showed me around and we had a chat. He is a great man. I am just glad he forgave me eventually for not signing for United that first time, but it took him six years to speak to me again.'

His own experience was clearly why Gascoigne would urge Wayne Rooney to remember what he had at Manchester United after the shenanigans of the autumn when it seemed he might be leaving the club, only for sanity to prevail after all the brinkmanship.

'The only thing I can think of it is that it was agents messing with his head,' said Gascoigne. 'Deep inside, I know he loves Manchester United. Why go anywhere else? He's got a lovely wife and family and the best manager in the world in Sir Alex Ferguson. Who would want to change that?'

And the money, reportedly £200,000 a week? 'The first transfer that had me shaking my head was a left back who went to Chelsea for £79,000 a week. That shows you what Wayne is worth. Just look at some of the goals he scores.' Gascoigne had less time for Carlos Tevez at Manchester City, however. 'I can't get my head around someone who's on £240,000 a week and gets homesick and wants to go home. What's that all about?

'When I joined Rangers, I told Walter Smith I wasn't bothered about the wages. I just wanted to play. Players have got to look at it financially but also where they want to be playing. There are players on half as much as Wayne and nowhere near the player he is. If Wayne has a long career the money will take care of itself. Coleen's got her work too, and it helps to have someone in a relationship working for their money'. Citing Rooney's goal of the season, an acrobatic volley against Manchester City, Gascoigne added: 'If he keeps scoring goals like that nobody will question the money. The good thing for Manchester United is, even if they are paying him

£200,000 a week, they can easily get that back from him from a transfer. They will be in profit.

'Sir Alex has had a good effect on him. Rooney's got that fiery head and that's good, you don't want to lose that, but he does have to lose that snapping at referees and upsetting everybody. He should take it as a compliment if he's getting kicked and whacked because that means they fear him.'

There were many who saw Rooney as the new Gascoigne: Wazza and Gazza and all that. The similarity was largely down to the pair's kindred-spirit working-class background and any excesses of off-field behaviour rather than talent on it. Gascoigne was the more natural and intuitive player; Rooney's game was more physical, less skilful. 'No one is as good as me,' said Gascoigne, that mischievous grin breaking out. 'No, I always say that. I wouldn't like to put pressure on him. There was only one Paul Gascoigne and there is only one Wayne Rooney. He's good all right.'

What about all the pre-season nightclubbing, Rooney being pictured urinating down an alleyway and with a cigarette in his hand; the exposé in a Sunday newspaper of him consorting with prostitutes; an earlier revelation that he owed £700,000 to a bookmaker friend of Michael Owen, his teammate now at United? 'Sir Alex Ferguson won't let Wayne get out of control,' Gascoigne insisted. 'He's got a wife and kid now. The press made me a celebrity. I liked going to premieres and to drink with celebrities but he is already a celebrity. He's got a wife at home that he loves. He's got to learn from his mistakes and if anything goes wrong now, it's his own doing. But Sir Alex won't let him go wrong.

'All these things in life you learn. If he did owe Michael Owen's bookie some money, well when you are younger you get bored and they gamble, but he shouldn't be bored now he has a kid. He's got himself through a sticky patch and can stay at the top. You have to be able to make mistakes to be able to learn from them and he's still a young man.'

What would be Gascoigne's advice to him now? 'Just keep on doing what he is doing. People will be jealous and envious of him. It's great when you become famous but then they knock you back down. But Sir Alex will keep him grounded.'

While Gascoigne may have had admiring and soothing words for Rooney, he was less forgiving of certain aspects of the modern Premier League that he now followed on television. 'One guy in a game I was watching made eight passes badly and I am thinking, "Fuck me. These are Premiership players." No wonder fans are getting frustrated when they see that kid on £80,000 a week and he can't even pass a ball straight. Not once but eight times.

'I don't think I have seen anyone really run at a player and beat them. You see Gareth Bale doing it to get a cross in but not someone going for goal. Sometimes I find it hard to watch when we are bringing in foreign players for nine million quid and they can't trap a bag of cement when we have got young kids not being given the chance to play.'

How would he fare in the modern game? 'Me? They wouldn't get the ball off me,' he said with another smile – as long as he had an old England teammate at Euro '96 alongside. 'I would just need a Paul Ince to do my work and get the ball for me.'

Gascoigne was now getting back into the game, had gone to the Carling Cup final at Wembley between Birmingham City and Arsenal – where he had not been recognised by a steward trying to deny him access to a hospitality area. 'It was good for my humility,' said Gascoigne, who had graced the national stadium, even disgraced himself, but never been anonymous there. Spiegel also took him to Madrid for Tottenham's Champions League quarter-final against Real, helping him with his fear of flying.

Also as his recovery was developing, with him now in aftercare in Bournemouth, not only was he getting his act together, he was taking it on the road with a series of evenings at theatres through the summer and autumn of 2011. They would feature him and Jimmy Greaves, another former England player in recovery from alcoholism with some 30 years head start on Gascoigne, in conversation and answering questions from the audience.

Part of the reason for the tour was down to putting right his tangled financial affairs, which had seen him be too generous with some people close to him. He was also coming to an arrangement with Her Majesty's Revenue and Customs over back taxes. His recovery demanded that not only did he sort it all out, but he also got over his resentment towards people he perceived as having taken advantage of him. 'I was on good money at Lazio but I gave most of it away,' he said. 'I drank a lot away, yes, but also the divorce cost me a lot and agents have taken a lot. I have been stitched up for millions but I can get it all back. I can take my time.'

After the tour, he wanted to get back into football in some capacity, he said, but was in no rush. He had played the game at a feverish pace, having seen things more clearly and quickly than others on the field, but now it was about putting his foot on the ball after having made a series of bad decisions. 'A lot of people have offered me work or help, including six Premier League managers,' said Gascoigne. 'Jose Mourinho asked me to go to Milan to see him. I was also an ambassador for the FA, going to go to South Africa, and working on the World Cup bid but I lost out on that. I didn't want to let anyone down. In the end, I let myself down most.'

There was also the offer of the manager's job at Garforth Town of the Evo-Stik Northern Premier League from owner Simon Clifford. 'Simon was a nice guy but I wasn't sure about it,' Gascoigne explained. 'A few things went wrong. It wasn't his fault but it got a bit messy. He was offering me £10,000 a month but for that I had to go to all the schools, do signing sessions, turn up two hours before kick off to do a talk-in. I can make £10,000 just for a talk-in. I wanted to be a manager, not part of a circus."

He still wanted to manage, but realised just how tough it was, and how much tougher it was getting. 'I applied for the York City job but 70 people went for that and if that happens, then what chance have I got?' he wondered.

You suggest to him that coaching elite young players, maybe at the FA's new national coaching centre opening at Burton, might be the answer, with the English game crying out for ball carriers and passers. 'Some of the stuff I did on the pitch, I don't know how I did it. If I try and explain it to kids, they say "how did you do that?" So I have to show them.' The problem, Gascoigne added, was his hip. He had not long ago had an operation to insert a metal joint but it was knocked out of kilter in the car accident and now needed to be reset. 'That's why I would get frustrated,' he said. 'I would say to kids, "I want you to turn and beat two" and have to show them how to do it. I need to get the hip sorted first.'

Otherwise, he was physically in better shape than he had been for years. 'My weight is 11 stone 10 pounds and I am starting to put muscle back in,' he said, showing me a stomach without fat. 'I like being around 12 stones. My playing weight was 12 stones 3 pounds. I've been training twice a day for the last three weeks but I can't go running because of the hip. It's only gym work.'

He genuinely, at last, seemed to be getting the message about taking his abstinence from alcohol – taking life indeed – one day at a time. 'I don't know if I will drink again but I am not drinking today,' he said. 'That's all I can do. I'm dealing with my problems better. I am not in a hurry to get there now. I'm very happy now. I know I have been in this situation of being sober before but then I stopped going to AA meetings. I am not one of those who say I have made it. I am a recovering alcoholic. I will never make it. I am always recovering. I have to put my own house in order.

'I have felt like I have had an enormous brick wall in front of me but I am dismantling it brick by brick. I am making life the way I want it now. If it's a bad day, I try to get through it without a drink. If it's a good day, I make the most of it. I do know what it's like to be sober. I don't want to mess it up this time.

'An old woman stopped me in the street the other day and started poking me in the chest. She said, "Hey you, I know who you are. Get it right this time."' At the memory, he smiled the smile of the cheeky chappie who once enthralled the country but a smile which could no longer excuse his alcohol-stoked excesses, as he well knew.

We were done, after two hours of conversation where once two minutes would have been an effort for such a restless soul. He stood up and offered a handshake. 'Chee-ahs, Ian,' he said in his Geordie brogue. 'I enjoyed that.' Gazza enjoying an interview? Something definitely had changed. You knew it was for the better. You just hoped it was for good.

He had been through the mill for two decades now and deserved recovery. His abilities and achievements on the pitch could never be decried nor underestimated despite the episodes off the field. They had been due to a sickness in his soul that he was now healing. As he took responsibility for his old excesses and errors, the goodness and humanity that was always in his heart was now ready to emerge rather than be submerged by the illness, with all its bitterness and resentment. Gazza was turning into Paul Gascoigne and the man he was intended to be before alcohol robbed him of his full potential.

In many ways, his had been the story of the English game over those two decades. There had been great events on the field – the only place, he once said, where he ever felt truly safe – and exhibitions that nothing happening off of it could sully. Away from the arena, however, a host of damaging events had occurred that made you wonder how much better it could have been for participant and watcher alike had the sickness been arrested earlier and better decisions been made.

In that time, had the Premier League been good for the game? It depended who you talked to; those who had benefited from it or those who had suffered. It had certainly been a huge success financially, the football slicker and quicker, if not always as skilful and entertaining as when it began 20 years earlier. Out of the dysfunction of the 1980s emerged a whole new ball game, with grand new stadiums and a place at the centre of the country's popular culture. Superficially, the game had never been healthier.

Then again, it had never been unhealthier either. Its biggest clubs carried huge debt to be serviced from revenue they hoped would not dry up, although many fleeced, cash-strapped fans were wobbling worryingly in their support. It was also sad to see so many clubs dining off the scraps that the gluttons of the Premier League let fall to the floor, heartening though it may have been to witness them soldiering on amid so much adversity.

When the Premier League was conceived, Gazza was still a simple lad from Gateshead who just wanted to play football. Then the bright lights turned his head, as did agents and hangers-on, and his illness was ignited. We watched it all, sensed that it would either implode or explode.

When it exploded, Paul Gascoigne at last, thankfully, settled into a less frenetic, less money-driven life where he reappraised his priorities. His recovery would need humility and daily nurturing of his abstinence to sustain him in a new healthy lifestyle, physically and emotionally. Perhaps the modern game he helped create could learn from the symbolism of his story.

POSTSCRIPT

THOUGH THEIR NEW STAND wasn't ready for opening day and they had to wait two weeks to play a home game, the 2010/11 season began so well for Blackpool. They amazed all by winning 4-0 at Wigan in their opening game and did what Gypsy Leah Petulengro said they would: went straight to the top of the Premier League. It only lasted for a few hours, however, until Chelsea beat West Bromwich Albion 6-0.

Still, 'Pool looked like surviving at Christmas after a first half to the season that included a win at Liverpool and in which they captured the country's imagination with their fresh air and fun. That Stanley Holloway monologue about *Albert and the Lion* was proving prophetic:

So straight 'way the brave little feller
Not showing a morsel of fear
Took 'is stick with the 'orse's 'ead 'andle
And pushed it in Wallace's ear!

Come the start of 2011, however, the Tangerines struggled and were finally, sadly, relegated on the last day of the season by one point after a 4-2 defeat by Manchester United. As the next verse had it:

You could see that the lion didn't like it
For giving a kind of a roll

He pulled Albert inside the cage with 'im
And swallowed the little lad... whole!

Manager Ian Holloway entertained us royally to the end, even when fined £25,000 for fielding an allegedly weakened selection at Aston Villa. 'The fat lady has sung and I don't like her tune,' he said at Old Trafford.

Charlie Adam was sold to Liverpool in the summer for £8 million, and other important players also departed, notably David Vaughan to Sunderland, and DJ Campbell to Queens Park Rangers.

Despite that, Holloway not only decided to stay at Bloomfield Road, but also built another promotion-challenging side in 2011/12 which beat Birmingham City in the play-offs and returned to Wembley to face West Ham in the Championship final.

During the course of the 2011/12 season, it was revealed that Owen Oyston was paid a staggering £11 million as a director's fee for the Premier League season. The club's players' wage bill was revealed to have been £13.5 million, compared to the best payers Chelsea's £189.5 million.

For Portsmouth, our season under scrutiny of 2010/11 was about regrouping and attempting to sell the club. Having offloaded the high earners, it did look early on as if Pompey might be Championship relegation fodder but manager Steve Cotterill steadied the ship and they finished a reasonable 16th. A takeover of the club was finally announced on 1 June 2011, when Convers Sports Initiatives, controlled by a London-based businessman Vladimir Antonov, bought out Balram Chainrai and his Sports Holdings (Asia) Ltd.

Coventry City sacked their manager Aidy Boothroyd in March 2011 after a run that saw them win just once in 16 games. He was one of 15 managerial changes in the 24-club Championship that season.

For both Pompey and Coventry, matters worsened over the next

12 months. At Fratton Park, administrators returned to ply their expensive services after the bank that Antonov owned was seized by the Lithuanian Government and criminal proceedings issued against him. Portsmouth were docked 10 points, which effectively relegated them to League One for the 2011/12 season. The Football League chairman warned that if no buyer could be found, Pompey could be liquidated in the summer of 2012. The same fate hung over Coventry, who were also relegated to League One with owners SISU no longer willing to bear losses.

England's qualifying campaign for Euro 2012 proceeded no more than adequately as Fabio Capello and his players sought to redeem themselves in the eyes of the public. There were wins over Bulgaria, Switzerland and Wales but a goalless draw at Wembley with Montenegro (population 625,000) told of enduring problems. Indeed, any time England came up against anyone decent, they continued to labour, being defeated at home by France and held by Ghana in friendlies.

In the end, draws with Switzerland and Montenegro and wins over Bulgaria and Wales were enough for England to qualify for Euro 2012. But before that, in February 2012, Capello walked away having been told to ditch as captain John Terry – whom the manager had reinstated after a year's punishment following the Wayne Bridge affair – due to a pending court case concerning an alleged racist remark towards the Queens Park Rangers defender Anton Ferdinand.

After a spring of clamour for Harry Redknapp to replace Capello, the FA opted for West Bromwich Albion's safe-pair-of-hands Roy Hodgson. The decision was based not only on his long coaching career that took in international spells with Switzerland and Finland, but also his greater suitability for involvement with fresh coaching initiatives based at the new national centre of St George's Park, near Burton.

It was a decision that failed to excite the footballing public but at least confirmed that the new chairman David Bernstein – who had laudably abstained during a laughable re-election process for the FIFA President Sepp Blatter – was ready to do the more thoughtful, rather than easy populist, thing.

The FA's travails continued. After losing their World Cup bid, and being roundly criticised for their handling of it, the FA lost their director of marketing and communications, Julian Eccles, on top of the departures of other senior figures in Lord Triesman and Ian Watmore. Few seemed to lament Eccles going and fewer probably even noticed.

The FA's general manager Alex Horne commissioned a confidential staff survey designed to get the organisation into the *Sunday Times* 100 best companies list. It backfired spectacularly. There was a 70 per cent fall in faith in him compared with his predecessor Watmore and a general discontent within the FA, as well as a call for more racial and gender diversity at senior levels. The move from Soho Square up to Wembley probably didn't help, with Olympic Way a wind tunnel of a walk to work in midwinter.

The only consolation for the FA was that FIFA was even more disgraced after the World Cup process. A host of allegations and counter-claims emerged that led to vice-president Jack Warner quitting and presidential candidate Mohamed bin Hamman being suspended for alleged bribery attempts. Sepp Blater came through a cursory internal investigation.

The Department for Culture, Media and Sport heard from all the major figures in the game during its inquiry into governance. Lord Triesman alleged that there had been corruption in the World Cup bidding process. In the end, the FA agreed to two new independent directors on its executive board: businessman Roger Devlin and former Millwall chief executive Heather Rabbatts CBE. Twenty years after deputy chief executive Pat Smith had played such a key role in the establishment of the Premier League, the FA finally had a woman in a position of influence again.

After watching FA Cup finals for years at the nearby stadium, Wembley FC had a cup final of their own in 2011, though sadly they were beaten 1-0 by Sandhurst in the Combined Counties League Premier competition at Farnborough FC. They finished 14th in the league. Things picked up a little the following year as they finished 10th. They also landed a sponsorship deal with the American beer company Budweiser, new sponsors of the FA Cup to replace E:ON, which involved the former England manager Terry Venables becoming Wembley's director of football. He insisted that it was more than a publicity stunt and he would be hands-on.

With three months of the 2010/11 season to go, Arsenal were in contention for four major trophies. They even beat Barcelona 2-1 in the Champions League last 16 at the Emirates. Then came a last-minute 2-1 defeat by Birmingham City in the Carling Cup final at Wembley and it all turned sour. The Gunners were beaten 3-1 in Barcelona in the return leg, lost 2-0 to Manchester United in the FA Cup and fell away in the league, finishing fourth in what had looked like a two-horse race between them and United at one point.

The mood began to turn against Arsène Wenger, who was urged to get out the club's cheque book and start buying some established players. 'In Arsène We Trust' turned into 'In Arsène We Rust'. It didn't help that amid a flurry of late-season defeats, the club increased season ticket prices by 6.5 per cent. Their lowest price of £985 made them the most expensive in the Premier League. Sadness off the field came with the death of the influential director Danny Fiszman from throat cancer in April 2011.

Ahead of the next season, having lost Cesc Fabregas to Barcelona, Wenger went on a late transfer rush reminiscent of an absent-minded gift hunter in a petrol station on Christmas Eve. Arsenal did recover from a bad start that included an 8-2 defeat by Manchester United, with Mikel Arteta – signed from Everton – finding his feet and youngster Alex Oxlade-Chamberlain both emerging as key players. They finished third, although silverware eluded them again. That is, except for Robin Van Persie, whose 30 league goals made him both the players' and journalists' choice for Player of the Year. He thus became the latest Arsenal hot property to give them a summer of anxiety as the more moneyed – notably Manchester City and Real Madrid – sought to get him on the cheap with just a year left on his contract.

Crawley Town's resources duly took them to the Conference title in 2010/11. AFC Wimbledon finished runners-up just ahead of Luton Town, who parted company with manager Richard Money in March and replaced him with his assistant Gary Brabin. The two clubs made it through to the play-off final at Manchester City's Etihad Stadium, the Dons squeaking into the Football League thanks to a 1-0 win courtesy of Danny Kedwell's penalty. Kedwell had turned down a move to Crawley the previous summer.

Rushden and Diamonds were expelled from the Conference after being unable to give the competition an assurance they would complete their fixtures the following season, due to debts believed to be near £1 million. The Northamptonshire club formed by the Dr Martens shoe manufacturer Max Griggs had risen up to the Football League since their formation in 1992 – the year the Premier League was formed in 1992, but were also refused entry to the Southern League and an AFC Rushden and Diamonds club was formed by supporters, who hastily entered a youth team into the Northants Senior League.

Luton again changed manager towards the end of the 2011/12 season, replacing Brabin with Paul Buckle. Buckle had previously been sacked by Bristol Rovers, whom he had joined after taking Torquay to the League Two play-offs. Buckle duly resurrected Luton's fading season and led them to the play-off final against York City at Wembley. Sadly for the Hatters, they fell at the final hurdle for the second year in a row, York winning 2-1 to return to the Football League after an absence of eight years.

Meanwhile, Crawley had another Cup run in 2011/12, losing to Stoke City in the fifth round, and won another promotion, to League One. Curiously, though, their manager Steve Evans departed with just a few games left to take over at Rotherham United of League Two.

Bradford City went on a decent run in League Two after their win at Barnet that 2010/11 season, including a 5-0 win over Oxford United, and it seemed as if they might be challenging for the play-offs. It was a mirage, however, and there was no hint of silver to mark 100 years since they won the FA Cup. After a 1-0 defeat in February 2011 at home to Chesterfield, who would win the title, manager Peter Taylor was sacked. He was replaced by former Valley Parade favourite, Peter Jackson.

Barnet looked for most of the 2011/12 season as if they would be relegated but chairman Tony Kleanthous sacked manager Mark Stimson on New Year's Day after a home defeat by Aldershot. From there, their fortunes gradually turned, first under caretaker Paul Fairclough, then former Bees manager Martin Allen, although he soon decamped to Notts County. He was succeeded by former Barnet striker Giuliano Grazioli, also once of Wembley FC and who had been working in Barnet's community trust department. With the input of Lawrie Sanchez, former Wimbledon and Northern Ireland manager, acting as a consultant, Barnet completed a remarkable escape from relegation by one point by beating Port Vale 1-0 – thanks also to Lincoln City's freefall. At the end of the season, Sanchez was appointed manager with Grazioli as his assistant. Sanchez was sacked with just a few games left of the next season in April 2012 with Barnet in trouble again, to be replaced by... Martin Allen. It worked, as he fashioned two final wins to keep Barnet up once more by the skin of their teeth.

Bradford City enjoyed a scarcely better season. Peter Jackson lasted just four games and was replaced by Phil Parkinson, formerly of Charlton, who took League Two's best supported club to 18th.

At the other end of the professional game, Manchester United won the Premier League in 2011 for their 19th top-flight title, surpassing Liverpool's record. Sir Alex Ferguson hit upon a striking partnership in pairing Wayne Rooney – who admitted during the season that he should not have questioned Ferguson's transfer policy – with Javier Hernandez. That partnership also took them to the 2011 Champions League final at Wembley, where they were beaten comfortably 3-1 by a magnificent Barcelona team. It showed that United were still some way short of greatness and needed new signings, perhaps even a marquee player who might excite as Cristiano Ronaldo once did. Lionel Messi was not about to leave Barca for Old Trafford, however. The game was due to mark the last appearances for United of Edwin Van Der Sar and Paul Scholes, who both retired with honour. Ryan Giggs signed another contract to make it 20 seasons of appearances in the Premier League.

In 2011 United became the first English club to take £100 million in commercial income in a financial year, up more than a third on the previous year. The increase helped compensate for a £5 million downturn in match-day revenue. At one point, just after Christmas, the club sent text messages to their supporters urging them to bring a friend to the game on 4 January against Stoke City. They remained ridiculously profitable, however, despite the servicing of almost £500 million worth of debt. They declared cash assets of £113 million, which Sir Alex had his eyes on as a transfer pot. The sizeable anti-Glazer faction continued to resent the costs of tickets – up 42 per cent in six seasons – and the servicing of debt; £400 million of interest payments made in the Glazers' tenure.

In the summer following the title win, Ferguson moved quickly to sign the Blackburn defender Phil Jones, Spain's Under-21 goalkeeper David de Gea and Aston Villa's Ashley Young for a total of £50 million. The moves – along with Ferguson summoning Paul Scholes out of retirement – were not enough to help United to a 20th Premier League title, however, and they were pipped in 2011/12 by Manchester City – those 'noisy neighbours' – on goal difference. City recovered from problems with prima donnas Carlos Tevez and Mario Balotelli to land their first title in 44 years as redemption for the often beleaguered, always cheerful, manager Roberto Mancini.

City did the double over United, by an astonishing 6-1 at Old Trafford and 1-0 at the Etihad late in the season. The hammer blow was struck, however, on an astonishing final day of the season when it seemed as if United had won the title by winning 1-0 at Sunderland only for Edin Dzeko and Sergio Aguero to score in added time for City to overcome QPR 3-2. There was significant financial disparity between the two clubs. It emerged that the amount going out of United, to debt-servicing and fees to the Glazers, topped £500 million while investment from City's new Abu Dhabi owners approached £1 billion.

Tottenham Hotspur enjoyed a wonderful run to the 2010/11 quarter-finals of the Champions League. Having trailed Young Boys of Berne 3-0 after half an hour in a qualifying round, they made it to the quarter-final but lost 5-0 on aggregate to Jose Mourinho's Real Madrid. The effort took its toll, and Spurs finished fifth in the Premier League and had to settle for a Europa, rather than Champions, League place. Despite missing much of the second half of the season with a hamstring injury, Gareth Bale was voted by his peers as the PFA's Player of the Year.

The next season, Spurs even looked as if they might win the title for a while, but amid speculation about Harry Redknapp as the new England manager, they faded and had to be content with fourth place, just seeing off Newcastle United, resurgent under Alan Pardew's management. Spurs did not even make the Champions League, despite finishing fourth. Chelsea winning the trophy in 2012 – of which, more later – meant that Tottenham were consigned to the Europa League. It cost Redknapp his job – the Spurs chairman David Levy deciding he wanted a change of manager.

Matthew Etherington enjoyed another good season in 2010/11 – and a season free from gambling as he continued his recovery, staying in close touch with Peter Kay and the Sporting Chance clinic. Stoke finished 13th in the League and reached the final of the FA Cup for the first time. Etherington recovered from a hamstring injury just in time for the final but Manchester City beat them 1-0 to take the trophy. Injuries too often intervened the next year, but Etherington had his life back.

The win over Aston Villa proved a rare highlight for Roy Hodgson at Liverpool and, after a 3-1 defeat at Blackburn in early January 2011, he was sacked by the club's new American owners. He was replaced by Kenny Dalglish, who interrupted a cruise in the Arabian Gulf to become a caretaker manager. Such was Dalglish's record thereafter, as Liverpool beat Chelsea and Manchester United to climb the table, that he was given the post full-time before the end of the season. They then lost their last two games of the 2010/11 season but sixth place gave them grounds for optimism that Dalglish would renew his rivalry with Sir Alex Ferguson of 20 years earlier on more equal terms at the top of the table.

That feeling was compounded by Dalglish being given £100 million to spend, including the £50 million banked from the sale of Fernando Torres to Chelsea. He recruited strikers Andy Carroll from Newcastle, for a club-record £35 million, and Luis Suarez from PSV Eindhoven, along with Jordan Henderson from Sunderland, Stewart Downing from Aston Villa and Charlie Adam.

Roy Hodgson was appointed WBA manager in place of Roberto Di Matteo and promptly led them away from relegation with a series of fine results – including a 2-1 win over Liverpool. Hodgson repeated the feat the following season of 2011/12, his competent and well organised Albion team winning 1-0 at Anfield to offer signs of why he was made England manager. It was a result typical of a poor Premier League campaign for Dalglish and his team, as they finished only eighth and saw Suarez banned for eight games after being found guilty by the FA of making racist remarks to the Manchester United full-back Patrice Evra.

Dalglish bought himself some time with Liverpool winning the Carling Cup, beating Birmingham City on penalties, and reaching the FA Cup final, thanks to Carroll, previously an expensive misfit, scoring the winner over Everton in the semi. Returning to Wembley, they were beaten 2-1 by Chelsea and soon Dalglish departed, with owners FSG making it plain that finishing so far off a Champions League place was not acceptable. In sacking director of football Damien Comolli a few weeks earlier, they had also shown their displeasure with the recruitment of players. In as replacement came the impressive and innovative young Swansea manager Brendan Rogers.

Gerard Houllier improved Villa's fortunes in the second half of the 2010/11 season as his training methods, disciplinary code and recruitment began to take shape. Darren Bent arrived from Sunderland for £24 million to score goals and lead Villa, after a brief flirtation with relegation, to ninth. However, Houllier struggled to recover in the eyes of the fans from his show of affection for Liverpool and fielded a weakened team in an FA Cup tie at Manchester City – something he admitted to me he later regretted.

Then in April 2011, he suffered a dissected aorta – a tear to the artery leading to the heart – and had to sit out the end of the season. It was nowhere near as serious as his episode at Liverpool and did not require surgery, but Villa were not willing to wait for him to recuperate through the summer before making decisions and they paid him off, to his great sadness.

After a messy recruitment process that saw former England manager Steve McClaren rejected due to fan protest, the Villa owner Randy Lerner hired Alex McLeish from relegated neighbours Birmingham City to even greater fan protest. McLeish endured a torrid 2011/12 season during which Bent was a long-term injury and Villa only narrowly avoided relegation, prompting the sack for McLeish. It emphasised the belief of Houllier – who continued to make a solid recovery – that the club needed root and branch reform. Norwich City's Paul Lambert became McLeish's replacement.

Sky Sports celebrated its 20 years on air by extending its portfolio with the acquisition of the Football League's television rights, the BBC deciding they could no longer afford them. Otherwise, the season for the satellite channel was blighted by the Andy Gray-Richard Keys sexism row involving their off-air comments about the assistant referee Sian Massey.

'Richard and Andy – key people in the early success of Sky Sports. Superstars,' said a sad Vic Wakeling, who was awarded a CBE in the Queen's Birthday Honours List in 2011. 'Andy in particular changed football commentary style forever and won a string of awards. Great shame they will be remembered for this.' The appropriately opinionated Gary Neville, having retired as a Manchester United player, was hired as a pundit and enjoyed a critically acclaimed first season. Neville was also recruited as an England coach by Roy Hodgson.

Within a week of my visit to Aldershot in early 2011, the club had sacked their manager Kevin Dillon after a fourth consecutive home defeat, at the hands of Oxford United. They moved quickly to replace him with Dean Holdsworth, the former Wimbledon striker, who had been in charge of Newport County of the Conference. Holdsworth took the Shots from 20th to a creditable 14th. They even looked a potential play-off team at one point. Marvin Morgan was suspended, fined and farmed out on loan to Dagenham and Redbridge. Hereford United climbed away from relegation in 2010/11, though were unable to do so the following year. Aldershot had a Carling Cup run that saw Manchester United come to the Rec, and finished the 2011/12 season a reasonable 11th.

Under Spencer Day, Chertsey Town finished runners-up in 2010/11 by three points to Guildford City in the Combined Counties League. They were allocated the one promotion place, however, due to Guildford failing to meet ground requirements, and placed in the Southern League's Division One Central. Day tendered his resignation at the end of the 2010/11 season and talked to a variety of other clubs about joining them but was prevailed upon to stay at Chertsey. He no longer wished to be involved in the finances of the club, however, but merely to manage the team.

During the next season, he accepted an offer from Conference South club Farnborough to become their manager. As well as leading them away from the relegation zone, he stabilised the club off the field, reluctantly agreeing to become the club's nominal owner and guaranteeing debts until new input could be found.

Blackburn Rovers were beaten in the fourth round of the FA Cup at Aston Villa in January 2011 and indeed struggled under Steve Kean through the second half of the season, saving themselves from relegation only on the last day by winning 3-2 at Wolverhampton Wanderers. QPR would thus be going back to Ewood Park to play Rovers in the Premier League after winning the Championship. Rangers promptly announced 40 per cent increases in season ticket prices – with the cheapest seat now £47, up from £20.

That following season of 2011/12 would be traumatic for both clubs. Kean continued to make regular 48-hour flying visits to India to meet with the new owners, and retained his job though many thought he would be sacked. Venky's declared him, 'unsackable', however, which simply rendered them hostages to fortune. Fan opposition to Kean reached a crescendo just before Christmas 2011 when the scale of abuse directed at him was graphically shown on TV during a home defeat to Bolton. He rode the storm with some dignity but Rovers were eventually relegated to great anguish within the town.

QPR just managed to survive on the last day – to the relief of their new owner Tony Fernandes. Fernandes had sanctioned the recruitment of expensive earners such as Joey Barton then sacked Neil Warnock and hired Mark Hughes as his replacement.

Sam Allardyce returned to the game just after the end of the 2010/11 season. He was hired by West Ham United, newly relegated to the Championship, and charged with getting them back into the Premier League, at least in time for their scheduled taking over of the Olympic Stadium in 2014. With Tottenham and Leyton Orient pulling out of the stadium bid due to the athletics track remaining as a condition of tenancy, West Ham had become preferred occupants, although a decision on the eventual occupancy was further delayed until after London 2012.

For much of the 2011/12 season, it looked as if Allardyce would lead West Ham straight back to the Premier League via automatic promotion but they lost out to Reading and Southampton and had to settle for the play-offs.

The fortunes of Ipswich Town initially improved under Paul Jewell's management – the Jewell in the Town, became the phrase – and they threatened at one point to make the 2010/11 Championship play-offs before tailing away to 13th place. There was not quite enough quality and depth in their ranks just yet but they joined a list of clubs who would be investing in promotion for the following season. Connor Wickham was sold to Sunderland for an initial £8 million. The money made no difference, however, and Ipswich struggled anew, finishing 15th.

David Sheepshanks stepped down from the boards of Ipswich, the FA and the Football League in order to concentrate on his role as chairman of St George's Park, the FA's new national coaching centre. Clearly he would not stop supporting Ipswich, though, and you sensed that he would be back in football politics at some point.

At its 2011 summer meeting in Cyprus, the Football League agreed 'in principle' to adopt a salary cap to try and stem the financial losses of their clubs. The Championship said it would 'work towards' a limit of 55 per cent of their income being spent on players' wages for the 2012/13 season.

In April 2012, the League also announced measures for their clubs to adopt financial fair play rules along the same lines as UEFA's relating to balancing income and playing budgets that might help clubs live within their means and save them from themselves. They were scheduled for the 2013/14 season.

On Hackney Marshes, Lapton were deposed after four seasons as champions of the Hackney and Leyton Sunday League and could only finish fifth. Black Meteors were runners-up to Real Romania. Sadly, a crucial game between Real and Lapton in March 2011 descended into a brawl amid allegations of racist remarks, and police were called. A few weeks later, police also returned to break up fights between Black Meteors and FC Metwin.

'It was a bit shocking and we can do without all that,' the league's chairman Johnnie Walker told me. 'Mostly people get on at the Marshes and we keep a lid on any racism but there is an undercurrent of it sometimes, I have to admit.'

I told the former sports minister Richard Caborn that Walker was not overly impressed with the new dressing rooms. 'Bloody hell,' Caborn replied. 'We put a million quid into the Marshes. I'll go down and have a look.' The building of the Olympic Park was duly completed for the 2012 Games despite Walker's reservations.

After their aggregate victory over Copenhagen in March 2011, Chelsea beat Manchester City 2-0 four days later and embarked on an impressive unbeaten run in the Premier League. Fernando Torres even scored a goal – but then most people did against West Ham. The Blues were beaten home and away by Manchester United in the quarter-finals of the Champions League, however. They also lost at Old Trafford in the league and finished 2010/11 runners-up. Almost inevitably it meant the sack for Carlo Ancelotti, who was fired in a corridor at Everton's Goodison Park ground by chief executive Ron Gourlay after a defeat on the final day of the season. In his eight years in charge of the club, Abramovich had now dismissed – or got someone to do it for him – six managers.

Make that seven. After hiring what he thought was Jose Mourinho lite in the 33-year-old Andre Villas Boas, Abramovich sacked the Portuguese in March 2012. His assistant Roberto Di Matteo took over and led Chelsea to the FA Cup final, where they beat Liverpool 2-1 to take the trophy, and a Champions League final against Bayern Munich after masterminding a remarkable semi-final aggregate win over Barcelona. He and they topped that in Munich, though, with a dramatic victory over Bayern on penalties after drawing 1-1. Didier Drogba, who had headed the late equaliser, scored the winning penalty. Chelsea thus became the first London club to become champions of Europe, Roman Abramavich's £1 billion project completed.

At Manchester City, their Italian manager Roberto Mancini had the last laugh on his critics who thought all through the 2010/11 season that he was one match away from the sack. He not only delivered the FA Cup, City's first trophy for 35 years – though it was overshadowed by United winning the title the same day due to bad planning by the Premier League and FA – but took them to third place in the Premier League and automatic entry to the Champions League.

He then topped that with the dramatic last-day Premier League title victory of 2012.

Three of the Crewe Alexandra Under-18 team were selected for the England Under-17s for the European Championship finals in Serbia in May 2011 – Nick Powell, Max Clayton and goalkeeper Ben Garratt. England lost 1-0 to Holland in the semi-finals. The three retained their places for the World Cup finals in Mexico the following month. The senior Crewe team finished 10th in League Two. Powell made one full appearance and 18 as a substitute for the first team, Clayton two as a substitute.

Both continued to enhance their reputations during 2011/12 season, notably Powell, who made 43 appearances and scored 15 goals to help Crewe to the play-offs. Powell proceeded to score a wonderful first goal in the 2-0 win over Cheltenham Town before make his summer move, with Manchester United the destination in a £6 million transfer.

After Manchester United's defeat by Barcelona in the Champions League final of 2011, Sir Alex Ferguson urged the footballing authorities to revamp the rules regarding the time English clubs were allowed to spend with elite young players if they were to come close to emulating the skills and passing ability of the Spanish.

In October 2011, the Football League reluctantly agreed to the terms of the Premier League's Elite Player Programme, which meant that they could no longer go to a tribunal to determine a fee for a 17-year-old who wished to move to a Premier League club. Instead, they had to accept £3,000 per year for every year of a player's development between the ages of nine and 11 and between £12,500 and £40,000 for every year from 12 to 16 depending on academy status. The threat if the Football League did not accept the scheme was that they would lose their £5 million a year grant from the Premier League for youth development.

Mark Halsey finished the 2010/11 season refereeing Newcastle United v West Bromwich Albion, a mostly meaningless mid-table fixture. When we had originally agreed for me to spend a day with him, it was for a Newcastle match, and the home club secretary had agreed to it. When the Premier League put the block on it, I received an email from them saying that Mark would not be doing another Newcastle game that season.

Relationships between managers and referees took a new twist. Sir Alex Ferguson had been given a five-match touchline ban in March 2011 for criticising Martin Atkinson after Manchester United lost a game at Chelsea. Bizarrely, he was then charged by the FA for praising Howard Webb ahead of the return league game in May. Carlo Ancelotti was also charged on the grounds that comments might be seen to be influencing the referee but such was the ridicule of the charges that they were dropped.

Standards were criticised again during the 2011/12 season after a raft of controversial decisions – notably over diving and balls crossing goal lines to reignite the technology debate. With demotions and retirements, the elite group of referees dwindled to 16, with few of calibre looking ready to step up. Mark Halsey continued in the top flight but was not awarded the 2012 FA Cup final that many thought he deserved.

Brighton and Hove Albion won League One in 2010/11 by three points from also-promoted Southampton and moved into their new stadium on a wave of euphoria, holding on to their manager Gus Poyet, who was much coveted elsewhere. Swindon Town were relegated, but bounced straight back in 2011/12 as champions under Paolo Di Canio's passionate management. Poyet went close to the 2012 Championship play-offs with Brighton, who were given permission by the local council to increase the capacity of the Amex Stadium by another 10,000.

In the inaugural 2011 Women's Super League, Birmingham City set the pace, with Arsenal and Chelsea chasing them. Doncaster

Rovers Belles lost their next two games but then beat Liverpool 1-0 at the Keepmoat Stadium for their first home win. The crowd was 261. It helped put the Belles sixth of the eight teams at the mid-season break ahead of England playing in the World Cup finals in Germany. There they performed only averagely. A splendid win over Japan was followed by a quarter-final defeat by France on penalties.

After that, Arsenal won the WSL title, clinching it with a 2-1 win at Liverpool, both goals scored by Rachel Yankey. Doncaster Belles finished seventh, Chelsea sixth. England captain Faye White announced she was retiring to have a baby.

For Truro City, 2011 was a summer of celebration and for once their location helped them. QPR may have been new to the Premier League but that was not going to stop their manager Neil Warnock, once of Plymouth Argyle and who had a house in Cornwall, from taking his squad to the South West for pre-season as he always did, and the White Tigers hosted QPR in a friendly in July. Weymouth manager Martyn Rogers resigned at the end of the 2010/11 season over a cut in playing budget for the next campaign.

Truro struggled to a mid-table position in Conference South in 2011/12, beset by two winding-up orders from the Inland Revenue over £100,000 in back tax, which City eventually paid. Cornwall County Council gave outline permission for a new £24 million 'Stadium for Cornwall' but it was a slow process. Weymouth narrowly avoided relegation from the Southern League Premier Division again.

Gradually, Paul Gascoigne continued to unravel his previously tangled life of active addiction and simplify things as he continued his recovery. He duly appeared on stage on tour with Jimmy Greaves and received a welcome lift when he reached an out-of-court settlement with Her Majesty's Revenue and Customs over the payment of a £32,000 tax bill.

Ten days after the final day of a 2010/11 Premier League season that had been the highest scoring since its establishment with an average of 2.80 goals per game, the last game of the domestic season pitted Swansea City against Reading in the Championship play-off final at Wembley. By winning 4-2 in another pulsating game, Swansea became the 45th club – and the first from Wales – to reach the English Premier League. A remarkable subsequent season they enjoyed, too, finishing 11th in the league thanks to some attractive passing football engineered by Brendan Rodgers, whose team's victories over Arsenal and Manchester City were clearly noted by the powers-that-be at Liverpool, who would go on to hire him.

One year on, and after the Premier League's 20th season had seen another record goals tally of 1,066 from the 380 games at an average of 2.81, Blackpool were back at Wembley to face West Ham in the Championship play-off final of 2012.

This time there was to be no romance as realism triumphed. a late goal by Ricardo Vaz Te gave West Ham a 2-1 win and took them back into the Premier League. Blackpool for fresh air and fun? Sadly not this second time.

Still, to comfort them they had the continuing parachute money from that previous Premier League season where our journey began – even if that was nowhere near what they might have been earning.

For in June 2012, the League signed a new domestic three-year TV deal with Sky and new players BT Vision. Taking effect in 2013, it would be worth £3.018 billion pounds, an increase of some 70 per cent on the previous £1.78 billion. It meant that even the bottom club would receive at least £60 million for a season, the champions around £100 million. While the League rejoiced, the rest of football looked on in envy.

When the Premier League began, we had been astonished at its new TV riches of £302 million. Twenty years on, it would be receiving 10 times as much. This when the rest of the country and its businesses were in recession. None could have guessed it in 1992. Can we guess what 2032 might bring?

ACKNOWLEDGEMENTS

MANY PEOPLE HAVE helped with the writing of this book by giving their time and expertise freely to help paint a picture of modern English football and how the game has changed in the 20 years of the Premier League. Their names will have become apparent as the story unfolds and my thanks go to all of them.

I am very fortunate, foremost, to have had the backing of my wife Vikki Orvice, who has not only had to endure much during the process of this book – with which she shared the whole of our first year of marriage – but has also helped with much sound advice through her own considerable knowledge of football. I am very grateful to her and just sorry that her beloved Sheffield United were relegated, then lost the play-off final the following season.

I would like to thank Matthew Engel for commissioning this book and Charlotte Atyeo at Bloomsbury for bringing it into being with her belief in it and sensitivity in editing it. My literary agent David Luxton has also provided much appreciated support.

Thanks, too, to my daughter Alex and son Jack who offered welcome company and encouragement.

As well as the many footballing figures who helped me, some top journalists offered me their much-valued expertise, including Malcolm Vallerius, Bill Bradshaw, Phil Shaw, Patrick Barclay, Henry Winter and Patrick Collins.

On top, I am fortunate to have such good friends and confidants to sustain me in Christine Foley and Bruce Lloyd. Finally, I would like to thank someone without whom nothing would be possible: Bill W.

Ian Ridley, St Albans, June 2012

INDEX